YOUR PRAECEPTA:

STEP VI

YOGODA SAT-SANGA

FORTNIGHTLY INSTRUCTION

...ALIZE THY SELF

YOUR PRAECEPTUM

No. 131............

Thy Self realization will
blossom forth from thy
Soulful Study

PARAMHANSA SWAMI YOGANANDA

PUBLISHED BY

Yogoda Sat-Sanga

(Self-Realization Fellowship & Shyamacharan Mission

Founder—Paramhansa Yogananda

President—Sister Daya.

Yogoda Math, Dakshineswar, P. O. Ariadah.

Dist : 24, Parganas, West-Bengal, India.

TABLE OF CONTENTS

The Editor's Notes are on the last page. As always editor Donald Castellano-Hoyt can be reached at dcastellano.hoyt@gmail.com for any questions, corrections, or suggestions.

This reproduction is intended as a facimile of the original Indian manuscript. Adjustments have been made to approximate the type face, size, and spacing allotment. Therefore, as in previous republications, some pages end with a sentence going partway across the page and then continuing on the next page.

Praeceptum	Page		Praeceptum	Page
131	003		146	085
132	008		147	091
133	012		148	097
134	018		149	104
135	023		150	109
136	030		151	114
137	037		152	120
138	042		153	125
139	047		154	130
140	053		155	134
141	058		156/1	139
142	064		156/2	144
143	069		156/3	148
144	074		156/4	153
145	079		Exam	160

YOGODA SAT-SANGA FORTNIGHTLY LESSONS
BY PARAMHANSA YOGANANDA

WE WANT TO BEHOLD THEE AS THOU ART

"Father, open the windows of the stars, open the windows of the blue sky, open the windows of scenic beauties, open the windows of minds and hearts, open the windows of our souls, and show us Thy face hiding behind all windows of Nature and human minds. "How long wilt Thou remain hidden, only partly revealing Thyself through the twinkling stars, through the winds and mighty sunshine and through our reason. Divine Father, no longer are we merely satisfied with Thy suggestions, We want to behold Thee as Thou art.

"Burst our souls, take away the veils of the sky and our minds. All the homage of our Being, the homage of our Soul, we lay at Thy feet. We worship Thee in the temple of the dawn, in the midday sun, in the portals of evening, and in the tabernacle of the night.

"Father, as we sit quiet, one by one we close the doors of our senses lest the aroma of the rose or the song of the nightingale distract our attention from Thee. Come into the temple to fulfill all our hopes. Thou art the salve of our lacerated hopes. Heal us of our sickness. O Eternal Salve of our Souls, heal us of our woes. Make us whole in Thee.

"Receive the devotion of our hearts. We worship Thee with the bouquet of devotion of all hearts. Father, bless us through Christ and through all great Saints. Saturate us with Thy presence, ignite our ignorance with Thy Divine Flame."

THE LAW OF REINCARNATION

Reincarnation means that the true image of Spirit, the immortal Soul, being superior to the perishable body, survives it and passes to another body for the fulfillment of its destiny and the working out of the effects or traces of former actions which are lodged in the subtle bodies accompanying the soul in the passage from one body to another.

Reincarnation is a scientific doctrine and a Christian doctrine, and so, in the Hindu Bible and the Christian Bible, we find that there is the same conception of reincarnation -- the same laws of finding God. It is one of the greatest doctrines because without it we cannot conceive the justice of God. The 379 million people of India, the Buddhists, the Persian Faith of the Magi, the Jewish Faith, the early Gnostics, the Christian Fathers, representing more than half the human race, all believe in this doctrine.

Evolutional reincarnation starts from crystals to the human sphere of existence. After many live from an animal body, the soul passes to the body of a man. Matter suppresses the Spirit as it is trying to reform it from within by evolutional coaxing. Reincarnation represents the retrograde stages through which the Spirit returns to itself from the many to the one (Itself).

SOUL IS IMMORTAL The conservation of energy is true in the physical world as well as in the subtle psychical world. Soul is immortal, hence the soul encased in a mortal body existed before and will exist in all future time. Reincarnation cannot be intellectually understood; one must consciously experience the state of sleep and death through Self-Realization -- the highest technique of concentration and meditation.

One life is not enough to contact spirit and to purify ourselves. We must have time to work out our imperfections. Our immortality must have time to retrace its steps back to God. We have come away from God and we must go back to Him. We cannot go back to the immortal state unless we become perfect, and to become perfect we must have several lives to work out our desires and get back to God.

The soul, being immortal, outlives the body, and the soul, being immortal and filled with imperfection, cannot go back to Spirit unless it has had those imperfections removed, and if the soul cannot do away with these imperfections in one life, it must reincarnate in order to conquer them, If, just by the virtue of death, a soul with imperfections can go back to God, then what is the use of being good? Why not do all the evil things you desire to do, if at the end of life you go back to God anyway?

Immortal souls are sent to a mortal school to enact a drama with the attitude of an immortal, but in this school they limit themselves to mortal desires. Why should you not have mortal desires? Because they contradict your immortal nature. But that doesn't mean that you should all live like hermits. The Bhagavad Gita says: "Do all things with the consciousness of God."

In the Bible we find the following Revelation, Chap. 3:12 "Him that overcometh, will I make a pillar in the temple of my God, and he shall go no more out."

He who overcomes the bodily desires will be a fixed soul (pillar) in the mansion of God's presence, and he will not have to go back to the earth in pursuit of the fulfillment of earthly desires.

THE TREE OF LIFE Revelation, Chap. 2:7: "To him that overcometh will I give to eat of the tree of life, which is in the midst of the paradise of God." He who overcomes the desires of the body will not come back to earth to taste the bitter-sweet fruits of earthly life, but will be able to enjoy God, or the "Tree of Life", which is ever-present in the paradise of ever-living, divine happiness.

The highest Hindu Scripture, Bhagavad Gita, says: "I, the Spirit, reincarnate myself again and again in order to uplift the oppressors and redeem the virtuous." As a man, forsaking one worn-out garment, puts on a new one, so also, the soul, leaving a tattered body, betakes itself to a new fleshly dwelling.

We do not improve all at once, but gradually; many births give our souls and subtle body a chance to improve. The difference in the tem-perament, nature, capacity and evolution of different members of the same family, having the same surroundings and the same training, cannot be explained except through the theory of reincarnation. God would be partial if He created one person prosperous and another person poor; they are what they are by their own action, but people with good opportunities should help those with lesser opportunities, otherwise they will develop apathetic Karma (action) which will spiritually degrade them and ultimately make them poor.

John 9:2: " Master, who did sin, this man or his parents, that he was born blind." You may ask: "Why does a baby die in infancy, or why is a baby born blind. The answer is that the baby transgressed some law in some other life. Where does a person with equal good and bad Karma (action) go? Reincarnation solves the problem of vicarious (sic) sin and other problems.

-Page Two-

AVOID FORCED REINCARNATION You want to live in the body free and not be thrown out of your bodily home Your home is omnipresence but you forget that. Some say this little cage will be broken whether you want it so or not. Why don't you follow the way by which you can consciously go out of one body?

God was in the spirit, but He said, "I want to be out," so He became the plant life. Then He thought, "I express life and beauty in the plant, but I must have motion, so His feet were released from the earth and He became the animal. In Nature God first realized His beauty and in the animal He not only realized His beauty but also His sensibility. His voice began to sing in the nightingale, but He said, "Well, I sing, but I do not know what I sing," so God became man. Then He began to express His reason. In man God's omnipresence is expressed greater than ever. Then God became the superman and said at last, "I am God who has become man." In the superman the omnipresence is expressed, whereby he knows that he is in all things present. That is what these Lessons teach you. How to reverse the searchlight of the senses so that you can be free to live as a master. When you can realize that, then you are free. If you persistently follow this path, you will know the Truth.

One life is not enough, one lesson from the world is not enough, but through appreciation of all good things and non-attachment, we can be free from forced reincarnation, which is a self-inflicted form of punishment. We should reincarnate on earth as Jesus did, of our own free will and not as a matter of compulsion. Free the soul from Karma's law (action) which binds it, and free it from the bondage of forced reincarnation.

THE APOLOGUE
THE DISCONTENTED MAN
Part I

A devout, rich bachelor, but also a "woman hater," thought he was free and happy in every way except for his destructive indigestion. He tried everything, but his money could not buy the remedy for has chronic ailment. At the age of seventy, when he lay dying from an attack of acute indigestion, he inwardly prayed: "Lord God, if I am to be born again, I shall be the happiest man in my next life if I am given a strong, healthy body free from indigestion, I shall not then care whether I have riches or not." The angel of God came in a vision while he was dying and whis-pered: "In thy next incarnation thy prayer shall be granted according to the sovereign command of the Most High."

The rich bachelor died peacefully and reincarnated in a very poor family, but he possessed a body as strong as a Sandow. His parents died early, which added to the intensity of his poverty. He was left with the inheritance of a muscle-loaded body, but with a gnawing hunger and no money to appease the demands of his strong hungry body. According to the latent wishes of his past incarnation, he would often say to himself: "Lord, I am thankful that I have a diseaseless, strong body, and it does not matter if I have no money." Years passed, but no matter what he did, he never seemed to get enough money to appease the demands of his strong appetite and adamant constitution.

At last, as he lay dying of starvation, he prayed: "Lord, I have had enough of muscles. What use are they if I have no money to buy food to keep them strong? Lord, If I must be born again prithee, give me money and health and I shall surely be happy." The angel of the Lord again granted his wishes, and in his third incarnation Mr. John was born a very wealthy, strong-bodied, healthy man. Years passed and he often said to himself: "I have everything; I am happy, but just the same I feel that health and money are useless with someone to share them with." So, as he lay dying of old age, broken-heartedly he prayed: "Lord, if I must be reborn again, do not make life so miserably lonely, but in addition to health and wealth give me a wife."

The angel of the Lord, as usual, granted the wish of this devout law-abiding Mr. John, so according to Divine decree, in the fourth incarnation he was born rich, very healthy, and in due course of time came to marry a handsome but very nagging, jealous wife, who even became jealous if he innocently happened to look at another woman. John passed his life virtually a prisoner of his wife. Years passed; with John wallowing in the mud of matrimonial unhappiness. As he lay dying from old age and a nervous breakdown, through constantly being nagged by his jealous wife, he prayed: "Prithee in the next life I want in addition to prosperity and health only a good wife."

The angel of the Lord again granted John's wish, so, in the fifth incarnation, he was born healthy and wealthy, and finally came to wed a very good, faithful, meek wife, who agreed with him in everything. After two years, at the acme of matrimonial happiness, his beloved wife died. John was grief-stricken and passed his life as a monk, constantly worshiping the gloves, shoes, and other possessions of his lost good wife.

(Continued in Next Praeceptum)

HEALTH CULTURE
THE SCIENCE OF NUTRITION
Factors Affecting Food Requirement

MIXED DIET   There is no one perfect food for the adult -- no one food that will meet all the requirements of the body. To be perfect "a food must contain all the food nutrients in their proper proportion in a moderate compass and must be easily digested and absorbed and yet furnish intestinal bulk." Since no one food will do this for the adult, a mixed diet is needed. Food should be so selected and prepared that each day's diet will supply all of the elements necessary to growth and health in the right proportions.

BULK For proper elimination it is necessary that the daily diet should include an adequate amount of bulk. This is furnished for the most part by green vegetables and fresh fruits.

LIQUID INTAKE Sufficient fluids are of great importance to the proper functioning of the body (see Praecepta 120- 125). Lack of the proper amount of fluids often causes chronic constipation.

FRESH CAULIFLOWER SALAD

1 small head cauliflower, uncooked 1/2 cup finely chopped celery
1 teaspoon vegetized salt
1 cup French Dressing

1/4 cup finely chopped green pepper 2 tablespoons finely chopped pimiento crisp lettuce or cress

Slice the cauliflower paper-thin, so that it will fall apart into tiny pieces. Mix all ingredients and allow to marinate in refrigerator for several hours. Drain off surplus dressing and serve on crisp green. The French dressing may be improved by adding a little tomato juice to it.

ASPARAGUS WITH MUSHROOM SAUCE

Steam asparagus. Wash and cut mushrooms into small pieces. Melt butter, blend in flour and seasonings, add milk slowly, stirring cons-tantly until smooth. Add mushrooms and cook slowly until they are tender. Place asparagus tips on buttered toast and pour sauce over it. Cream of asparagus soup may be used if fresh mushrooms are not available.

Asparagus with mushroom Sauce (Contd.)

Asparagus tips
1/2 pound mushrooms
4 tablespoons butter

1 teaspoon celery salt

4 tablespoons whole wheat flour
1/2 teaspoon paprika
2 cups milk
Whole wheat toast

PRAECEPTUM   INSPIRATION

WATCH YOUR THOUGHTS

Thoughts are like words and they send out vibrations, both good and bad, according to the caliber of the thought. When you can remain without thinking as long as you wish; when your mind is always still, and when you can remain without breath and be calm as long as you wish, and when you are happy in the consciousness of God, then you have perfect self-control.

You think you are just a mortal ready to be shattered with the hammer of death. Pluck that thought of death out of your mind and realize your immortality. The easiest and the best way of experiencing resurrection is by doing good and meditating regularly every day,

Most people are spiritually idle. They are filled with the consciousness that spiritual problems are too big to be solved and therefore they leave them entirely alone. However, if you mean business with God, He will surely answer you. Only be persistent, deep, unbaffled in your demands to learn.

If you live for God alone, if money, or health, or wealth is not your goal, but if God is your goal, then all else will come to you, Contact God first in the Temple of Silence, then health, prosperity, and wisdom will be added unto you.

Praeceptum Affirmation

"I Am the Prince of Perpetual Peace, playing the drama of sad and happy dreams on the stage of experience."

YOGODA SAT-SANGA FORTNIGHTLY INSTRUCTION
BY
PARAMHANSA YOGANANDA

FORGET US NOT

Beloved God, no more with words will I pray unto Thee. I sit in the temple of silence.

One by one I shut the doors of the senses lest the aroma of the rose or the song of the nightingale distract my thoughts of love for Thee. Come out of the stars, come out of the blue, come out of doors of silence. Take away the veil of Nature, take away the veil of mind.

Before Thy wisdom my wisdom is naught, before Thy power my power is little, but behind the wave of my power is Thy power, behind my life is Thy life, behind my thoughts is Thy thought, behind my reason is Thy reason, behind my love is Thy love.

Beloved of our hearts, we are all kings, masters of our souls, but be Thou the only king reigning on the throne of our devotion. Forget us not, though we forget Thee; remember us, though we remember Thee not. Unite our hearts into one great altar wherein Thy Omnipresence may rest evermore.

WHAT IS IT THAT REINCARNATES?

The physical body is composed of 16 elements, which can be found in any drug store. You are worth about 98 cents in chemical value when you are dead, but within this body are hidden two other bodies -- the astral body composed of nineteen elements, and spiritual idea body composed of 35 elemental ideas. The astral body,plus the unfulfilled desires of past lives and their traces,is what reincarnates into a new body.

If a pound of salt water is put in a jar and corked, and then this is put in another larger jar and corked, and these two jars are put in a third larger jar and corked, and if the three jars are put in the ocean, the salt water In them cannot mingle with the blue brine because of the confining jars. If the inside jar is broken, the salt water still cannot mingle with the ocean water. The three imprisoning jar must be broken in order to allow the water contained in them to become a part of the ocean. Likewise, the physical body has the astral body and the idea body within it. and within the idea body the soul is encased but corked with ignorance.

That is why, when the physical body is destroyed at death, the soul is not released. The soul can only find freedom when the corks of ignorance from the other two bodies are removed so that it can mingle with the ocean of Spirit. As we put on three sets of clothing, namely, Undergarment, suit, and overcoat, so the soul at death loses only the overcoat of the physical body.

The 16 elements of the physical body are iron, phosphorus, chlorine, sodium, iodine, potassium, calcium and so forth. The physical body is also made of tissue and cells and contains feeling, will, ego, soul, and so forth.

The astral or subtle body of 19 elements (Mind, Ego, Chittwa Intelligence, ten senses, Five Pranas) with the traces left by actions reincarnates,but the physical body does not. Desire causes rebirth. Performing actions with desire leaves traces, whereas,actions performed without attachment do not leave traces. Desire in connection with the earth brings one back to the earth.

The 19 elements of the astral body are the receiving sensory mind, the discriminating facility of intelligence,the feeling,ego,(pseudo soul) or the consciousness of the soul as the body, and the five electric life forces which help to carry on the crystallizing process(flesh building) and the metabolistic (organ creating) circulating, eliminating and assimilating functions of the body. If the crystallizing current of the body refuses to function properly, tuberculosis starts. If the circulating current works irregularly,an anemic condition prevails,affecting the subtle senses dwelling in the ten organs of sensibility, the power in the eyes, the listening, tasting, smelling and touching powers, the power of action in the hands,feet,and speech,and the genital and rectal muscles. So remember, 19 elements plus 35 elements go from the physical body at death.

Where does the soul go? To the astral world. Then the soul again takes a physical body in order to work out all desires that are not fulfilled. If you are sick, you will attract a sick body. If you are healthy, you will attract a healthy body. If you are wealthy, you will attract a wealthy home, and if you have a consciousness of proverty,you will attract a poor home. The best of all is to be born in a spiritual home.

Then comes the question; when people die are they all re-born immediately? The answer is —No. Some people sleep a long time and other(s) sleep a little while. Normal people come back to earth quickly. Sinful people take a longer time to return. Spiritual people can do as they please. They can remain in the astral world or take a body.

DIFFERENCE BETWEEN PHYSICAL SENSES AND SUBTLE SENSES   The ten senses of the astral body are the replicas of the ten physical senses. The

Physical eyes may be blind, but the astral eyes are never blind! For instance in a dream you may see, even though your physical eyes are blind. You are then using your astral eyes. It is the same with your hearing and so forth.

What is the difference between the physical senses and the subtle senses? Physical senses are the physical instruments but the subtle senses are the real organs. Only the mode of expression is gone. The power of the eyes, and the power of the hearing are still there: only the Physical telephone is gone. We can work all theses ten senses in the astral body. Dreamland is copy of the astral world. The dreamland is the proof of the astral world. Everything can be performed by mind and subtle sense crystallizing power, assimilating power, circulating power and metabolistic (sic) power.

The astral body is made of life force, only different kinds of life force, plus ego or I. Ego is Pseudo soul. It isn't the real soul. When awake the ego is recognise(d) by such expression as: "This is my body this is my name, this is my country." But as soon as you go to sleep you forget all this. God has then taken away all your traial (sic) and titles. So remember the consciousness of the soul in connection with the body is the ego. The ego ascribes to itself all the different conditions of the body. The body is like a chariot drawn by ten horses. The ego is the charioteer: the body is the chariot;the intelligence is the driver;the mind is the reins,and the ten senses are the ten horses.

Page Two

his prayer. So in the sixth incarnation, John was not only wealthy and healthy, but he found a long-lived, good wife. He and his wife had celebrated the anniversary of their silver wedding in happiness and satisfaction when one day he decided to engage a nineteen-year-old, good- looking girl secretary in place of his dead man secretary.

At first sight, John fell madly in love with his new secretary He thought; "My good wife must not know this. I love her with all my hearts, and I would never dream of divorcing her, but alas, although I love my very good wife, she has grown old and homely, and the young face of my secretary is vital, beautiful, and fresh like lily. Thus infatuation got the upper hand, and John divorced his good wife and eloped with the nineteen-year-old girl, who lived with him until she secured the bulk of his money. Then the young girl, who loved someone else, left the withe red rich man cold and dry, without much money, and without notice.

Broken in spirit as the years rolled by, in misery and deep meditation he earnestly prayed for a vision of the Lord. The Lord appeared in a golden aureole and said: "John, in the first incarnation you prayed for the curing of your indigestion without riches; in the second incarnation you were granted a strong body without wealth. Later on when you became tired of health without money in the third incarnation you were given health and wealth. Then you became tired of your loneliness and prayed for a wife; and so in the fourth incarnation you received- riches, health, and a nagging wife. So you prayed for a good wife. In the fifth incarnation I granted you a good wife in addition to health and wealth, when after two years your wife died. Then you said you would be happy if you could have a good long-lived wife: so, in the sixth incarnation, I granted you a good long-lived wife in addition to health and riches; but what a mess you have made for yourself trying to find different ways of making yourself happy in this delusion-ridden earth of mine. Now tell me: do you want the young girl back or your old wife back, or do you want to go on repeating the drama of lives as before, full of variety, heartaches, and thrills.

John reverently answered: "Lord, I want nothing but your constant contact. O lord, it doesn't matter whether I am rich or poor healthy or unhealthy, married or single, living or dying on earth or in heaven, so long as you teach me Your way to be happy, everywhere, anywhere you place me, in any circumstances of life, using my own free will to do your will alone.

God replied: "Son, this earth is but a movie house, where I all of you, my immortal children, to play the various ever-changing drama of life, to be entertained and to entertain, with an immortal attitude. It grieves me to find that most of you forget that the tragedies and comedies of life are only my unreal dreamplays, and thus tarnish your immortal Souls with the temporal desire of earth life. You can never find changeless, immortal happiness in my mortal, ever-changing earthly land,

"Do not build the mansion of your happiness upon the treacherous quicksands of earthly existence. If you want to be perennially happy, look within, play your drama in the world as I the Director, want you to play, not in the way you want to play and muddle up my drama, and I am sure you will know that you only dreamt that you were unhappy and desired material things. Now you know that you are My ever-happy, ever-perfect, ever satisfied child wanting naught of this imperfect dissatisfying, delusive earth but me, and to fulfill My desire here."

10

DIETETICS   Dietetics is the science which teaches the correct feeding of individuals in all of their various states of health and disease. Right food builds up resistance to disease and the ability to contend with favourable physical conditions when they are encountered. It has been thoroughly proved by research workers in the field of nutrition that a carefully regulated diet which supplies all the essential:elemen(t)s including mineral salts and vitamins,produces stronger, better formed physical bodies and higher mental types of individual with more stable nervous systems and more equitable dispositions. Nutrition experts are agreed that, "In the development and maintenance of health,in preventive medicine,and in corrective and therapeutio treatment of nearly all abnormal conditions and diseases,dietetios is today of greater recognized value than any other one factor,

SCALLOPED POTATOES WITH CELERY

    2 cups sliced raw potatoes   Vegetized salt
    2 cups sliced celery   1 tablespoon chopped pimiento
    1 1/2 cups milk or thin white sauce

        Mix ingredients and bake for 1 hour and 20
        minutes

APPLE
PUDDING
        3 cups grated tart apples 1/4   3 teaspoon cloves
        cup lemon juice 1/2 cup raw   1 teaspoon vanilla
        or brown sugar 1 teaspoon   3 table spoons butter melted
        cinnamon 3 egg yolks   3 egg whites

Mix all ingredients except egg whites together lightly. Beat the Whites and fold in. Bake 25 minutes in a buttered baking dish in moderate oven. Serve warm or cold with cream.

P R A E C E P T U M   I N S P I R A T I O N
FIND YOUR OMNIPRESENCE IN MEDITATION

To be one with God is to own the entire kingdom of Omnipresence This earth is a little dot in the sun and the sun is a little dot in the sky,and how small is this sky compared to God's Universe. This is Gods kingdom.

To be earthly king is to be a slave but to be a king of infinity is to be a real king,for then you are free. The king of possessions is only king when he has these possessions, but the king of infinity is king without any wealth at all. The real king is he who loves God. When you wear crown of peace then you will have everything. Unless your heart is pure,unless you find your soul in attunement with God, you never reach this state.

The more you meditate, the more you can do service for others, the more you are in tune with God. Selfish people remain hide-bound in spirit but the unselfish expand their consciousness. God has buried Himself in matter and when you find your omnipresence in meditation you will go back to God. If God is pleased with you, all Nature will work in harmony with you Learn to talk to Him with all your soul

P R A E C E P T U M   A F F I R M A T I O N
In the temple of of my earthly mother's love I will worship the incarnated Divine Mother's love.

Page   Five

YOGODA SAT-SANGA FORTNIGHTLY INSTRUCTIONS

BY
PARAMHANSA YOGANANDA

BLESS US WITH THY PRESENCE

Come Thou, O Spirit, on the altar of our hearts; come on the altar of our calmness; come on the altar of our love. The altar is ready with new-grown flowers of devotion, saturated with the musk of our age-long love. Come in the temple of silence; come in the temple of quietness; bless us with the assurance of Thy presence.

Father, naughty or good, we are Thy children. Alone we came on the earth and alone we go. Thou, the spiritual Hunter, have always pursued us but we have fled from thee through dark, titanic gloom. All things have betrayed us because we have betrayed Thee. Open the stars; open the portals of the moon; show us Thy beauteous face.

O, Tremendous Love, hiding behind the dark of the evening and behind the gloom of the night, hiding behind the mighty dawn, come out, receive our soul's devotion. With the toil of passions, with the glory of the mind and the depth of our devotion and the burning language of our heart, we pray Thee come unto us.

Reveal Thyself, for we are Thine. No more worshiping Thee behind the flowers of the veils of nature; show us Thyself as Thou art. Crossing the sky and earth and the billows of the sea bounding over the vast thoughts with in, O Thou Silent River of Life, show Thyself. Teach us to swim in Thee.

EVOLUTION AND REINCARNATION

All matter is composed of living intelligent electrons. All minerals, plants, and animal bodies are made of intelligence and electrons. The clod reflects intelligence, for some soil grows plants and minerals and transforms the earth into plants in order that we may live. The soil is alive. The plants support animals and human beings. They are alive. The sensitive plant, or Mimosa plant, when you touch it, closes its leaves and branches.

According to the theory of evolution, all the animal bodies are inter-related, just as fish were changed into birds when they were chased by larger fish. We have the flying fish. The lung fish develops lungs instead of gills when their native rivers dry up. The tadpole starts out as a fish with gills and becomes a land animal with lungs. But we have not yet seen an ape change into a man. The missing link is a myth. The earth's lowest strata reveals sea shells first, then vegetation, then animals, then different kinds of primeval man, namely, Neanderthal, Piltdown, Crommagnon, and modern man, but we do not find any missing links of half-man or half-animal skulls in the strata where animal skeletons are found, and the strata where human skulls are found.

MAN IS A SPECIAL CREATION Man is a special creation, and yet we find man's body made after the pattern of animals. Human ears resemble sea shells, and the tail at the end of the human spine reminds one of the tail of primates. The Darwin point at the top of the ear is the vestige of the long ears of the donkey, and our intestines resemble the snake. The quick movements, restless eyes, and grinning face, resemble the monkey. The running power of man reveals the racing power of the horse. Man is brave like the lion, foxy like the jackal, cruel like the tiger, meek like the lamb, hypocritical like the quiet cat who has just eaten a tame canary, and he can sing like the nightingale and is ferocious like the wolf.

A solution of the dispute between the evolutionist and the special creationist is reached by a medium view in the following way: The scientist is right when he declares that all animal bodies are inter-related, such as baboons and horses, and that they came from the lemur, and the lemur from the fish family. But since the scientist cannot find the missing link, he must admit the special creation of man, but then he might ask: "How is it that there are animal characteristics in man?" The answer is that the animal Souls, for further advancement, were made to reincarnate in the specially created human bodies, beginning with Adam and Eve.

The transgression of Adam and Eve shows that, although their bodies were specially created by God, yet their Souls were once in animal bodies. That is why Adam and Eve, instead of immaculately creating their own kind by will power, by freezing Cosmic Energy into the form of children, they ignored the warning of God not to awaken the sex instinct in the Tree of Life, which they remembered from their past lives. God told them to enjoy all other fruits or senses of sight smell, taste, and hearing, but not to indulge in the sense of touch. When Adam and Eve ignored the warning of God, they had to create their own kind in the human way.

MEMORY IS NOT THE TEST OF PRE-EXISTENCE because we do not remember our former lives does not mean that we did not exist before. We do not remember the nine months of our embryonic existence, nor do we remember when we were six months old. Hence, how could we remember when we lived in a different body with a different brain and nervous system, and a different appearance.

It is well that we do not remember the hard experiences in the school of our past lives, for we would not again like to struggle with them. If we remembered all our hard knocks of prenatal life, we would feel disinclined to be good again, and would be bored by repetition. If we remembered our childhood days, our youth, and our old age, we would not like to live over again the pranks of childhood, the comedies of youthful life, and the tragedies of old age. Think what a blessing Reincarnation is, for it smashes our old rickety car of life and gi(v)es us a brand new model in which to try to win the race of Life.

It requires years of investigation to know one's former incarnations. You can know about reincarnation not by reading books or hearing lectures, but through scientific, metaphysical research. Reincarnation is the only logical solution to our lives. If we are immortal and we die in imperfection we cannot go back to God. We must work out that imperfection.

The first tendency that you had up to the age of five came from your past lives. After that age it becomes diluted with this life. Think as far back as you can remember, then enumerate your first unalloyed tendencies. Did you love incense or oriental philosophy, or pictures of saints, or did you love mechanisms and mechanistic instruments? Those early tendencies, separated from the acquired tendencies of this life, reveal your past. Materialistic occidental can develop spiritual oriental characteristics in this life, and vice versa, and when they are reborn they can change their race and nationality.

Some wise children are born of ordinary parents, and sometimes moron offspring come from intelligent parents. Those vagrancies in life show that different Souls are born in the same family. Sometimes, when you find a family in which the members fight most of the time, it indicates that they knew each other in a previous life and were arch enemies, concentrating and establishing hatred in their hearts for each other. So, Nature, due to the law of concentration involved in hatred, brought the fighting Souls together, so that they could get enough of the long-missed and eagerly-waited-for opportunity of the joy of fighting with one another at close quarters, within the arena of a small home. So, beware, do not bring your enemy near you nor attract his bad qualities by constantly concentrating upon him through the channel of hatred.

BE FREE FROM DESIRES AND ATTACHMENTS   God sent perfect Souls to earth to behave like immortals -- calm, desireless, and happy -- and to watch earthly moving pictures, and to act in them, but, during the acting and watching of mundane moving pictures, Souls, through contact and ignorant behaviour, develop attachments in the intricate dramas of earthly life. Unless these desires are cast off before death, the Soul must return to another body in the same earthly moving picture house in order to work out the desires born there. For instance, if you die with the desire to possess an expensive automobile, with Eternal gas, you won't go to heaven where Souls glide without vehicles, but you will have to come back to earth where that particular desire can be fulfilled.

Even the highest earthly desire of the Soul is limiting when compared to the Eternal Kingdom of the Cosmos, which it loses due to concentration upon little things.

Every action performed to please God leaves no attachment. For instance, if you eat strawberry pie or make money to please God, or with the consciousness of pleasing God, you will not carry the desire with you when you die, but if you act with greed or thought of gain for self, and then suddenly die with the unfulfilled desire, you will have to come back on earth to fulfill that desire. This does not mean that you must be without ambition. The lazy, negligent person is not ambitious to please God by good actions on earth, so he has to come back until he learns to work with the one purpose of pleasing God. The Egotist, who works only to please himself, becomes involved in an endless net of desires, from which he can extricate himself only after many incarnations. Therefore, you must neither be idle nor absent-minded, nor egotistically ambitious, but you must be divinely ambitious to work and play on earth with the right attitude of mind, in the way the Divine Director wishes.

To leave the world and go to the forest to meditate is extreme, for your earthly desires can follow you to the forest. To be merged in the world causes misery and increases desires, but to be in the world but not of the world, or better still, to enjoy the world with the pure joy of God, brings lasting happiness. Then everything that you do will be right. To leave the world without conquering desires, produces hypocrisy , and to be in the world without training gets you mixed up and makes you hard-boiled and worldly. To do everything in the world to please God is the highest ideal, according to the Hindu Scripture, the Bhagavad Gita, the teachings of which are compatible with Western life, as well as with Eastern life. If you go to the forest and do not live hygienically, you will die of disease, and if you live in the world without peace, you will die of mental worry, but with God in your heart, and a smile on your face, let your hands ungrudgingly work for Truth alone.

YOU MUST PASS ALL GRADES IN THE EARTHLY SCHOOL   The physical body is the tenement and the   Soul is the tenant. The fleshly house is perishable and the Soul, being the image of Spirit, is imperishable. That is why Jesus said: "I (the reflected individualized Soul) and my Father (Omnipresent Spirit) are One." When the body dies, the Soul has to go somewhere else for shelter, but due to the Soul's intimate contact with the body it develops imperfect physical desires. These imperfect material attachments cling to the disembodied Soul and prevent it from returning to Spirit. Thus, the immortal but imperfect soul has no other alternative but to come back to the mortal school of life to work out its imperfections.

When a child, sent to school, fails to make the grade, he has to go back again and again until he passes his examinations. So, also, Souls who fail to preserve their perfection while in the mortal school of educative entertainment, have to go back for many incarnations until they completely bring out their hidden spirit nature. The immortal Soul must win several prizes in order to maintain Spirit-endurance, self-control, detachment, morality, calmness, and spirituality before graduating, and must pass all grades in the earthly school in order to be ready for Immortality.

Immortal soul children are sent to the movie house of Life to make pictures or to watch pictures of Life, both tragedies and comedies, with an unruffled equanimity. When these divine children can go back to God and say: "Father, I enjoyed acting in and watching Thy earthly moving pictures, but have no more desire for evanescent amusements, " they are no longer forced by their material desires to come back to earth.

THE A P O L O G U E
SAGE BYASA AMD THE GOPINEES
PART I

Sage Byasa was the far-famed author of the greatest Hindu Scripture -- The Bhagavad Gita. Once upon a time, long, long age, he was seated in lotus posture by the sacred, dancing blue waters of the River Jamuna, in deep contemplation. A few clouds had been playing havoc in the sky and had squirted lots of water into the peacefully-flowing Jamuna and made her boisterous like an excited stallion, so much so that she threatened to sink any boat that ventured to ride upon her.

The rains had ceased their pattering dance with their myriad feet on the watery floor of the river and the angry roar of the rain- taxed and trampled river could be distinctly heard, when the melodious voices of lady saints, the exalted Gopinees, distracted the Sage from his meditations.

The Gopinee devotees sat around the Sage, after laying down their baskets full of milk-made sweetmeats, looking helplessly at the raging river which they wished to cross. The Sage addressed them in a musical voice, saying "Sacred Souls, what can I do for you; please command.

The angellic Gopinees answered: "Honored Sage of almighty power, please do something so that we can get to the other bank of the turbulent Jamuna, as no boat will take us across. "

Again the sage spoke: "But what's the hurry to reach the other side of the Jamuna during such a storm-tossed state of the river. Can't you wait and go tomorrow when the river displays a calmer mood?"

"Ah, no, we must go, Christna's magic flute of Divine Compassion is calling us. We must get there some way for we are carrying freshly-made milk-sweets made for Him."

Now there appeared on the face of the Sage a mysterious, mischievous little smile and He retorted: "Ah, ah, I see you all think of Christna alone and not of me. I won't do anything until you have allowed me to share in those sweets."

Some of the Gopinees shouted: "How dare you blasphemously taste the sweets first when they are meant first to be blessed by the sacred lips of the Sovereign Omnipresent, our Lord-God Christna."

Byasa was stubborn, however, and kept repeating; "Nothing will I do, unless I participate in the pleasurable taste of those delicate sweets."

At last, seeing no other way, and possessed with an irresistible desire to pay their respects to Christna, the holy mothers -- the Gopinees offered some of the sweets to the Sage, who kept on eating until he could eat no more. Some of the Gopinees were inwardly criticizing the too-healthy appetite of the Sage and his blasphemous act of eating the sweets before his Lord and Master, Christna, had tasted them.

Finally, Bysa (sic), stuffed with food and followed by the Gopinees, somehow carried himself to the brink of the boisterous river and loudly exclaimes: "O River Jamuna, made holy by the sacred of my Omnipresent Christna, if I sure have not eaten any thing, divide and part". And behold the Jamuna obeyed and parted, revealing a beautiful road running up between two blue walls of waters and reaching up tp the other bank of the river.

The Gopinees were amazed at the miracle and still more bewildered by the sage's contradictory exclamation: "If I did not eat" after he had gorged himself with sweets, and they were still more bewildered at seeing the river obey the sage's request, based upon an apparently untruthful plea. However, although puzzled and excited, the Gopinees raced pell-mell through the water-walled path way to the other side of the river, even as the followers of Moses passed through the miracle-made road between the sea-walls when chased by the angry Pharaoh.

The Gopinees, upon reaching the other shore safely, found the river Jamuna calmly flowing down the silvery sandbanks, and they waved their thanks to the meditation-merged sage Byasa.

The Gopinees finally reached Christna's side and found him lazily dozing, apparently after a heavy meal. Slowly He rose and welcomed them without uttering a word of thanks for the delicious sweetmeats presented to Him. The Gopinees were quite surprised and inwardly hurt because Christna did not display even the slightest degree his usual keen interest in his favorite sweetmeats. Unable to understand all this after a long pause and while still looking at the half-sleepy Master and the untouched sweetmeats, the Gopinees finally exclaimed: "How strange Lord, after we took so much trouble to make and bring these sweets, knowing how well you like them, you are not a bit interested."

(continued in Next Praeceptum)

HEALTH CULTURE
THE SCIEI CE OF NUTRITION

AN ADEQUATE DIET   It is difficult to convince people of the great importance of an adequate diet because the lack of some of the essential elements is not always immediately evident, and the ill effects may not be readily or promptly recognized. However, "Any diet lacking in any essential cannot be continued for any length of time without producing abnormality and often irreparable defects. The deterioration is not only visible but it affects the inner and vital organs so that the entire organism suffers." (No citation)

To have an adequate mixed diet it is not necessary to have a great abundance of all of the protective foods and there is no excuse except laziness and ignorance for any one going without them. Reliable information can be secured free from late books by authorities on diet(tet)ics in the public libraries. There are also any number of modern magazines devoted to health and even some of the daily newspapers print up-to-date information on the subject.

To repeat again, the protective food mentioned above are milk, eggs, fruits, leafy vegetables and vitamin D products. All the new discoveries add to the importance of these foods which should be included in the diet of every person every day.

ANDALUSION ASPARAGUS

2 bunches asparagus
2 sweet red or green peppers chopped
1 clove garlic minced

2 tablespoons olive oil
6 eggs
vegetized salt

Steam asparagus. Cook Pep(p)ers and garlic in olive oil until tender. Poach eggs. Put asparagus on hot platter, cover with sauce and arrange poached eggs on platter. Asparagus may be sprinkled with a little lemon juice if desired.

PINEAPPLE ICE CREAM

2/3 cup sweetened condensed milk
1/2 cup pin(e)ap(p)le juice
2 tablespoons powdered raw sugar
1 cup heavy cream, whipped

1 cup crushed canned pineapple

grated rind of 1/2 lemon
few grains salt.

Combine condensed milk, salt and pineapple juice. Mix well and stir in pineapple, sugar and lemon and chill thoroughly. Fold in stiffly beaten cream and pour into freezing tray. When frozen to mushy consistency beat until smooth and return to tray to finish freezing.

PRAECEPTUM   INSPIRATION
GO BACK INTO THE   OCEAN OF GOD

Again and again you are bound by the wheel of desires. You are living in a cocoon of ignorance and have surrounded yourself with false desires. You must break those threads and become the butterfly of eternity and fly away to the shores of immortality. You were sent here to watch these tragedies and comedies of life with an immortal attitude. It is when you watch these dramas with a mortal attitude that you are conscious of failure and disease.

Do not crave things; enjoy them in an unattached way. Do not form desires for anything, but enjoy all things without desiring them so that you will not miss them when they are gone. When the storm is on, the wave separates from the ocean, but as soon as the ocean is calm, the wave goes back into the ocean. So it is with us. As soon as this storm of desire is gone, then we can go back into the Ocean of God.

When God comes to you, you will have so much to be happy about that you will not mind the burning up of all desires. It is only by knowledge and wisdom that It is only by knowledge and wisdom that you can emancipate yourself.

PRAECEPTUM AFFIRMATION

I shall watch Thy working Hands in the laws of gravitation and all other forces. In the feet of all living creatures I shall hear Thy Footsteps.

YOGODA SAT-SANGA FORTNIGHTLY INSTRUCTIONS
BY
PARAMHANSA YOGANANDA
ETERNAL BLESSEDNESS

May Thy light be established evermore, O spirit in the sky, O Spirit in the blossoms, teach us to seek Thee in Thy temple of Nature, in the Temple of mind and in the Temple of great souls; Unite our hearts on one great altar; unite our souls in Thee; unite our hearts into one heart. We are all Thy children. Dispel the walls of caste, race and color so that the sunlight of Thy presence may shine within us in the fullness of Thy glory.

O Spirit in the fragrance of the flowers, in the perfume of minds, show us that Thou art on the altar of Nature and in our souls. Teach us to worship Thee through all our desires, through all our pursuits, for Thou art the only reality. Without Thee nothing exists. O Light of Lights, O nectar of Nectars, Joy of all Joys, permeate us within and without; dispel the gloom and inharmony in our bodies, minds and souls.

Heavenly Father, lift our consciousness from the senses and matter to the supernal bliss within. Make our super-consciousness predominant, that we may always live in eternal blessedness.

DISEMBODIED SOULS

Part I

METAPHYSICAL DEFINITION   A disembodied souls (sic), metaphysically defined, ought to mean a soul liberated from the bondage not only of the physical body but also of the other two bodies -- causal and subtle. Usually a disembodied soul is thought of as a soul who has lost the physical body due to the phenomenon of death.

All souls cannot go everywhere in space. Just as people cannot enter everyone's home in the material world. The physically disembodied souls with different qualities from different clans, consciously or unconsciously, remaining huddled up in different groups in their assigned different quarters. Good souls who learn to consciously watch sleep and death, go out of the body consciously and can keep their consciousness in death. Virtuous souls have the option to change their bright vibratory residence in spirit world whenever they want to reincarnate. Reincarnation is not forced upon them; people with deep realization may come to or go from earth as they wish.

These living beings that we love, they are our family. When we grow attached to them, suddenly they are torn from us without any explanation from the Infinite. We feel like rebels. Why is it that souls come and then are taken away? What is the reason? If anyone wrests your possessions from you, you fight, you bring law suits against him, but you

S-VI * P-134

only helplessly weep when the dearest of all your possessions your loved ones are suddenly, unreasonably and timely taken away from you. You break your heart when your most loved ones die; you cry bitterly, you suffer silently and then after a time, you forget more or less and you accept the decree of the destiny.

WHAT GOVERNS HUMAN RELATIONSHIPS   Is there any reasonable explanation as to why you were given certain ones to love and then, perhaps, before your love had fully matured in them, they are taken away mysteriously from you by the cruel hand of death? Is Nature a circus jester who takes pleasure in seeing people love and then torn apart? Is Nature the great Jester who mocks at all the sacred vows of loyal love and loyal friendship? Is paternal love just instinct-instigated? Is conjugal love Nature and Sex Instigated? Is friendship emotion-born? Is the dream of eternal love between souls a mockery of imagination?

Is it through the vagrancy and whim of Nature that some souls are thrown together so that they may become attached to one another? Or is it due to similar actions of previous lives, similar dispositions, like tendencies, or is it pre-natal acquaintance, friendship and love which brings (sic) souls together? Is it that he makes us intelligent tools to suit His life's dreams, and destroys us at will? Or is it that this world is a playhouse of God's Whims. Is it that He makes some of us poor some of us rich, some idiotic or wise, in order to fill His stage of life with variety, so that at death He can pull us back into His bosom? Is this life the beginning and the end? Is it that souls are created as types of mentalities who are attracted to each other through similar likes and dislikes but not through any pre-natal ties, only to part forever in death? Is love just the chemical combination of souls with mutual affinity, so that after a certain period of temporary union they fall apart never to meet again? Is Nature or destiny jesting with friendship and with true love between souls?

HUMAN LOVE MUST BE EXPANDED INTO DIVINE LOVE   The answer lies in this explanation: The Immortal Divine love is trying to awaken the all-perfect Divine love in souls through various processes of Divine, conjugal, parental, friendly, brotherly, sisterly, fatherly, and motherly love.

It seems that individual human souls, and families, societies, nationalities, and animals, birds, and flowers -- all living creatures are but chemicals of life to purify and convert human love into Divine love. When the friendship and love of souls gets mixed up with pois(o)nous chemicals of selfishness, mechanical family relations, sex madness, physical attachment, emotional excitement, utilitarian barterings, sudden loves, sudden hates and sudden deep friendships followed by sudden deep enmities, then human love dies a temporary earthly death.

This human love of the heart can remain asleep for awhile intoxicated with mental poisons of selfishness, attachment, and imperfection, but it can never die. If human love fails to purify in one souls it will be dissatisfied and it will keep on seeking other souls in this life or beyond the portals of this life in the land of incarnation until it meets the soul in which it finds the expressions of all the perfections of Divine Love. Until perfect, unconditional, undying, pure divine love is expressed in a friend, there will be no liberation.

HUMAN LOVE CAN FIND THE DIVINE ANSWER I N PURE FRIENDSHIP   The immortal perfect love in us is madly roaming in the pathways of incarnations, trying to find a perfect human channel through which, without destruction, it can express itself. When perfect pure love and friendship are expressed between two souls, that love will be registered as One Divine Love. That same love defies destiny, mocks at death and time, for that love will be two co-mingled founts of love ever playing on the bosom of God. This type of human love will never be satisfied with substitutes of body attachment, eye attractions, or sex lures. It can only be satisfied when it expands itself into unselfish, unconditional, Divine love.

Page   Two

19

When you feel that you can be a friend to an individual unconditionally; when you feel that all your most exacting demands of perfect and pure Divine Love have been amply expressed through this person, and when you lose all desire to seek the Divine Love in anyone else, then will the friendship-thirst of your soul be quenched.

Human love may find its perfect Divine answer in a pure friendship with some one of your own sex, or your human love may behold the Divine love in pure conjugal friendship with some one of the opposite sex. Human love in the latter case can only perfect itself by the predominance of soul affinity and less of the physical attractions. Human love may find satisfaction in all types of human relationships. This human love of yours may find the Divine Love in your mother or father, or son or servant, or in your Spiritual Preceptor. Remember, your human love must be converted into Divine, impersonal love before it can ever be satisfied.

KEEP ON SEEKING UNTIL YOUR HUMAN LOVE FINDS DIVINE LOVE   Remember also that until your human love finds Divine Love in someone, so long will Nature keep mocking your friendship through the agencies of fickleness, temperaments, emotions, sudden partings, and death. Do not deceive yourself until you have found the Divine perfect love, and keep on seeking; in this life and in all incarnations until you find it.

The Divine Love-thirst of your soul will never be quenched until you find Divine Love in some one. Then, after finding Divine Love in one, you will suddenly find that your heart will feel the same Divine Love for all the members of your family and for anyone who belongs to your country or to your world. You will feel the same Divine Love even in the flowers, birds, and beasts.

You now know what we mean by saying that you should try to know the truth about your dear ones, sometimes it happens that after a long search of incarnations, or a long search of years, almost at the very end of your life, you may find the dear one in whom you want to perfect your human love into Divine Love. Then you must realize that there must be sufficient time for your human love to be perfected into Divine Love. What happens if death cuts you off from your dear ones and you are unable to convert your human love into Divine Love? Then you will find that you will be born again with the heart of a faithful, true friend, seeking only the one who also is born after the pattern of your dreams of Divine Love.

This must happen to complete the perfection of human love into Divine Love which you started in your last incarnation.

THE A P O LO G U E

SAGE BYASA AND THE GOPINEES Concluding Part

With a smile and an understanding look in his eyes, Christna calmly replied: "Why, I have eaten them already."

"How and when," quickly asked the Gopinees in chorus.

"Why, that hoary fellow on the other side of the river has already fed me too much of those sweets which you gave him. Why, it was I who ate those sweets through his mouth. He is very naughty. While he pretended to taste those sweets by his own ego he transplanted my omnipresent consciousness to his taste in his own mouth. So, I have been eating those sweets, not he. I will eat the rest tomorrow. I am quite satisfied at present."

Then the Gopinees understood what Byasa meant when he said: "O Jamuna, if I did not eat, divide and part," and why the River Jamuna obeyed, being commanded by the Omnipresent God, who was consciously appealed to through the deep devotion of Byasa.

When in a high state of divine ecstasy, the devotee finds his complete Oneness with God, so that he realizes God as seeing, smelling, touching, hearing, and tasting through him. In that state he no longer like the ordinary mortal man, feels that his ego is responsible for all actions.

Jesus knew that He was One with the Father; that is why whenever He said: "The Heavenly Father make thee whole," or, "I say unto thee, arise," he did not feel any difference.

When Jesus said: "I say unto thee, arise," He didn't refer to His limited ego, but to the "I" that was One with the Father ("I and my Father are One.")

So, in the state of Divine Oneness, it matters little whether one says: "Heavenly Father in me, make thee whole," or "I (as One with the Father) command thee to be whole."

The above story of Byasa teaches the moral that all true lovers of God must so meditate upon God and be in such ecstatic joyous communion with Him that God will be considered responsible for all actions.

Of course, before this Divine union is attained, it is wrong to say: "God is doing everything and not I," for, by this way, one may approve of all his wrong actions as being the actions of God. One's conscience must not be made blunt -- when your conscience tells you that an action is wrong, it is wrong. If you are One with God, you will see God working through you in everything. It is all right to pray in the following way:

"O God, I know the sacred bliss-producing laws of virtue, but I cannot always follow them, altho(ugh) I may be extremely willing to abide by them, and I know the terrible effect of vice but I cannot always stop being influenced by it, even though I abhor it, and now, Celestial Father, the Employer and Lord of all my senses, I commend all my good and evil actions unto Thee and I will act as Thou dost inspire me. I will perform good actions with Thy thought and I will think of Thee and with Thy thought perform evil actions actuated under the spell of temptation-compelling-charm of will-paralyzing evil.

"Thinking of Thee equally in good and evil activities, my evil activities will change into good activities and evil habits will change into good habits. Then, at last, when I would see, hear, smell, taste, touch, think, reason, will, and feel all surrounded by the protecting walls of the Omnipresent Goodness -- then I would behold Thee reigning in that sanctuary forever. Receive my perpetual prayers of gratefulness."

HEALTH CULTURE THE SCIENCE OF NUTRITION THE MINERAL SURPLUS   mineral elements consumed in excess of the body's needs must be excreted or they cause trouble. Some minerals cause this surplus to be acid and some cause the chemical opposite, or alkali. Both classes -- in the right proportion -- are necessary to the wellbeing of the individual.

Equal amounts of acids and alkalies present at the same time neutralize each other. They form a salt and its reaction is neither acid nor alkaline. If there is more of either than is used in forming the salt the resulting mixture is either salty and alkaline or salty and acid.

Excessive alkali in the system is fairly rare for the alkaline surplus is readily excreted from the body. An acid surplus is also excreted if it is not too large.

(Continued in Next Praeceptum)

SCALLOPED EGGS AND TOMATOES

3 1/2 cups cooked or canned tomatoes
2 tablespoons minced onion
2 teaspoons vegetized salt
2 tablespoons raw sugar
4 tablespoons melted butter

1/2 teaspoon paprika
6 hard cooked eggs
1 cup grated American cheese
2 cups soft whole wheat bread crumbs

Cook tomatoes, onion, salt, sugar and paprika. Shell and slice eggs. Place layer of eggs in bottom of buttered glass casserole, cover with a little tomato sauce, sprinkle with cheese and then crumbs. Repeat layers until all ingredients are used having crumbs and melted butter for the top. Bake in moderate oven for 30 minutes.

MAPLE ICE CREAM

4 eggs
1 tablespoon whole wheat pastry flour
1/8 teaspoon salt

2 cups evaporated milk
1 1/2 cups whipping cream
1 1/4 cups maple syrup
(Highland Brand is 100% Maple)

Beat the eggs, add sugar and flour mixed together. Slowly add heated evaporated milk and cook in double boiler until thick, stirring constantly. Cool, add salt, maple syrup and whipped cream. Place in freezing tray.

PRAECEPTUM INSPIRATION
OMNIPRESENT CHILDREN OF GOD

Reincarnation teaches Souls to travel through the mineral, plant, animal, and human life of all the brown, white, black, yellow, and red races, so that they may not become attached to the confinement of one body or one race, but may learn to perceive themselves as Omnipresent Children of God, (present in everything).

As long as one has hatred and repulsion in his heart, so long must be keep roaming through the corridors of incarnations. After about eight million lives, the human life is finally attained, according to the Hindu Masters. So, do not waste your previous life in foolishness, wading in the mud of the senses and ignorance, but realize that in this life you have the chance, by conscious trance-unity with Omnipresent Spirit, and by realizing your brotherhood with all Creation, to know yourself as not wholly belonging to everything and every Being.

When you feel that the stars, clods, birds, beasts, men, and outcasts are all your blood relatives, and when your heart throbs in them, then the compelled imprisonment of reincarnation will be enforced no longer, but you will freely go everywhere to open the gates of rainbows (sic) wisdom, so that all sorrowing, groaning animate and inanimate life may make a rushing exodus into the everlasting freedom in God.

PRAECEPTUM   AFFIRMATION

"There is no space between minds and souls. Though far away in thought; our loved ones and all things are really ever near."

YOGODA SATSANGA FORTNIGHTLY INSTRUCTIONS
BY
PARAMHANSA YOGANANDA

HEAVENLY FATHER, COME TO US

Heavenly Father, we feel Thy presence within the cave of our minds, in the nook of our feelings, in the garden of our love. Fill us with the aroma of Thy presence. Break the stars, break the blue, break the thoughts and feelings and show us Thy presence within us, around us everywhere.

Centuries and centuries we have been searching for Thee in the pathways of ambitions.

... we know that it is Thy presence that we have been seeking. Hide no longer behind the roses and our feelings, hide no longer behind our thoughts, behind our soul.

In the glory of nature's robe come to us, decorated with all the wisdom of the centuries cone to us with the ocean breeze of Thy presence Take away darkness that hides Thee from us.

Thou art just behind the stars, just behind the blue heavens, just behind the atmosphere, just behind every human being. Thou art just behind our thoughts and feelings and our love for Thee. Teach us to feel Thee just behind our thoughts, just behind our feelings, just behind our love.

Peace!   Joy!   Peace!

DISEMBODIED SOULS

THE METAPHYSICAL TECHNIQUE OF CONTACTING LOVED ONES Let us not bury the souls in the grave and call death "annihilation" but let us see it as a door through which bravely-marching souls of earthly life can enter to find the all alluring, all-charming region of our ever-luminous, ever-peaceful common cosmic Home. Mortal fears, heartaches, dreams, and illusions fade, but the darkness of death changes into a beautiful universe. Why pity the "dead?" In wisdom, they pity us. They can see their super-region and us at the same tine with their spiritual eyes, while we cannot see then with our gross spiritually-blind physical eyes.

Death is not annihilation. It is the switching off the nerve current from the entire body bulb. Death is a state of passive involuntary relaxation brought on by sudden accidents, disease, sorrow.

The forcible, sudden, and permanent disconnection of the life current from the body-bulb is popularly called "death" or complete annihilation of life. In reality, it is only a temporary state. It is not the end of things but merely the transfer from the domain of change able, ugly matter to the realm of infinite joy and multi-coloured flashing lights.

Souls with causal and astral bodies tainted with the seeds of evil karma (or action) and saturated with obnoxious desires, becomes extremely afraid at the call of death and struggle very hard to be deaf to it. Death or the law of change has to expel them by force from the apartment house of flesh because they want to stay even when their lease on the bodily house has expired. Such souls become unconscious through extreme grief arising from the forced expulsion.

It takes a long time for such souls to be reborn. According to the quality of the subtle body, disembodied souls are allotted different vibratory regions of pranic or life energy mansions, in infinite space to live in.

Body is composed of organised motions revolving around an ego motions of sensations (physical body) motions of energy (subtle body) and motion of ideas (causal body). The soul does not come back to its own consciousness as long as the ego rules the three bodies. This ego is present in the state of body consciousness which says "I am walking" etc. It is also present in the dream consciousness which knows "I am dreaming." It is present in the Turia or deep sleep state, also. Hence the the soul does not get a chance to know itself owing to the active presence of ego. Salvation lies in completely freeing the soul from its identified three bodies. Soul may reincarnate in the three bodies without being attached to them,

FREE YOUR SOUL FROM THE BONDAGE OF DEATH   Why not learn the method by which you can switch off the current from the entire body through conscious will by the steady, conscientious practice of the Praecepta instructions, thus freezing the soul from the bondage of death. Besides, just as electricity does not die with the breaking of the bulb into which it flows, but merely retires into the big dynamo behind it, so our real self is not destroyed but retires into the Infinite Omnipresent Self when our life forces are switched off from the body bulb.

Whether we are awake in this life or dreaming in the astral life, there is no death. We are still in the lap of God. When you go to the Astral life, this life becomes unreal and that becomes real, and when you come back to this life, that life becomes unreal and this life is real. But you must know that both of these are nothing but the dreams of God. Some day, when you find Him, you will wake up from these dreams of life and death. The idea of Utopia comes from the astral land, but even when you get there, you will not be satisfied because you will have to get out of both the astral and the physical before you can be eternally happy in God.

When you have had a day of worries, you are apt to have nightmares, and so after death, if you have had worries and have not lived a good life you will have nightmares in the astral world and your soul will not be at rest. The physical body is a dream of God, but even then you see it as rea. So, when you are dead, even then the astral body will become real to you. AS this body seems real to you now, so the astral body will become real to you when you have left this body,

"Insult not my death with tears, ye who are left on this desolate shores to moan and deplore. It is I who pity you." Do you see? You pity them and they pity you.

Page two.

YOU CAN REACH ADVANCED SOULS THROUGH LOVE   The contact of Souls is possible by the power of passivity and concentration. It is possible to invoke them in the physical body by making it sleep, which practice is dangerous. They can and should be invoked consciously. In the negative passive state, only stray truant disembodied souls possess the body into which they are invited, and may harm it by over-staying. Highly developed souls can only be invited by prayer, love, and meditation; other means do not attract them, nor do they satisfy the curiosity of the mediocre.

First, you must have the desire and the patience and the strength, and then follow the law. How? The Spiritual Eye is the instrument. This is the radio by which you broadcast and it is the receiving set by which you can tune in with the other world. First of all, many of you know that if you love someone, you may see them in dreams. It is not always the reflection of your own mind. They try to get in touch with you.

It is also possible to tune in with those who are gone and have been reborn again if you know how to handle the different forms of consciousness. In dreams you can't commune with them. They only talk with you, but in the superconscious state you can know how to contact them and also talk to them. This is what happens: The heart sends vibrations out. Certain electrical impulses come in the brain and then, when all other thoughts have gone, the image appears. But what you want to learn is how to tune in with superconsciousness.

Unless you have love for a person, you cannot find that one. And if you are sad and grieve for the person who is dead, you will keep that person earth bound. That is selfish. You do not cry because you have lost that person; you cry for yourself -- cry because you miss him. You can help much more if you just send your love. Send loving thoughts; such thoughts travel through the ether and departed souls get them. When you send an intelligent thought through the ether, even if you do not know where that person is, if the thought is continuous, it will finally reach that Soul.

If you lose through death some one very dear to you and you find it impossible to forget him, even though you travel far away from him, through the arches of thenyears, proceed to find him in the following way; practice for two hours each day, for months, or if necessary, for years. Sit on a straight chair, practice the highest technique of concentration that you know, for one hour, then lift your hand and concentrate upon the finger tips. Then concentrate upon the point between the eyebrows, and see the Spiritual Eye, and continuouslywill to contact the Astral body of the departed Soul. Keep on turning your hand very gently in a circle toward north, south, east, and west, or northeast, southeast, and so on, at every direction in the circle around which your hand moves, and try to feel the presence of the Astral body of the departed Soul. When your fingers feel that you have touched him as you used to touch him while he lived, your heart will be thrilled. Then keep on visualizing him in the Spiritual Eye and you will see him. Then ask your fingers and heart to indicate in what place your friend is reborn, according to the direction you felt him through your fingers. When you feel him through your fingers and heart, and can see him and talk to him, he will tell you where he is in the Astral world, or the place where he is bom. Then there will be great rejoicing.

You must not feel helpless; you must not accept the decree of fate and begin forgetting your real perfect friend. If he has gone before you, then throughout your life broadcast your undying love to your friend until you see his or her Astral body or until he or she appears to you with the conventional garments of a human body beautiful, during your sojourn in the garden of life.

-Page Three-

If you had a perfect friend who met a so-called untimely death, make the following affirmation after meditation. Look at the point between the eye-brows, seek the light, and broadcast your message: "Dear one, be comforted, receive my vibrations of ever-living love. Meet me again soon." If you perform this exercise faithfully, you will find that right through your Spiritual Eye there will pour into you living, loving vibrations, and the realization of the presence of your lost perfect friend. Even if your friend has been reborn, his Astral body will respond and be projected in you.

Disembodied Souls can be consciously contacted by those who can "live without breath" or consciously watch and disengage themselves from the physical body, or by those who can retain their consciousness during sleep and the deep sleep of death. Only advanced Souls who can live with out breathing or heartbeat can consciously realize the state of death in which the breath and heart-beat stop. Undeveloped Souls become unconscious when they lose their breath. Advanced Souls can consciously go to the Astral world, which follows after earthly death, and there, by intuition, can detect the Souls they seek. So, practicing breathless silence is almost a condition, a passport, required to enter the Spirit world.

THE APOLOGUE
THE WISHING TREE

Once upon a time there was a hermit of Hindustan named Hari, who wore the soles off his feel traveling through the rocky regions of the Himalaya Mountains in search of a certain wishing tree. The Indian legends describe this wishing tree as grown by fairies and endowed with magic powers, and with great and trusting qualities. Such miracle-making trees are said to have been grown by divine fairies for the benefit of true hermits who might happen to seek them.

Hermit Hari was spiritual, devoted, and firm in his determinations. Long had he searched for God but had received only glimpses of Him in meditation. Next to God, the coveted object which Hermit Hari searched for was the wishing tree, which was supposed to grant the fulfillment of any or all desires to the one who sat under it.

It seemed that, although Hari had failed to commune with God at will, nevertheless he had grown great occult powers due to his austerity, self-discipline, and occasional contacts with God. It seemed that the time had at last arrived when Hermit Hari's determined search had culminated into the accumulation of good Karma (action.) Through the magnetic power of the stored-up good Karma and Latent divine power manifested in Hari, he felt that he was going to be rewarded through the possession of a wishing tree.

Hermit Hari's bud of a wish seemed to grow into a flower of fulfillment when he apparently accidentally came across a great bushy tree in the course of his travels in the interior snow-walled valleys of the Himalayas, where very few people were able to desecrate this virgin magic land with their sordid footsteps. His strange intuition at once led him to recognize at first sight that the large bushy tree was a wishing tree. Suddenly, inspired by untold delight he raced toward the tree, and standing under it as per the magic directions, he wanted to test the occult powers of this famous "wishing tree."

Hermit Hari said to himself: "If it is a wishing tree, I desire the instantaneous materialization of a mighty castle." No sooner had he expressed the wish than the great castle suddenly materialized beside the

-Page Four-

tree, spreading out over a vast area as if it had always been there.

After dinner, Hermit Hari retired to a secluded room on the ground floor of the castle. This room was rather dark and dreary, and as Hermit Heiri lay there looking toward the open window which overlooked the forest, he sent forth another strong thought: "I am protected here by an army of soldiers but the window in my room is open and without bars. If a tiger comes and gets me, that will be the finish. "

Just then, as Hermit Hari continued in his attitude of fear, a big tiger bolted through the open window of the castle bedroom, and carried off the fear-frozen Hermit Hari, It was too late for him to realize that he was under the influence of a wishing tree which would grant both his good and his bad wishes, irrespective of whether they were actuated by good or by undesirable motives. The business of a wishing tree is to grant wishes, and it was true to form, according to the strength of the thought, whether negative or constructive.

My great Master often used the above story to illustrate that we all are living in this world beneath our magic-all-desire-fulfilling wishing tree of will power. Our will, being a reflection of the Almighty- Divine Will, has in it the seeds of almightiness.

Most people rejoice if, as the result of a continuous will and effort in an unknown past life, they suddenly succeed in this life, but most people, by continuously misusing their will power, suddenly reap evil consequences and forget that they were created by their own wishing tree of almighty will power. It is wise to wish for good things while you are standing beneath the almighty wishing tree of your will, and be careful that you do not concentrate upon fears, failures, diseases, ignorance and lack of God-contact. They might suddenly loom out of the unseen and cause you unending troubles.

Remember, you were born beneath the boughs of the wishing tree of high accomplishments and achievements and you must not think evil, as that will bring nothing but harm to you. Since you are under the Invisible Wishing Tree of the Divine Will in you, use it all the time to learn of God and attain Self-realization. In this way you will forever quench the thirst of all your desires.

HEALLTH CULTURE

THE SCIENCE OF NUTRITION

THE MINERAL SURPLUS (Continued) An acid surplus is sure to be harmful especially if it continues over a period of time. Prolonged weariness, a tired feeling upon waking in the morning and frequent colds are some of the conditions which indicate too much acid in the system. The necessity for a well-balanced diet is therefore evident. Besides the consumption of too great amounts of acid forming foods, excess acid in the body may be caused by overwork, lack of rest, lack of enough fresh air or sunlight, etc.

It is generally agreed that in order to keep the chemical balance of the body it is necessary for the normal individual to consume 80% of alkaline-forming foods and 20% acid-forming ones.

-Page Five-

The principal acid-forming elements are chlorine, sulphus and phosphorus, and the ones forming alkalis are sodium, potassium, calcium and magnesium. (These were discussed in detail in Inner Culture, Diet and Health page, each month from May 1935 to October 1936)

(Continued in Next Praeceptum)

OMELET WITH ASPARAGUS

5 eggs, separated	2 Teaspoons lemon juice
2 tablespoons whole wheat pastry flour	2 tablespoons butter asparagus, steamed
1/2 teaspoon vegetized salt	grated cheese
5 tablespoons evaporated milk	

Beat egg yolks until thick and lemon colored. Add flour salt and evaporated milk. Beat whites until foamy, add lemon juice and beat until stiff but not too dry. Lightly fold in yolks until thoroughly mixed. Heat butter in large frying or omelet pan. Pour in egg mixture and cook over a low flame until bottom is well browned, about 20 minutes. Set in a moderate oven to dry top. Put drained asparagus on heat proof platter and sprinkle with plenty of grated cheese. Place in oven until omelet is ready. Fold omelet and slide it into platter beside asparagus. Garnish with sautéd mushrooms.

RASPBERRY SHERBET NO. I

3 cups fresh raspberries or two cups canned raspberries 1 cup water	2 tablespoons lemon juice 1/2 teaspoon grated lemon rind

1 1/3 cups (1 can) sweetened condensed milk

Rub berries through strainer to remove seeds. Stir in water, lemon juice and lemon rind. Add sweetened condensed milk and blend thoroughly. Freeze in freezer. Makes one quart.

PRAECEPTUM INSPIRATION
HOW TO OVERCOME SORROW

By knowing the difference between hallucinations and subconscious suggestions, you can develop the super consciousness through which you will receive the messages of those who have gone. Say a prayer for them and they will receive your message. Always concentrate between your eyebrows when thinking of them, but never keep your mind filled with sorrow.

If Mr, Sorrow comes, do not give him strength by acknowledging his presence. If you feed him with the nectar of your tears, he will stay. He will soon spread all over the bedroom of your life. The minute he arrives, laugh at him. Apply the fists, limbs, and elbows of your will power and throw him out of the chamber of your life. Thus you will win a physical bout against sorrow. Then, too, this will be a metaphysical victory over sorrow.

Resurrect your real smiles from beneath the tomb of sadness. Smile when the storms of suffering shriek around you. Say: "I have launched my boat on a dark sea; I have heard Thy call. Thou knowest that I am coming." God knows that you are on the sea of trials; He knows that you are moving your bark. He knows that you must battle the storms that are around you. You are clouded by ignorance. You do not see the Spirit in everything.

PRAECEPTUM AFFIRMATION

"I want secretly to remain in the caves of Divine love in souls and silently serve them with invisible thoughts of helpfulness."

-Page Six-

आत्मानं विद्धि

REALIZE THY SELF

YOGODA SAT-SANGA

FORTNIGHTLY INSTRUCTIONS

YOUR PRAECEPTUM

No. 136

Thy Self-realization will blossom forth from thy Soulful Study

TO BE CONFIDENTIALLY RESERVED FOR MEMBER'S USE ONLY

YOGODA SAT-SANGA FORTNIGHTLY INSTRUCTIONS
BY

PARAMHANSA   YOGANANDA

(To be Confidentially Reserved FOR MEMBER'S USE ONLY)
EELECTRIFY US WITH THY WISDOM

"Heavenly Father, Giver of Life, we are floating oon Thy
cosmic bosom, we are dancing on the waves of life and death, but
behind all these Thou art the motion of Immortality. Teach us
to behold the waves of eternal life. Take our consciousness
away from change to the changeless; take our consciousness away
from the passing joys of life.

O Thou Beloved Spirit, behind the waves of the sky,
bbehind the waves of light, behind the waves of life, behind
the waves of changing scenery -- O Infinite Beauty of all
beauties, O Joy of all happiness, O Immortality, reveal
Thyself unto our consciousness.

Make us feel that we are Thy Immortal children come
hhere just to play and show our immortality which comes from
Thee. Rejuvenate our bodies, minds, and souls with Thy
eternal light; electrify us with Thy message of immortality;
electrify us with Thy message of wisdom.

O Christ, O God, purify our consciousness with Thy living
luminosity. Saturate our souls with the fragrance of Thy glory,
and may we manifest Thy consciousness in the cradle of all
space and in the song of the birds and the Song of the spreading
dawn over the hills.

THE LAW OF KARMA

Your physical body was not manufactured by God alone. You have done lots
of work on it. God made you in his image, but some of you have desecrated that
image of God. Some faces reflect godliness and others reflect evil and cruelty.
It is all due to your actions of this life and past lives. What you have sown,
you must reap now or in the future. There is no escape save through God-contact
and God-realization. There is no God punishing you or rewarding you. You are
your own judge. Either you are punishing yourself through evil or freeing
yourself through God.

Karma is the law of action. Mind or body in a specific form of movement is
termed "action." Every action mentally or physically performed, consciously or
unconsciously, has a specific effect on the life of man. These effects, good or
bad, of actions in this present life remain lodged in the subconsciousness, and
those brought over from past existences are hidden in the superconsciousness,
ready like seeds to germinate under the influence of a suitable environment.
Such traces, or effects, are not left in the subconsciousness or
superconsciousness if the actions are not identified with feeling or personal
attachment. The ideal is not inertia, but is rather to cognize experiences
without desire for the fruit of action. Action is necessary but must be
performed with unselfish ambition if karmic chains are to be avoided.

"Purushakar" is the term used for seeds produced by present actions.
"Samskar" means seeds produced by past actions. Action that is performed by free
will and intelligence is called "free action" or

"Purushakar," which means action performed by free will. "Samskar" means action performed by influence. Those actions which come under "Samskar" are those past habits, or actions of past lives, which come as the instincts and habits of this life. That is the inner environment which governs your life. Then there is also the outer environment -- the planets, world, nation, family, neighborhood, books, and so forth. These all influence man's actions.

Freedom doesn't mean to be able to do anything you please. You must understand to what degree you are free and how much you are influenced by bad habits. To be good just because it has become a habit to be good, is not freedom. To be tempted is not bad, but to be able to overcome temptation is great, and is freedom, for then you are guided by free will and free choice only. To be good, not being good just from habit, but acting only because you think you should be good, and because you have the will power to be good -- that is freedom. That gives you real freedom.

THE LAW OF ACTION IS BASED UPON THE LAW OF CAUSE AND EFFECT   The Law of Karma, or action, is scientific (subject to the law of causation), philosophic, moral, and practical.

"The Lord is a God of Knowledge, and by Him actions are weighed." -- Samuel I, 2:3.

Karma exists for man so that he may return from multiplicity to unity. Man's transgression of Karmic Law delays his evolution.

Reasons why all should know the Law of Karma:
To avoid future mistakes.
To escape or minimize the results arising from errors already made.
To be able to act rightly, free from external influence and desire.
To understand the various influences that may be employed to modify the effects of Karma.
To be able to consciously and independently create Karma, in accordance with right judgment.
To be liberated from the clutch of Karma by understanding it; knowledge is freedom.

Springs of Action:
Impartial reason of man.
Acquired habits of present life.
Impulses acquired in previous states of existence. Influence of environment.

We are held responsible for the acts of our innate impulses, because even though we do not remember them, we ourselves have created them.

Examples of enigmatic karmic results:
The virtuous and vicious man.
Solving the paradoxical manifestations of Karma.

CHART OF INFLUENCES OPERATING UPON HUMAN ACTIONS

1. Present World Civilization	2. Present Family Influence	3. Hereditary Influence	4. Specific Environment Influence

World influence, national Karma, family influence, influence of impulses, those acquired in previous lives, hereditary influences, influences at birth, those acquired through reason, effect of independent will upon action, superstition and repeated affirmations of mothers or other close childhood companions, such as "John is a bad boy."

Decrease the percentage of undesirable karmic action and increase the percentage of your independent action. Individual as well as collective action produces vibrations in the ether that affect the world in good or bad ways.

Act according to the Law of Karma and thus rise above it.
Think before you act.
Conscious Karma.
Roast karmic seeds of past actions in the fire of desireless action.
Diagnose all paradoxical events of Karma.
Control so-called "fate."
Above all, act lawfully to rise above the law.

KARMA IS NOT FATALISM   The law of action, or karma is not fatalism. Whatever you have done may be changed. Why does one become ill? Because he has transgressed laws in this life or a a past life. Many people confuse Karma with what they call "fate," When you forget the cause of something that you were responsible for, and when the effect of that cause comes after a long time, and you are unable to explain why that effect has come to you, then you call it "fate."

The idea of fate springs from ignorance of the real causes that operate in the production of an event. The effects of actions are generally forgotten; but they remain hidden, ready to germinate into further effects. We mistakenly think these sudden and unexpected events of life are caused by an external fate, but there is really no such force as fate.

Our lives are governed by our past actions. Different habits are controlling our different lives. Everything comes from the past.

This Lesson is not given to try to make you a fatalist, and go through life fooling beaten, thinking that everything disagreeable is happening to you. Nothing rules you. You are the architect of your destiny.

YOU REAP WHAT YOU SOW   Those who acquired riches, health, prosperity, wisdom, or spirituality in past lives are born with specific advantages from the beginning of their present lives. Likewise, those who created poverty, disease, and ignorance, through negligence in past lives, will meet those conditions from the very beginning of their present lives.

This law of action, namely, that you reap in this life what you sowed in a past life, is a just law. It takes away from God the stigma of being an autocrat who creates some healthy brains and some moron brains just for variety. This law of action explains the apparent injustices from the very birth of human life. It also gives hope to all, for the sinner is a sinner not because his parents gave him a sinful brain, but because he created it in a past life and thus attracted sinful parents.

Medical doctors would say that John inherited insanity from his insane father, but the metaphysician would say that John attracted an insane parent in this life because his Soul brought back the tendency of insanity from his former life. This latter doctrine alone gives faith in the justice and wisdom of the working of God's laws in the lives of men.

If a person lives one hundred years, he has time to struggle against evil and become good, but if a baby dies at the age of five he is given reason and free choice, but no time to use them, in order to win the battle of life. Such a baby must die because of a former transgression, and must be born again and again in various schools of life, until he educates himself to right behavior.

The main reasons for people having various grades of latent health or ill-health, or good or bod tendencies, can only be satisfactorily explained when records of former lives are sought. Besides, for one hundred years of sin one cannot have eternal punishment, and what would be done with Souls whose lives are equally good and evil? The latter's Astral bodies cannot be sawed in halves and half sent to heaven and the other half to hades.

We reap what we sow, hence all the visitations of ills are not due to our parents of this life or to grandparents, but are due to our sins in this life or past lives. We are never sinful enough to deserve eternal hades. Sin is a graft, a parasite. Essentially we are perfect Souls. Hence, to work out sins, Souls must come to earth. After they work out their error-yielding sins, they become free to become One with God again.

Souls who reach perfection never need to come back to earth again. A bandit, when he dies, does not become an angel just by the virtue of death. Those who live a desultory life, and are yet expecting to be angels by the virtue of death, will have a long wait and a disillusionment. We are the same after sleep as before it, so, sinful or virtuous Souls are the same after death.

Since millions of people die in imperfection, they cannot remain forever in heaven, but have to come back to regain the lost perfection of their Souls. As Souls, we are already rays of God's fire. We can remain hidden in sin just as the sun hides behind a cloud, only for a little while, but not forever. All the sins of the Cosmos could not destroy our luminosity, only we must remove the torturing, choking clouds of ignorance and manifest our everlasting light. We must not reason this way: "Since we must be redeemed some day, let us tarry on the way." That is foolish, for sin is very painful and one must not willingly let the Soul suffer for aeons of time through one's ignorance.

All effects or seeds of our past actions (Karma) can be destroyed by roasting them in the fire of meditation, concentration, the light of superconsciousness, and right actions, free from desire for the fruit of action.

THE APOLOGUE

KING KUVERA AND BUDDHIMAN

King Kuvera had a favorite minister named Buddhiman. The King was a great connoisseur of human personality. Much jealousy prevailed among his courtiers, all of whom highly resented his attention to Buddhiman, which they construed as nothing but extreme blindness and partiality on his part. The king had waited long to find an occasion in which he could show his other courtiers the real reason for his respect for Buddhiman's judgment.

One Evening the King and his courtiers were sitting in the parlor when they all heard outside in the distance a noise which sounded like a marriage procession.

So the King asked his first courtier to go out and find out all about the procession. The first courtier returned after fifteen minutes. The King asked: "What did you find?" The first courtier replied: "Your Majesty, it is nothing but a marriage ceremony."

Then the King again asked the first courtier: "Who are the bride and the bridegroom?" "Well, your Majesty, I didn't ask that. Shall I go and find out?"

The King became displeased and sent a second courtier to find out all about the marriage procession. After the second courtier returned after one-half hour, his Majesty inquired: "Tell me now, who are the people."

"They are the son-in-law and daughter of the neighboring prince." Then the King asked: "What are their names?"

The second courtier failed to answer the question of the King. So the King sent a third courtier and when he returned after three-quarters of an hour, the King asked: "Please tell me the names of the parties getting married."

"Prince Rama and Princess Sita, your Majesty." Then the King asked: "How old are they?" The third courtier remained silent and could not reply to the queries of the King.

So at last the King, displeased, called Buddhiman, who was sitting in the next room, unaware of all the King's questionings. The King casually asked: "Buddhiman, will please find out about the procession which is playing a band in the distance."

After an hour and a half, Buddhiman returned. Then the King asked him:
Question 1: "What is the procession about?"
Answer: "It is a marriage procession."
Question 2: "Who are getting married?"
Answer: "Neighboring Prince and Princess."
Question 3: "Who are they?"
Answer: "Rama and Sita."
Question 4: "How old are they?"
Answer: "Prince Rama is 25 and the princess is about 20 years old."

Question 5: "How much dowry did the prince get according to Hindu law?"
Answer: "One hundred thousand, your Majesty."
Question 6: "When will they pass by this place again?"
Answer: "In the third morning early."

The the courtiers saw the difference between their personalities and that of Buddhiman. They, in spite of repeated questionings, only inquired partially about the marriage procession and hastily returned, whereas Buddhiman took enough time and gave enough thoughtful attention to find out all about the marriage procession, so that no matter what the King asked, he could reply to his questions.

So in this world there are people of various personalities. Every business man should desire an employe with an intelligent personality, and every person should study himself in order to remedy all his defects of personality, to emerge gradually as a balanced, all-round developed character.

HEALTH   CULTURE
THE   SCIENCE   OF   NUTRITION

THE MINERAL SURPLUS (Continued) In general the foods containing a predominance of acid forming eelements are meats, fish, eggs, and the grain products such as breakfast cereals, bread and marconi (sic). Most of the fruits aand vegetables contain more of the alkali-forming elements. While lemons, ooranges, grapefruit and limes are acid to the taste, their final result is alkaline. This is because the acid which is tasted is organic acid and this is so completely changed by oxidation during the process oof digestion and absorption that their ultimate reaction is due to their mineral content which is predominantly alkaline.

The use of plenty of milk, vegetables and fruits will keep the ddiet balanced for the normal individual. However, it is well to note wwhat is meant by "plenty" for it requires "the alkaline surplus from one quart of milk, four or five vegetables, and two or three fruits to bbalance the acid surplus from an egg, a dish of cereal, one portion of meat, and two or three slices of bread. " (No citation)

P R A E C E P T U M   I N S P I R A T I O N

DO NOT BUILD YOUR HOPES UPON THIS LIFE
I

What is death? When you close your eyes, it is dark, but when yyou open them again It is light. Death is similar to that state. God is everywhere but your eyes are so closed that you do not behold the beauty of the Beloved. Break the cords that bind you.

This earth is not meant for heavenly manifestation, but to llook into the futility of life. Gloom after gloom, delusion after delusion, this mirage on the desert of our consciousness must be destroyed and we must find our True Selves beneath the veil of reality.

Do not try to build your hopes upon this life. Where is yyour safety? You are safe only when you are castled in the realization of God. Oceans cannot drown your fire for God. You are the wave that shall become the ocean. There is no death, but only life. The living testimony of the life of Christ must be the guiding eevidence that reincarnation does exist.

Jesus Christ was the product of his own efforts. That is the cconsolation before you and me, that every moment of life must be filled with the consciousness of God, so that as we go along we may some day reach the shores of eternal freedom.

P R A E C E P T U M   A F F I R M A T I O N

I am enveloped in the aureole of Thy all-protecting Omnipresence in birth, in sorrow, in joy, in death, in activity, in meditation, in ignorance, in trials, and in final emancipation, all the time -- ALWAYS.

PUBLISHED BY

Yogoda Sat-Sanga

(Self-Realization Fellowship & Shyamacharan Mission

Founder—Paramhansa Yogananda

President—Sister Daya.

Yogoda Math, Dakshineswar, P. O. Ariadah.

Dist : 24. Parganas, West-Bengal. India.

YOGODA SAT-SANGA PRESS

YOGODA SAT-SANGA FORTNIGHTLY INSTRUCTIONS
BY
PARAMHANSA
YOGANANDA

WE OFFER UNTO THEE THE DEVOTION OF OUR HEARTS

Divine Father, receive the devotion of our hearts. We have brought a bouquet of minds and a bouquet of devotion of all Souls to offer unto Thee. Receive the bouquet of our devotion in the temple of OM.

Thy vast temple dome includes all temples, all churches. In the walless temple we worship Thee with the love of our inner Being. Receive the offering of our hearts. Tear away the veil of silence and show us Thy Face of Power. Tear away the veil of matter and show us Thy Face of Energy.

O Spirit, we behold Thee through the windows of stars and the doors of the moon and the sun. We behold Thee through the portals of ignorance and devotion. We behold Thee through the portals of all prayers, but we find Thee in the portals of our love.

Father, naughty or good, we are Thy children; receive us in Thy temple. Burn away our grossness our weakness, our disease, and our ignorance. Be Thou the only King on the throne of our desire. Be Thou the only ambition on the throne of our ambition. Be Thou the ocean in which the rivers of our desires meet.

KARMA'S RELATION TO
HEALTH AND PROSPERITY

Success in this life depends upon the ratio between past success tendencies and present judicious will efforts for success.
If the tendency of a past life of success was weak, and the efforts for success are weak, then financial success in this life will be meager, almost negligible, but if the success of a past life was strong and the present life is marked by inactivity and inertia, then, in order to be successful, one must be born in a rich family or suddenly inherit a fortune. Some individuals who grew tired accumulating riches in a past life, due to the repulsion developed against money before death, might be born in poverty and struggle but might inherit lots of money by a so-called stroke of good luck, or through a sudden inheritance or lucky small investments.

No one can be a financial success or a failure in all lives, for human consciousness changes by its own weakness or strength or through the changes of environment. Real financial success of all lives, until emancipation, consists in the ability of one destroying all the seen tendencies of failure by the power of super-concentration.

A Yogi may not possess much, but through his ability to focus his mind he learns to create at will the financial success he needs for himself. Of course Yogis do not entertain any desires for themselves but only the desire that "God's love shall reign on the shrine of their soul forever. " They also pray: "Heavenly Father, may we kindle Thy love in the flaming altar-hearts of others. "

Blind selfishness in the root cause of unbalanced prosperity.
Rich people who acquire success fighting failure, but later become lazy ignoring the agonies of others who fail, may lose their wealth by wrong investment or may attract poverty in the next life. Many are the romances of Dame Fortune with her consort, the Lord of Judgment -- Karma (law of action, or law of Cause and Effect).

If one has not been prosperous for many lives, he should know that he has buried somewhere in his sub-conscious mind the success tendencies of some past lives, which if roused, can help him. The chronic failure must remember that he has his almighty, all conquering will, only it might be sleeping and lazy due to lack of initiative or undaunted repented efforts. The chronic failure must not waste time neglecting and paralyzing his will. By the repeated efforts and knocking of his will power, ultimately he will surely rouse the success tendencies sleeping in the dark chamber of subconsciousness.

Most people start out to adopt a career or profession without considering the influence of pre-natal karmic habits. That is why born artists fail when they attempt to act the role of business man. That is why the born Spiritual man does usually not succeed as a business man. A man cannot be an absolute failure unless he hypnotizes himself to think so; a man is an absolute failure when neither his judgment nor the judgment of others can convince him that he can be a success.

TYPES CLASSIFIED AND EXPLAINED   There are different degrees of health and many kinds of diseases. Some people are so healthy and shining that they belong to the waterproof fireproof "Asbestos clan. " The health of some is like a fine watch which goes well when proper care is taken but at the slightest neglect it begins to suffer. They are the "Mechanical Type. " Some are healthy all the time, but when they get sick, they get very sick. They are the "Born Healthy Type. " Some are healthy but weak. They are the "Medium Healthy Type. " Let us trace the past karmas of these types. Let us diagnose their prenatal and post-natal habits.

(1) The "Asbestos Type" of health is born of the accumulated health habits of many lives (including the last incarnation) plus natural health habits and habits of exercise of this life. This Type of individual was probably a Yogi in many lives and he can destroy all the post seed of ill health if he practices Yoga principles (scientific union of body mind and soul with God by scientific psychological methods of meditation and discipline) in this life. If he just undergoes physical exercise and proper diet, but does not practice yoga principles, he may retain his health with chances of losing it late in life. The person who properly practices Yoga principles (Yogic concentration as taught in former lessons on concentration and meditation) overcomes little health transgressions and the accumulated, unhealthy seed tendencies of the erroneous health habits of this life. The aspirant after the "Asbestos Health Type" must not depend only upon past health tendencies and the physical exercises of this life; he must also keep burning away the accumulating seeds of the unhealthy actions of this life, no matter how small they may be.

(2) The "Born Healthy Type" lives on his accumulated past health seed tendencies, plus fairly right living and exercises, but no Yogic practice, and gets sick when the principles of acquired health wears

off and the little unroasted ill health transgressions of this life get strong.

(3)   The "Medium Type" is acquired by the past seed tendencies of health acquired by will power and not by the power of the mind plus physical exercise. That is why this type is born healthy but weak. Physical exercise in this life would remove that weakness.

(4)   The "mechanical Health Type" is born of the mechanically healthy man in the past, who obeyed health laws through fear and nervous caution. That is why these Health Types have health only as long as they follow rules. Too much dependence upon law and not enough upon God and self reliance makes one become "Health-law bound. " Do not be a slave to law; use the law to serve you.

(5)   The "Die-Hard Type" is born due to the equal power of sickness and health tendencies. That is why they have health and sickness alternately. If you have great devotion and are obedient to God, you will have a great devotion but all the time broke God's hygienic, mental, and spiritual laws.

To destroy sprouted chronic disease seeds and lurking disease seeds, it must be remembered that the recharging body-battery exercises, given in early lessons, must be practiced with deep concentration, followed by the concentration and meditation lessons. When practicing these lessons, the consciousness of health, energy, and power must be kept predominant. When this power is felt all over the body as an incessant influx of vitality, then the ray of vital sense must be switched to the brain and held there for a long time. In this way the vital power will roast out all lurking past disease tendencies.

During meditation, the Yogi feels the power of concentration in between the eyebrows, and peace all over the body. Whenever he specially wants to rid the brain cells of past failure or sickness seeds, he must switch on that peace and concentration power to the brain. The entire peace feeling of the body and the power of concentration between the eyebrows must be continuously transferred to and felt in the brain.

FAILURE AND ILL HEALTH TENDENCIES Removed by WILL POWER

Every business man should know that good fortune is dependent upon the law of successful action of the past and also continued successful activities of this life. A man striving for permanent success must meditate every morning and night, and when the super-conscious peace and concentration rays burst out, then the nocturnal blackness of restlessness will disappear; then he must turn those rays on the brain and scorch out the lurking seeds of past failures and stimulate the success tendencies. He is the really prosperous and healthy man who can remove failures and ill health by his power of will, and all failure and ill health tendencies which might have, without warning, entered the cells of the brain due to slight negligences of this life.

The best way to escape the effect of a specific action is to destroy it in this life. You must destroy now the undesirable things you have created. To fight Karma, you have the good forces of all lives plus God, and contact with Him eternally.

When all the evil seeds of tendencies are roasted in the brain, each microscopic brain cell becomes the throne of brilliant king of wisdom, inspiration, and health, who sings and preaches the glory of God to the intelligent body cells. Such people are rally free. Such people can be free-born in other incarnations. They only reincarnate in-order to wipe away the tears of others. Such people carry halos of invisible healing light. Wherever they go, they scatter the light of prosperity and health.

THB APOLOGUE
THE CULPRIT AND THE JUDGE

A Mohammedan judge, called Kazi, who was squatted on a large wooden divan, looked comfortably important as he gazed at the awe-struck clerks, chaprasi (office bearers) policemen and chained criminals who surrounded him. The clerks and policemen of the village, being ignorant, were afraid of the all-powerful all-wrathful much dreaded decree administrator, the honorable Kazi. The criminals waited, trembling in their clanking chains, anticipating a dire fate at the hands of mood-governed Kazi, but on this particular day, among all the criminals to be sentenced by the Kazi, there was one who was dauntless.

Mr. Ali, the village Kalu (oil dealer and cultivator) not only did not tremble, he smiled at the judge, whose sacred authority was horribly mutilated, and red with rage, he bellowed "Sirrah, criminal Ali, you will hang for your laughter unless you proceed forthwith to confess your guilt. " Smiling again, Ali with his vocational craftiness said: "Honoured Kazi, your two-horned ox wandered on my pasture lands and fought with my ox and broke both of his precious horns. I have a damage suit against you, sir, and I want prompt redress."

The Kazi scrached his head and tried to wiggle out of this trap of dilema. At last assuming his momentarily forgotten authoritative mimicry of fierceness, he shouted, "Office clerk, bring hither my Lal- Pothi (red leather law Book). " The law book was brought. The Kazi quickly opened it at the centre pages, and even though, it was upside down, he pretended to the ignorant people that he was reading from the unquestionable authority of the law book, the absolute judgment in connection with the case brought against him by Ali.

The Kazi just used the open law book as a ruse and started to read his then and there made-up-law: " The red book says that the oil dealers are slick and slippery like oil, and because of this proverbial cunning, they should live by there wits, and this one should not have been foolish enough to lose control over his own stupid ox and allow it to fight with my powerful ox. Beasts are non-intelligent. My beast broke the horns of your beast because both were beasts. Case dismissed.

The village onlookers, in the little court room, became wrathfully bewildered at this unjust judgment, and even as they were muttering their thoughts of injustice done to the oil dealer, clever Ali, with a smile on his face, launched forth as follows: "Honoured Kazi, I beg your pardon, I made a little mistake in my statement to you, which I must correct. " "What do you meant? " asked the Kazi. "Why, Honoured Dealer of Justice, my beast, fighting with your beast, broke the precious horns of your beast. "

At this the Kazi was red with wrath and shouted: "Hey clerk, bring the second Lal-Pothi (red book). " The second red law book was brought in. Forthwith the Kazi pretended to read from is "The red book says: "Proverbially slick oil dealers should only live by their wits and should never be foolish enough to breed stupid beasts which break the horns of intelligent beasts owned by intelligent law makers. " Mr. Ali, you should have lived only by the display of your intelligence and you should never have harboured a vicious beast. The penalty is that you must provide an intelligent ox with two horns in place of my hornless animal and one hundred dollars fine for all the trouble you have caused me, and for telling an untruth in the beginning. "

This story illustrates a common fault in our daily life partiality to ourselves. Personal interest should never bias, warp, or prejudice our judgment. Though we love to forgive ourselves, we find it difficult to forgive others.

Most people think that they themselves, like ancient kings, can do no wrong, or at least are very blind to their own faults. It is customary with most minds to magnify the faults of others, whereas those same minds minimize, or resolve to nothingness, their own errors. If one demands justice from others, he must also be just enough to demand justice from himself. If he hates the fault of others, he must learn to hate his own faults too. If anyone feels the pangs of injustice done to him, he must also be commiserative about the injustice he perpetrates against others. If your feelings are hurt easily, you must not indulge in hurting the feelings of others. If you want to be justly treated, you must learn to treat others right. Abuse of your authority may stifle the voice of your enemies for a time, but it can never destroy the dynamite of hatred against you which might be secretly piled up to explode under you and blow up at some unexpected moment.

HEALTH CULTURE

THE SCIENCE OF NUTRITION THE MINERAL SURPLUS (Continued)

Besides keeping the daily diet balanced, modern nutritionists consider it wise for normal people to go on an alkalinizing diet for a few days once in a while. This means using only fruit and vegetable juices, and vegetable (sic) mostly uncooked.

This may be done to suit individual convenience. At all times it is important that care should be taken to keep the diet balanced.

PRAECEPTUM INSPIRATION
HOW TO PLAY THE DRAMA OF LIFE

In each life time, man is given many chances to play comedy, tragedy, or the joyous drama of life, according to the wishes of the producer Karma past action) and then he has to go out of that particular picture forever. In spite of the phenomena of reincarnation, each person lives as the same individual but once, because he does not recall his previous lives.

It is wonderful that each soul, although immortal, is able to remember only his present life. It is well that he knows only that he is to play this drama of Life once and is then to be called back to the place from whence he came. Many people would postpone the efforts to do their best if they knew that they were to have another chance, and many would have the courage to try to play the drama well if they knew that they had played very poorly in their former lives.

Your Karma cannot be destroyed without the contact of God. When you realize that you and your father are one, then all the seeds of Karma must go. You must roast the past seeds of bad Karma with the fire of wisdom and then they will not germinate. Bring in the light of wisdom and you will drive out all the darkness of undesirable past actions and be free in God.

PRAECEPTUM AFFIRMATION

"I am beholding, through the eyes of all. I am working
through the hands, and I am walking through all feet. The
brown, olive, yellow, red, and black bodies are all mine. "

YOGODA SAT-SANGA FORTNIGHTLY
BY
PARAMHANSA YOGANANDA

UNITE OUR HEARTS ON ONE ALTAR

Father, destroy the imaginary barrier walls that separate brother from brother and show us that Thou art the Spirit ever- existing on the altar of our hearts. Bring all nations to an under standing. Unite our hearts on one altar; unite all temples to be Thy Church.

Father, electrify our health with Thy perfection, electrify our souls with Thy wisdom, electrify our minds with Thy power. No more forgetfulness. Through centuries of wandering, at last on the pathway of remembrance we behold Thee. Open the windows of our hearts, behold us everywhere, and teach us to behold Thee everywhere. "He who watcheth Me always, him do I watch always. He never loses sight of Me, nor do I lose sight of him."

Father, reveal Thyself through the portals of the dawn. Teach us to feel Thy muscles in the rays of the sunshine. Teach us to behold Thee through the pale portals of the moon, and through the portals of the evening and the twilight. Teach us to behold Thee through the temples of night. Enter Thou in our Souls through the portals of our hearts' devotion and through our prayers. Inflame our Being, ignite our ignorance. Vanish darkness evermore from our minds. All our love and devotion, everything that is noble, we lay at Thy feet.

SOURCES OF REJUVENATION PART I

All forms of motion, like waves, rise, remain for a tim, then dissolve. The human body, which looks so compact and solid, is, in fact, nothing but a bundle of motions. Motion signifies any moving power. The human body is a bundle of forces whirling together in ultra-rapid motion. As the ocean has dancing waves on the surface and a second strong undercurrent beneath, likewise, the body is not just one kind of motion; it is a conglomeration of forces and motions, whirling within motions.

First of all, the solid flesh is made of very tiny cells, blood corpuscles and particles. The bones are made of small cells, portions of water, and various chemicals. All the tiny cells are grouped together by a strange chemical force. By knotting the cells in various mysterious ways, the different kinds of cerebral, nervous, connective, osseous, and muscular tissues and organs are formed.

HOW LIVING CELLS ARE REJUVENATED   Tissue is the general name for all the different forms of materials of which the body is composed. Then again, the same invisible force biologically arranges the cells so that some form into hard bones wonderfully worked into a skeleton frame, around which flesh can cling. This superstructure of flesh and bones has, on the external side, been made dependent upon the ultra-violet rays in the sunshine, upon oxygen and good food, and upon pure liquids, such as water, fruit juices, and so forth. Oh the internal side, these living cells, which constitute the flesh, bones, and all tissues, are kept rejuvenated by thoughts and by biological forces.

-Page One-

The body is a combination of cells which are made of moving molecules These cellular molecules are made of whirling atoms, protons, and electrons These cellular and molecular atoms and electrons in turn are made of semi-intelligent sparks of biological vital forces The vital sparks are condensed sparks of God's thoughts Therefore, we see that the physical body is a bundle of motions On the surface of this body are found the chemical motions and the dance of cells Below the surface of the waves of chemical and cellular motion are found the dancing waves of molecular motion.

Below the molecular motion move the waves of atomic motion. Below the atomic motion is found the electroprotonic motion Below the electroprotonic motion are found the dancing, waving sparks of vital forces.

Below the surface of the vital sparks lie the waves of sensation Below the waves of sensation lie the waves of thought, feeling, and will force Below all the above layers of waves, the Ego is found to remain hidden.

VITAL FORCE IS THE MANIFESTATION OF A VASTER FORCE   Now we find the body like an ocean of motion containing various layers of motion On the surface the body appears to be a solid mass, occupying a small portion of space, but we see that these cellular waves are manifestations of a vaster area of dancing molecular waves Likewise, the molecular waves are manifestations of a vaster area of atomic waves The atomic waves are manifestations of vaster waves of vital force The vital force is a manifestation of the vast force of all forms of subconsciousness, super-consciousness, Christ Consciousness and Cosmic Consciousness.

On the surface, the body as chemical motion is small and dependent upon chemicals drawn from the earth, and upon food, water and sunshine, but on the internal side the body and its chemical cellular motions are nothing but condensed waves of Cosmic Consciousness Therefore, the body as a solid substance occupies a very small space, but since the body on the internal side is condensed Cosmic Consciousness, it is vast and omnipresent.

SPIRIT IS CHANGELESSNESS As the wave cannot exist without the ocean, so it can be said that the ocean has become the wave In the same way, the body must not be isolated and spoken of as existing in Spirit, but it can be said that the ocean of Spirit, or Cosmic Consciousness, has become the motion body, or the waves of all finite manifestations The body is constantly decaying Decay does not mean annihilation It means certain changes of motion which we, as human beings, fear and dislike.

The nature of matter is change The nature of Spirit is changelessness. The body is born It changes through growth from babyhood to old age and then degenerates and dies During all this time, the tissues are passing through continual changes Human beings like the changing dancing waves of vitality called "youth."

In the inner spiritual source the body motions are constantly flooded and rejuvenated by the motions of consciousness, including subconsciousness, superconsciousness, Christ Consciousness and Cosmic Consciousness On the external, or material side, the body is reinforced with floods of chemicals, oxygen, and sunshine.

It is very strange that the chemical motions of the body have to be kept alive and dancing by the forces of food, chemicals, and sunshine, while it would be entirely possible to keep them alive and flooded with vitality from the inner source of Cosmic Consciousness The body, being motion, cannot live without motion Therefore, it has to be kept stirred with life externally by food forces, and internally it has to be kept dancing with vitality derived from Cosmic Consciousness.

YOUTH CAN BE MADE STABLE   It is evident that a certain bodily motion, called "youth," can be made stable by reinforcing it with a harmonious supply of power from the internal energy and from external sources which keep stirring life in the body.

-Page Two-

Death is not cessation of motion forever, but only cessation of the temporary body state, until the inner motions of the vital forces of Ego, Soul, and Karma can reappear as materialized motion in a new body.

The Soul, by processes of incarnation, rejuvenates the body into a new body by changing the atomic vibrations and tendencies of a decayed body, or by transforming new vibrations of energy and chemicals into a new body. If the soul is powerful enough, it can re-change an old body into new instead of discarding it entirely, weaving another garment of flesh out of new electro-vitalic threads.

THE INFINITE SOURCE OF ENERGY   God's omnipresent electric energy is flowing into your body all the time, but you are not conscious of it. Remember, all Nature pays highest respects to God. Remember that God's power is with you, but the trouble is, you do not make connections. Realize that you are living directly by God and every other power becomes weak without the power of God.

Food, oxygen and sunshine can only give you health to a limited extent. You must know how to receive perfect health from the Infinite Source. Why? Because the physical sources are like little batteries, which play out quickly, but the Infinite Source contains the infinite dynamo which can continuously pour strength, happiness, and power into the soul. That is why it is so important to receive everything from the Infinite Source.

THE MIND AS A SOURCE OF ENERGY You must know the law by which you can receive power and strength from the Infinite Source. First you must convince yourself, that thought is reality. Everything you see is the thought of God. He had to first think of this earth before He made it.

Many people think that mind is the product of the body. The design and intellectual arrangements in the body clearly show that the human system is the product of a Superior Mind. Hence, the mind is the chief factor which governs the body.

The mind must never have suggested to it the human limitations of sickness, old age, and death, but it should be constantly, inwardly told: I am the Infinite, which has become the body. The body as a manifestation of Spirit is the ever-youthful Spirit."

The mind, being the brain, feeling, and perception of all living cells, can keep the body alert or depressed. The mind is the King, and all its cellular subjects behave exactly according to the mood of their Royal Master. As we consider the nutritive value of our daily menus, so must we consider the psychologican (sic) menus which nourish the mind.

Metaphysicians say that the body is not only an electro-magnetic wave, but it is a wavelet of consciousness floating in the sea of Divine Intelligence. Every day you must increase the strength of your body, the strength of your mind and Soul, and make your body, mind, and Soul a temple of eternal power, where God may reign.

SHORT APOLOGUES
ONE METHOD OF CURING A WAYWARD SON

A man once said to me: "Don't you think that we are all great sinners? And because of this, won't God send us to the region of fire and brimstone?" I replied: "Why do you say that?" He answered: "Because I know it." Then I said: "Listen; you are a very happy man, but there is one problem that is bothering you. You have a very wicked son. "

-Page Three-

He said: "Are you a fortune teller? " I answered: "No, but I tell people how to overcome misfortunes, and I have a wonderful solution to your problem of how to correct your son."

Then I said: "Can you find three confidential friends who will bind your son from head to foot? Then heat an oven very hot and slip your son in the oven. In this way you will end your misery and your son's too."

He said: "Why, that is terrible! How dare you think such a thing."

I replied: "My dear man, a little while ago you said that God was punishing us and that we were all wicked and would be thrown into fire and brimstone. Although your son is bad, still you can't stand the thought of hurting him. Don't you think that God is a little better than you are? He would'nt hurt us, His children, would He?"

THE MAN WHO COULDN'T Be BEATEN

A and B are fighting. They are both almost done for. A says, "I cannot fight any longer, " but B says, "I will give just one more punch even though I can hardly move. " And B wins the bout.

If you think that you cannot go on any longer and then you make an extra effort, then you will see that Divine Will will take care of your will. When man's will refuses to acknowledge the limitations of the human will, then his will becomes Divine Will. Whenever you meet resistance, do not give up. If you go on exercising your will power, you will suddenly find that your will has become dynamic. When it becomes linked with Divine Will.

THE SAINT AND THE GREEDY MAN

A saint and a greedy man were eating. The Saint said: "This is fine; I enjoy food." The greedy man said: "Well, I never ate this before," so he eats and eats until he Fills himself. The greedy man, when he dies, was greedy for food so he had to come back again to work out that greed. But the Saint said: "I enjoy food but I don't miss it when I don't have it because I know that I live by Spirit." Do you see? The idea is not to renounce but to do everything with the thought of God.

THE POLICEMAN AND THE SAINT

One day a policeman cried out, "stop!" to a Saint, thinking that he was a thief for whom they were looking, disguised as a Saint. The Saint, engrossed in his own thoughts, did not hear, and kept on walking.

The policeman slashed at him with his sword and cut his upper arm badly. When he saw his serious error, he was very sorry, but the Saint said: "Oh, never mind, it is nothing. It will be all right in a few days."

In only three days it was completely healed, and no soar was left. Such is your power and your consciousness when you know that God is with you. Make the contact and see the magic. Contact "Om. " Change your consciousness from the body to feel that you are the Cosmic vibration.

THE ANT AND THE SNOW PILE

Altho (sic) we think that our possessions are marvelous, they are not big to God at all. Once I saw a big pile of snow and a very little ant crawling on it. I thought the ant must be thinking that it was scaling the Himalaya Mountains. It was the Himalayas to the ant but not to me. A million of our years may be a couple of years in the mind of God. We must think everything in terms of bigness. Eternity! Space!

HEALTH CULTURE

THE SCIENCE OF NUTRITION

THE MINERAL SURPLUS (Concluded) Nearly all fresh fruits have an alkaline reaction, except plums, prunes, and cranberries, when eaten in the natural state without the addition of sugar.

-Page Four-

Some of the best alkalinizing (sic) foods are: fresh apples, apricots, fresh lima beans, green beans, fresh beets, all berries, buttermilk, cabbage, cantaloupe, carrots, cauliflower, celery, chard, cherries, fresh cucumbers, dandelion greens, dates, figs, grapes, lemons, lettuce, milk, oranges, parsnips, peaches, pears, fresh green peas, pineapple, potatoes with skins, spinach, summer squash, tomatoes fresh or canned and watermelon.

Sweet corn has a neutral reaction when first plucked from stalk. After 24 hours it becomes acid-forming.

When sugar is added to fruit it becomes acid-forming, hence the necessity for eating it in its natural state.

Rhubarb produces an alkaline ash but it is too high in oxalic acid to be really wholesome.

PEAS IN CREAM

2 cups cooked peas, 1 cup evaporated 1 tablespoon butter milk, undiluted (or cream), 1 small Smoein seasoning powder onion, minced; vegetized salt.
Cook onion slowly in melted butter, add seasoning, milk and peas. Simmer until slightly thickened.

FRESH PEACH ICE CREAM (Freezer method)

1 quart table cream, 1 teaspoon lemon 2 cups crushed peaches juice, 1 cup raw sugar or honey,   2/3 cup raw sugar; pinch salt. 4 teaspoon almond extract. Combine cream, sugar, salt, lemon juice and almond extract. Partially freeze. Add peaches which have stood in 2/3 cup raw sugar and finish freezing. For a crank freezer, use one part salt to four parts ice. If using a vacuum freezer, use one part salt to three parts ice.

PRAECEPTUM INSPIRATION

PEACE FLOWS INTO THE SOUL THROUGH MEDITATION

Peace is the altar of Heaven. Whenever you are disciplining yourself, you feel the presence of God. It is He who disciplines you through your own conscience. Whenever you have pure love in your heart, you are in the presence of God. When you are quiet, then you are with God.

When you are really happy, remember that God is smiling through you. When you have good and noble motives, then you have God with you.

When peace comes, you are One with God. Peace is not something which is negative; it is something which stabs the heart of worries. Peace can kill quicker than anger.

Peace is everywhere. It is an ocean of peace that you are swimming in. Without peace, your whole mental life will be poisoned. Just as blood goes through every tissue, so peace flows through every cell of the body. When you are peaceful, everything is beautiful.

Meditation is the process. Peace is the breath of stones, stars, and service. Nothing can live without peace. If God didn't hold His peace and harmony, the whole world would collide and be thrown out into space.

PRAECEPTUM AFFIRMATION

I am thinking with the minds of all. I am dreaming through all dreams. I am feeling through all feeling. All the flowers of joy blooming on all heart soils are mine. I am the eternal laughter. My smiles are dancing through all faces, I am the wave of enthusiasm in all hearts.

-Page Five-

BY
PARAMHANSA YOGANANDA

O Mighty Beloved, O Wine of the Centuries, we found Thee in the bottle of our devotion. Mighty Being, mighty Spirit, bless us that in our thoughts and actions, in our understanding , and in all that we do, we may spread Thy glory on earth to establish Thy temple in the Souls of men.

Bless us, that we do not become sidetracked from Thee. Bless us, that all our thoughts, actions, perceptions, and consciousness may be converted to one end -- to establish Thy temple in our Souls and in the Souls of our forgetful brothers.

Continuing to love all those whom we love now, and loving all those whom we loved before, we come to give the blossoms of our love unto all. We carry the blossoms of the love of incarnations in the basket of our heart and we strew them n the hearts of others of all nations, of all things living, that we may give all to our Father.

A heartful of devotion, all the blossoms of our love, we bring unto Thee. We pray unto Thee in the burning language of our love. Reveal Thyself. No more sidetracking by us. We shall follow the path that straightway leads to Thee. Unite our love with Thy love, unite our life with Thy joy, and our consciousness with Thy Cosmic Consciousness.

SOURCES OF REJUVENATION

Part Two

Most people live this life in an unconscious state. They come, strugle, eat, earn, and then jump into the abyss of the unknown. Very few people awaken themselves from the stupor of delusion and try to find the way of right living.

Do you wish to improve yourself? Then you must, first of all, take care of your health. The rattlesnake is a gentleman. He rattles before he bites, but the disease in you does not let you know until it suddenly pounces upon you. During the season of youth, you should he making life beautiful, but instead you are more likely to sow the seeds of disease.

Many times health has smiled upon you and each time you have kicked it away through wrong living! Many times you have eaten wrongly! How many of you exercise every day? Very few. You may think that sweeping the house gives you sufficient exercise, but it does not, because most of you do it with a grudge. Everything you do, you must do with your whole heart, do joyfully in order to get the best results.

Why is it that two people of the same ago, sex, and vitality look different? One may look young, with a smile, while another may look quite old, with worries written upon his face.

You must take care of your body machine in the ways taught in these Instructions. Do not give up as the years roll along as so many people do. Always have interests. Keep the mind busy creating new things. You must find the way. The Infinite powers are at your command.

-Page Two (sic)-

The ocean can help any wave to retain its form if it keeps pushing it from within its bosom, so man can retain youth by asking the unchangeable, ever lasting ocean of Immortal Power behind the wave of his mortal form to continue manifesting itself as that youthful vital form.

ENERGY FROM FOOD: Food is nothing but condensed atomic energy. The action of the chemical, vital, and mental forces upon the stomach and intestines change food into energy. It is this energy which externally repletes the body wave of life. Millions of people eat anything they please. Only a few live according to dietary laws and scientifically look after the body.

The correct diet is very important in building vitality. Eating plenty of ground nuts, ground carrots, and fruit juices will help. Fasting one day a week on orange juice and takinga suitable laxative that day will help to keep the body cells firm and free from disease, A three-day fast once a month on orange juice with alaxative each day while fasting will expel almost all poisons and will do much to make the body strong, healthy, and youthful to the last days of life. Orange juice is very good because it counteracts the acids in the body which are caused by eating meats and heavy foods. Do not make a practice of eating fish, eggs, and meat. Your kidneys will not stand it. You must balance diet by eating alkaline foods.

Energy From Exercise: Whenever you have a headache, or any other kind of pain, direct energy to that place, and hold the thought that God's electric energy is flowing through you. God's energy is holding your body together. You must know how to connect your will power with God's energy in your body.

Slowly tense to medium the affected part and hold the medium tension, (charge) counting 1 to 10, and then relax. Repeat nine times. Do this three times a day on a light stomach. As an exhausted battery takes time to be recharged from a dynamo, so the holding of the tension in any body part recharges that part. The Life Force is the all healing Soul X-Ray, without which no healing is possible.

While walking every day, slowly inhale, while counting one to twelve. Hold the breath for twelve counts, then exhale while counting one to twelve. Do this twenty four times every time you go for a walk. Every one must have at least a half hour sunbath twice a week, or, preferably, every day. Do not overdo this. Be careful of severe sunburn, which does more harm than good.

Every time you move your hand, you are producing an electric current, and all the ether is filled with Cosmic Light. Because you do not see it does not mean that it does not exist. It is that light which is giving you life. Just as ships are being operated by radio without any crew, so God is pouring energy into your body. The fingers are marvelous things. They are your antenna and you can very often feel the energy flowing into them.

Now comes the method. Relax your hands and arms. You do not feel any energy in them, but as soon as I teach you the method you will feel the energy flowing through them. It is a power that has always been within you but you have not been aware of it. I will teach you how to connect the body and the mind and the will together so that the energy can be evolved in your hands and arms. You can do the same with your feet and eyes, but that requires more advanced development.

Close your eyes. Concentrate upon your arms. Can you feel any energy there? Just a little bit. Do not tense your arms at all. Keep your arms perfectly relaxed at your side. You are now feeling as if silently just a little energy is flowing through them. Now lift your hand. You must send energy by will power. Keep relaxed with eyes still closed. Feel that there is a tremendous amount of energy passing through your hands and arms. Can you feel a little bit of current in the forearms and hands? Now feel that more current is flowing through the forearms and fingers, Gan you feel it a little stronger? This is just a mental or imaginative process.

-Page Two-

Now comes the physiological processes. First, will continuously that the arms are two batteries and take one hand and rub the opposite arm. Feel that you are charging your arm. Now remove your hand. Do you feel the current? Now bring your arm down gradually. That current was felt much stronger than in the first exercise, was it not?

Now rotate your hands around each other. Keep your eyes closed. Rotate faster. You do not feel the current yet, but your hands soon will be filled with current. Keep your mind concentrated upon the current and think that it is going from the medulla into the hands. Can you feel it? Go on rotating faster. Do not cease concentrating. Raise your hands then bring them down slowly, all the time thinking of some one you wish to send the energy to. Don't you find this exercise stronger than the first and second ones? Keep perfectly relaxed as you bring your hands slowly to your side. Can you feel the current going through your arms and hands and fingers?

Rub your palms together quickly. Concentrate with closed eyes, feeling energy in your hands and all around your body. Concentrate, charging your arms with immortal energy. Do not tense; keep perfectly relaxed. Remember, this energy is flowing along the entire arms and hands. Now, forget your arms and hands and feel the current only. Now lift your hands in front of you and bring them down gradually. Think of some one who is sick and send the current to that person. Can you feel the tremendous current moving now? Do you realize how powerful it is? Can you deny that power? No. It is going to the point between the eyebrows and through the spine into your arms and hands.

REJUVENATION THROUGH MEDITATION Last of all, man should depend more and more upon the limitless supply of the inner source of Cosmic Consciousness and less and less upon the other sources of body energy. The highest form of rejuvenation is to unite the human consciousness and Cosmic Consciousness through meditation.

By constantly holding the peaceful after-effects of meditation in mind, by feeling immortality in the body, by believing in eternal life instead of beholding the illusory changes of life, and by feeling the ocean of immortal Bliss God underlying the changeable waves of the experiences of past lives and the waves of perceptions of childhood, youth, and age in this life the soul can find, not only perpetual rejuvenation in the Soul, but also in the body. Just as soon as the body is found to be, not isolated from Spirit, but a number of rising falling waves of vibrating currents in the ocean of Cosmic Consciousness, then the perpetual rejuvenation of the Spirit can be implanted in the body if so desired.

THE APOLOGUE
THE GREATEST LOVER

A long time ago there lived in India, a God-loving Saint and his wife. The Saint loved his wife, but he loved God more than her or anything else. In fact, he had married in order to discover whether his love for God was greater than his conjugal affection. He had married with the understanding that he would leave his wife, possessions, and all if the love of God possessed him and he had an urge to leave all for His sake. He was continually checking up in his mind to discover whether he was loving; anything else more than God. He thought: "If at any time I stoop to begin to love anything more than God, I am going to remove that obstacle.

Time is a great trickster and delusion is subtle and penetrating, so after a while the Saint went on a pilgrimage with his wife, who was about to give birth to a baby. Both the Saint and his wife thought that the birth of the baby in the holy land of Benares would be auspicious and be good for the future of the baby.

-Page Three-

On the way, as they passed along the outskirts of a certain city, the wife was stricken with labor pains. The Saint hastily took his wife into an old dilapidated deserted house. As the wife writhed in agony, she said to her husband: "Saintly one, promise me that you won't desert our new-born babe under a Divine impulse, for I feel that I am going to die."

The Saint although extremely touched by the words of his stricken wife yet felt that he was between two fires – the child to be born and his paramount love for God. The Saint thought to himself: "I could not love my wife or the baby unless God made them lovable and gave them to me to love with the very love which came from Him." So he thought, no matter what happened, he would never let anything come in the way of his Divine love and he would forsake anything to appease his love-thirst for God. He resolved to cut off his hand or pluck out his heart or his eye, or otherwise maim himself, and forsake everything if by so doing he would become worthy of God's love.

Altho (sic) he was inwardly resolved to forsake all for God, by way of consoling his wife and not causing her any heartache, he replied to her repeated entreaties: "I will see what I can do. I will try my utmost to carry out your wishes." But hard are the tests of God and subtle are the ways of delusion. It happened that the wife died, leaving behind her a beautiful baby boy, whom the saint and his wife always prayed would be sent to them.

The baby was crying piteously, while lying near the dead mother and the stunned saintly father, when there was a great rumble in the ether, a light burning the bush of all ignorance, and a Presence possessed the Saint. He heard a voice say: "Beloved, come to me. We will remain in the ecstasy of Divine Love in the caves of the Himalayas."

The Saint was shaken with the love of God on one hand, and the love of the helpless baby on the other hand. But he thought: "I could not know what love is nor have the baby to love without God's love, so, if I cannot forsake father, mother, wife, child, and life for God. I am not worthy of Him."

Thinking this, he prayed: "Lord, Master of my life, you can take my life away now, and I won't be here to love or take care of the baby, as I must hasten to depart for the bower of the Himalayan caves, where I wish to commune with You."

As if in response to his prayer, his eyes suddenly rested on the floor and he saw a lizard give birth to an egg and silently slink away, leaving the egg behind her. The egg broke; a little baby lizard was born. I opened its mouth in hunger and suddenly a small insect flew in its mouth. The little lizard closed its mouth and its hunger being satisfied it began to move away to a hiding place.

Seeing this, the Saint thought: "If the Lord feeds the baby lizard, forsaken by its mother, so also He would take care of my baby, forsaken by his mother and father too. "

Thinking this, in the deep ecstasy of God's love, the Saint ran out of the house, all the while hearing the cries of the baby. But his heart was shaken and his human love suffocated him. He stood under a tree and prayed: "Lord, although my love for you is greater than my love for the child, you gave me a human heart and I feel worried about the motherless, fatherless, helpless baby. Lord, I beseech you show me something by which I can know that my baby will be cared for.

As if by magical response, the Saint saw the emperor's coach stop by the deserted house, attracted by the cries of the forsaken child. The barren Queen stealthily walked out of her husband's royal coach, entered the ruined house, lifted the baby from the side of the dead mother, then sprang into her coach and swiftly departed for her palace.

Later, as the Saint loitered in the city for a day or two, he heard that the King and Queen, having no children of their own, had adopted the Queen's foundling as their child and successor to the throne. The Saint, much pleased, left the city to keep his tryst with God in the Himalayan caves of Hindustan.

MORAL: Love God with all your heart and soul. Seek the Kingdom of God first, then all your desires will be fulfilled. "If thy hand" prevent thee, out it off." Cut off all difficulties which lie in the path of Self-Realization and supreme freedom.

It is better to enter into eternal life having maimed your fleshly comforts than to burn in the hell fire of satiety and discontentment through over-indulgence. Love God more than you love anyone or anything else, for you cannot know what love is nor use that love to love anyone or anything without first receiving that love from God.

HEALTH CULTURE
SCIENCE OF NUTRITION

GELATIN   Vegetable gelatin is much to be preferred to any kind of animal gelatin for the principal base of animal gelatin is glue. This is extracted from the bones, tendons and sometimes skins of slaughtered animals.
In order to whiten it and make it attractive the animal gelatin is treated with sulphurous acid and other mineral acids. Minute amounts of these acids may remain in the finished product. Taken all together, from the hygienic standpoint at least, animal gelatin does not seem to be a very wholesome food.

However, since there are so many delicious salads and desserts to be made with gelatin, it will pay you to consult your health food dealer and find out about the vegetable gelatin products.

SWISS CHEESE SOUFFLE WITH CELERY

2 tablespoons butter	1/2 teaspoon dry mustard (optional)
2 tablespoons whole wheat flour	1/2 teaspoon vegetized salt
3/4 cup hot milk	1/2 cup grated Swiss cheese
1 cup finely minced, cooked, well-drained celery	4 egg yolks, well beaten
	4 egg whites, beaten.

Make sauce with butter, flour, hot milk and salt. When thick and smooth, remove from heat and add cheese. Stir until cheese is melted. Add beaten egg yolks and then celery. Cool mixture, then fold in stiffly beaten egg whites. Pour into buttered casserole and bake in moderate oven 40 minutes.

PERSIMMON ICE CREAM

1 cup cream	1 cup persimmon pulp
1/2 cup nut meats	1/4 cup powdered raw sugar
sprinkle of nutmeg	pinch of salt

Whip cream, fold in nuts and persimmon pulp. Add sugar, salt and dash of nutmeg. Freeze in automatic refrigerator.

Page Five-

PRAECEPTUM INSPIRATION
YOU MUST LIVE A FULL LIFE

Why live an aimless life, without recognizing your powers, without understanding the ways that you can develop those powers. In order to be known of God, you must live a full life.

Try to please God in everything you do and you will live rightly. The best way to please God is to satisfy your reasoning, your logical reasoning. We have been gifted with reason, and when we do wrong, our reason will tell us so. Whether you think you believe in God or not, if you have reasoning power and a conscience, there will be a belief in God.

Eat right, exercise properly, keep good company, perform good deeds, keep a clear conscience and live in healthy surroundings. You should especially learn to smile when things go wrong and thus learning to smile alway; you will instil new life into your body cells, which are the builders and sustainers of your fleshly mansion.

Drink happiness from minds saturated with joy, and from the fountain of a daily twenty minutes of perfect silence, both morning and night. These are some of the best recipes for rejuvenation and for the maintenance of lasting youth.

PRAECEPTUM   AFFIRMATION

I am the Wind of Wisdom which is drying the sighs and sorrows of all Souls. I am the Silent Joy of Life moving through all Beings.

YOGODA SAT-SANGA FORTNIGHTLY INSTRUCTIONS
By
PARAMHANSA YOGANANDA

INITIATE US WITH THY ETERNAL ABUNDANCE

Heavenly Father,Thou art our cosmic house of supply. Bless us all that we may manifest Thy blessings in our health,in our mental aspirations, and in our soul expressions. Thou art the life in the stars Thou art the fountain of power. Heavenly Father, teach us to charge our selves with Thy unlimited power, with Thy unlimited wisdom,and with Thy unlimited expression. Forgive us our transgressions, forgive us our wanderings in the land of errors. Bring us to the right path.Show us that you are the supreme fountain of health; Show us that Thou art the ocean of life; show us that Thou art the fountain of all our wisdom. Shake away our ignorance; shake away our diseases;shake away all our suffering,and let the flame of Thy wisdom burn away the dross that is within us.

Destroy the veil which hides Thy face from us. Come as a burn-ing light,come as a glory in the stars,come as the immortal power of our thoughts. Father, we will not be satisfied with anything except Thee. We want Thy guidance,Thy strength,Thy counsel in every thing. As often as we think wrongly,l et Thy whisper in the temple of silence and wisdom guide us to the right path which leads to Thee, Come Father,Come; Come: Father, Come; Come,Father, Come; initiate us with Thy power of eternal abundance.

Peace! Joy! Peace!
HOW TO CREATE AT WILL WHAT YOU NEED

Lost people do not try to understand life at all. They go on living without any aim or goal. We must find the purpose of life. The great man and the small man have to struggle. Lost people say: "How can we adjust our actions to an ideal? We do not know How." But you know that you must eat and think in order to live,so you must find peace in eating and thinking. We can build the temple of our prosperity from our existing needs. By analysis we find that every human being is a physical being,a mental being and a spiritual being,but most people spend their lives in supplying the needs of the physical being only. However,true prosperity lies in supplying the needs of the mental and spiritual beings as well as the physical being.

Knowledge as to how to become prosperous is always important. The word "prosperity" plays a very important part in our consciousness. We must know in what lies real prosperity and the surest way of attaining it. Lost people come to this life, live in a mechanical way, they leave the shore of this world unconsciously. Very few people know the right way of living. Lost people imitate other people in their way of living, and before they get over the struggle,t hey pass on.

Real prosperity means supreme happiness, mental efficiency, and some material advantages. Real prosperity lies in increasing the power of your mental deficiency, by which you can create at will the things you need. There is a difference between things that you need and things tint you want. Things that you need are things which are absolutely necessary in life,a nd the others are things which you can get along without but which you think you must posses. All the time you must con-centrate upon the things that are absolutely necessary and not upon what you see that others have and feel that you must have.

Page One.

53

True success is another expression for all-round prosperity. Those who have perfect health, prosperity, happiness, wisdom and understanding have true success. If you know how to withdraw your attention and energy from all objects of distraction and place them upon one object of concentration, then you know how to create at will what you need.

WHAT IS "PROSPERITY?"

All of us love prosperity, but do we all find it? No. It is the will-o'-the-wisp which is always hiding from us. Lost people do not know the meaning of the word prosperity. Some will say: "Well, prosperity means health." But health without money to satisfy your hunger is not prosperity. Some one else will say: "Lots of wealth is prosperity," but if you you have lots of wealth and lots of indigestion, then that is not prosperity. When you are able to perfectly adjust yourself to the world then you are called "Prosperous." But beyond that we wonder who is the maker of reason in u s for unless we find all the answers to everything we are not prosperous. When you no longer doubt, but know everything, then you will be prosperous. When you find the answers to everything within yourself, then you can say I am prosperous."

IS MONEY "PROSPERITY"   Lost people think that you are prosperous only when you have lots of money, but real success means when you have all things at your command -- the things that are necessary for your entire existence. But very few people understand in what lies real necessity. Very few people know the real meaning of "needs." If the need is boiled down to certain definite things, then need can be easily satisfied.

Money is not a curse. It is the manner in which you use money that is of importance. You take a dollar bill and you ask it: "Shall I buy poison with you?" It does not answer, but if you misuse the brainless dollar, it will punish you. When you use it rightly, it gives you happiness. There is no Saint, no Savant who does not use money in his work. Whoever eats has to pay for the food, and it is better to be able to buy your food than to have to live on charity. There is a value to all things.

Lost people spend their entire mental energy in trying to make money, and some who are successful find out that they die of heart failur e when they are about to secure happiness. If you have lots of health and lots of wealth and lots of trouble with everybody and yours elf, you have very little. The entire purpose of life becomes futile when you cannot find happiness. When wealth is lost, you have lost a little. When your health is lost, you have lost a little, but when your peace is lost, all is lost.

You must increase the strength of the body and then increase the strength of your mind. The best way to increase mental power is to try to accomplish something worthy everyday. The things that you have been told you could not do, try to do. The more you improve yourself, the more you can be a friend to man. Reform yourself and you are reforming everybody around you. Everyday try to accomplish something which you thought you could not accomplish.

HOW TO CHOOSE A VOCATION   When you make up your mind to do some thing, let the earth and sun fly away from you, but do not give up. You are child of God -- You are as good as the greatest man on the earth. Before God one is not greater than another You must absolutely have your will power so balanced that you will stick to a thing until you succeed. First, carefully chose your work. You must like your vocation if you expect to succeed. If you have not found some thing that you like, then you must search for it.

When we think that we have to do too much at one time, we become very discouraged. Instead of worr)(iyng about what should be done you must say "This hour is mine. I will do the best I can." As the clock cannot tick 24 hours away in one minutes, so you cannot do in one hour what you can do in 24 hours. Live one present moment completely and the future will take care of itself

Fully enjoy the wonder and beauty of each instant. Practice the preserve of peace. The more you do that,the more you will feel the presence of that power in your life.

Take your time in making up your mind what vocation to follow then when you make up your mind,stick to your resolution. But if anybody shows you that you are wrong about something,accept their correction. Obstinacy is bad. You must first know that what you are doing is right then stick to it. Success gives one a tremendous ha ppiness.It does more than bring material wealth.

Every line of business is an art for dispelling certain human miseries. Getting a job is the art of satisfying our physical needs. Intel(l)ectual study nourishes our mind and intelligence and makes them better fitted for all good works.

YOU MUST BE GUIDED BY GOD WHO IS THE SOURCE   God has given you independence to shut out His Power or to let it in. Make your mind like the diamond, so that the power of God may flow through you. God tells you to create and will the things that you need, but do not beg; do not pray. Contact God first then: you will see that God's power is working with you if you have the faith that prosperity is control(l)ed by God and not by man, and then you must look after others as well as yourself. God does not tell you that you should not think. He tells you to use your initiative; but if you cut off the source, then you cannot receive help. If you, are guided by God, your mistake will be revealed to you.

Very few people realize that all our actions and destinies are governed by certain laws. Nothing happens just because of chance. Nothing is the result of certain circumstances. Every event of your life can be scientifical(l)y traced to a certain cause and because you do not know that the law of Cause and effect governs your life, that is why you believe in chance or fate.

The sunlight shines equally upon the charcoal and upon the diamond. So remember, the light of God shines equally in each of us. God made us his children, but we chose to be beggars, and that is why the law of cause and effect has been keeping us in its path, torturing us with materiality,

Repeat: "I will reason, I will create, I will do everything, but Father guide my creative abilities to the right thing which I should do."

And be fair with God. Perhaps He has something better for you. Talk sensibly to God and you will see that He will work with you.

S H O R T   A P O L O G U E S

VICTORY THROUGH FOLLOWING THE CORRECT METHOD

In Boston a young man came to me and said he wanted help, that no matter what he tried, he always failed in his business ventures. I said: " Go and meditate and say: every day I am getting richer and richer. " He tried to follow my instructions, but in about a month he came back and said: "It does not work. I am getting poorer and poorer. "

I said to him: "isn't it true that as you were affirming this, always in the background of your mind a little voice would say: "You poor simpleton, you know that you are getting poorer everyday." He said: "Yes."

I said to him very emphatically: "you must be deeply in earnest about what you are affirming. You must charge your mind with its importance; you must continually affirm it. That will greatly stimulate your will power, but in addition it will be necessary for you to work out the plan step by step, as you are guided by divine law. Remember, it is your creative ability, your present congenial environment, and your good Karma of the past that can bring your prosperity. Otherwise you will be limited. If you take the divine law and use it, all other laws of bad karma and wrong environment will be destroyed.

-Page Three-

(He) replied: "I do not believe it will work."

I said: "All right, in two weeks I am going to make $5000 through you." "$5000 through me? " he shouted. I said: "Yes. Let us meditate and ask God how we should invest our money in order to make $5000. So we sat in meditation until the divine contact was made. When the contact came, I said: "Father, tell me what to do. " After a while during meditation I saw two houses. So it came to pass that we invested in real estate; we bought those two houses and soon after we had bought them someone else wanted those houses and paid me $5000 more for them than I had paid.

You must always be guided by divine power, which is unfailing. As I perceive, so may you perceive; as I behold so may you behold the ethereal power that flows through you, through your speech, your brain, your cells, your thoughts. Every thought is a tube, a channel through which the divine light is passing. Open your hearts, that the Divine Flood my pass through you.

A SAINT'S WISDOM   One day, as I was starting on a pilgrimage, a Saint said to me: "Do not ask for anything to eat from anyone, and do not accept money from anyone, not even from your father." But I said: "Suppose I do not get anything to eat and I die?" He said: "Then die: die to know that you live by the power of God and not by bread." You are living by the power of God. Can man make the fruit and the other food that you eat? Remember, we are all living directly by the power of God. When you know that, the whole world will be at your command Claim your divinity first. Unite yourself with God. Receive your blessings from the hand of God first. Open your bankbook with God, that you may realize that all power and blessings and wealth and health come from that source.

HEALTH CULTURE THE SCIENCE OF NUTRITION

Scientific research has proved that it is possible not only to prolong life but to lengthen the period of youth and maintain maximum health and vigor for a longer time by the proper care and intelligence in the selection and preparation of food. It has been demonstrated that diet can increase the normal "life expectation" which has been inherited.

Of course, there must be sane living - proper exercise and rest, fun, friends and interesting work. The diet is also important in all of these activities for food affects the disposition as well as the physical body.

It is absolutely necessary for everyone to have plenty of milk, leafy vegetables, oranges, tomatoes or tomato juice, and other fresh fruits and vegetables every day. See that these foods are made so attractive that large servings are desired. With these as the base —always on the "must" list - other foods suited to individual appetites may be added. Serve some raw vegetables in salads every day and see that your bread and cereals are made of whole grain products,

HONEY DEW AND CHEESE SALAD
Sliced pineapple   3/4 cup cream or soft American cheese
honey dew melon,   1/2 teaspoon vegetized salt
        scooped out in balls
1 cup whipped cream   salad dressing, lettuce

-Page Four-

Place slice of pineapple on lettuce leaf. Combine cheese, whipped cream and salt and pile in center of pineapple. Surround cheese with melon balls and serve with pineapple dressing. Garnish with fresh cherries.

PINEAPPLE-STRAWBERRY SUNDAE

| 1 | medium can crushed pineapple | 1 pint cream |
| 2 | tablespoons raw sugar | 1 cup strawberries |

Drain juice from pineapple, add sugar, and chill. Whip cream, fold in chilled pineapple, and freeze.

Crush and sweeten berries, add pineapple juice and serve as sauce on frozen pineapple mixture. This is delicious and not as rich as some of the custard creams.

PRAECPTUM INSPIRATION
HOW TO REMEDY YOUR MISTAKES

Your success or failure now is more or less due to influences from the past, but you can remedy your mistakes because reason and will have been given to you. There is no difficulty that cannot be solved provided you believe that you have more power that troubles. You must use that power to explode your difficulties. Very few people try to scientifically succeed. We often hear someone say: "I am lucky", or, "It is fate," but there is no luck, or good fortune that you did not attract to yourself in the past, and there is no misfortune that has come to you that you did to yourself due to your wrong actions here in the present, or else away back in the past. That is why some people are born poor and some healthy, rich, and so on. Otherwise, if God made us his children, all equal, and then put some in good homes and others in bad homes, and so on, where would be His justice?

Remember, the greatest of all things is to please God first. If the whole world is pleased with you and God is not pleased, you. have nothing, but if the whole world forsakes you and God is pleased with you, then you have everything.

PRAECEPTUM AFFIRMATION

In the heart,
In the star,
In the body cell I love Thee;
In the electron I play with Thee.
I wish to worship Thee
In body, star, star-dust nebulae.
Thou art everywhere; everywhere I worship Thee.

-Page Five-

YOGODA SA(T)-SANGA
FORTNIGHTLY INSTRUCTIONS by
PARAMHANSA YOGANANDA

THY PEARLS OF WISDOM

O, Almighty, Beloved One, teach me how to wear the suit of silence and dive through the measureless cold blue ocean, and pierce the cave of stars -- if Thou art hidden there. Teach me how to swim over the waves of wind and light, and waft me to Thy measure less shore. I swam through many seas of desire and divided in Thy many seas, yet I found not Thy most sought for treasure.

I travelled deep in Thy ocean of Knowledge for the pearl of Thy power; for the pearls of Thy love, but when I did not find the pearls of Thy love and power, I blamed Thy ocean. Father, Thou hast taught me since to find fault with my diving,s o I dived again and again until I found the pearl of Thy power, the pearls of Thy love.

Teach me never to say that Thy ocean of wisdom is lacking the pearls of Thy power, but teach me to find fault with my diving. Teach me to dive again and again with the armor of Self-realization. Teach me to dive again and again until I find the pearls of Thy power. Decorated with the pearls of Thy power I shall enter into the mansion of Thy understanding. I dive through the measureless sea of the love in all things, in all hearts; I shall at last find the priceless pearl of thy presence.

CONFLICT BETWEEN THY FINITE AND THY INFINITE

Spirit is ever-existing, ever conscious, ever-new joy. He is. He was and ever shall be joy from the human point of view of time. In Spirit there is no past or future tense but only the present because spirit consciousness, like that of man, is not contradicted by death and oblivion. Spirit is ever-conscious. His superconsciousness does not cease to actively operate like that of man in sleep. Spirit has no al-ternating consciousness of wakefulness or subconsciousness like that of man, but has perpetual,e njoyable active and inactive wakefulness combined within himself.

Spirit was Joy, but there was no one to taste Him so He divided Himself into the Knower, Knowing, and Known. Enjoyer, Enjoying and the thing enjoyed. This Triune division of spirit into Knower, Knowing and Known was accomplished by the law of relativity and cosmic delusion, which are the same spirit, being one and indivisible had to will and willingly imagine himself to be many. Spirit, being independent and self- contained, everything evolving out of Him had his qualities of indepen dence. The desireless desire of spirit to create Himself as many was not real desire because it was not a necessity to Him. If creation was a necessity to spirit,t hen He is imperfect. He just differentiated Him-self as the Knower, Knowing, and Known in order to make Himself appre-ciate His almighty Bliss through himself as many. Also the many were to find that Bliss by self-seeking, independent effort. Spirit just created and differentiated Himself for a Cosmic Entertainment.

-Page One-

SPIRIT AS KNOWER, KNOWING, AND KNOWN IS INFINITE   Spirit has one
consciousness, that of Bliss. Individually, Spirit or souls encases in bodies,
behold solids, liquids gases, energy, feeling, and thought as relatively
different things. This is illusion, for solids, liquids, gases and feelings are
nothing but different forms of consciousness, and those can be duplicated and
perceived in a dream. Spirit's imagination to dream himself into knower,
knowing and known is infinite. Anything coming out of spirit has the essential
qualities of spirit, hence cosmic delusion, or Satan, is the willing conscious
imagination of spirit to make Himself look like finite when in reality He is
infinite. This desireless Desire, this Infinite cosmic Dream of finitude does not
affect Spirit, but it affects all individualized spirits or souls evolved out of
Him. What is play to Spirit is death to us.

        This Satan, or the conscious force of Delusion, which makes the Infinite
look like the finite, receiving independence, began to constantly transform the
Infinite into the Finite. This force unable to perpetuate the finite forms of
created minerals and species of animals, began to try to perpetuate species by
the law of sex propagation. Defect and misery arose from this. All things and
creatures began to suffer. The finite things and created living creatures,
instead of finding themselves as living waves of the cosmic seas of life,
unchangeable and essentially immortal, were made to believe, by the cosmic Law
of Satanic Delusion that they were isolated, separated from the cosmic Dream of
Life, having origin and decay. Finite Souls were further deluded into the
feeling attached to their passing states of existence; suoh attachment is the
real cause of all suffering, and suffering, born of the ignorance of attachment
is evil.

HYPNOTIC SPELL OF SATAN, OR DELUSION   All finite beings, instead of
observing with the eyes of the Infinite the superficial and formal changes they
undergo, began to behold these transitional states through the deceiving eyes of
cosmic delusion, or Satan. If all finite things acted in tune with the ordinary
mortal way, but only as the illusions of a person witnessing death, fear, and
disease under a spell of hypnosis. An outsider cannot make a person working
under a spell of hypnosis, believe that he is seeing or feeling something which
has been suggested to him to see or feel. A dreaming man does not know that he
is dreaming. So it is that individuals under the hypnotic spell of Satan, or
Delusion, do not know that all evil, disease, inharmony, and wars are created by
Cosmic Delusion and their wrong imagination born of that Delusion.

        Why is the tiger the enemy of man, and vice versa. Why does the cat eat
mice, and the big fish devour the small, helpless fish? Why is it that the
mosquito is not satisfied with just drinking human blood but also injects poison
into it? Why are there earthquakes and sudden accidents? Why do sudden famines
and epidemic visit man? Why is it that destructive forces lie side by side with
the harmonious division of seasons, night and day, health, oxygen, sunshine, and
human reason. The reason for this paradox, it seems, is that if God is goodness,
or harmony, and all things are created by Him, then how can inharmony,
suffering or evil exist? Certain it is that man did not create all evil.

INORGANIC SUBSTANCES ARE CONSTANTLY CHANGING The Conscious Cosmic Delusion,
or the desireless desire of Spirit, empowered by the Infinite to independently
create finite things through Divine imagination began to pull everything away
from the Infinite and evolved the law of propagation by cellular division and
sex creation, or law of repulsion, to keep everything vibrating away from the
Infinite, or small individual units. Law of sex creation or any law of
reproduction is the effort of Cosmic Delusion or Satan, to preserve his kingdom
of inharmonious finitude in order to fight against the divine law of evolution
by reincarnation.

        In spite of Cosmic Satanic Power influencing everything to remain finite,
the Power of the Infinite is trying to call back everything to merge into Him
by the law of evolution and reincarnation. All inorganic substances are
constantly changing into finer substances; that is, the earth is changing.

-Page Two-

into minerals, minerals are changing into trees, trees are evolving into animals, animals are changing into super-animals or man, and man is changing into superman and God. In spite of earth changes, such as bad weather reversed seasons, Nature's catastrophes, disease, and immorality all ignorance born of Cosmic Delusion and man's intelligence acting under its influence, the divine law of evolution and reincarnation is trying to cause all inorganic and organic matter to be reconverted into Cosmic Consciousness.

The constant war between the Satanic Delusion and God forces is marked everywhere in human lives and in all things. Nature, or satanic Delusion, tries to glorify itself and through its misguided independence hide God, which produces bacteria, and in man disease and trials, the tiger with its instinct to kill and various other inharmonies and discords. God's power, through the law of natural death, or change, (as against sudden untimely change or premature death) is constantly trying to release finitely influenced Souls to infinite freedom. Self-defense and the cruelties born of self-defense and the desire to hurt and kill in order to eat were suggested to man by the Cosmic Law of Delusion, which broke away from the Infinite Nature of God to become finite, unreasonable, and harmful.

WE MUST DEPEND DIRECTLY UPON GOD AND NOT UPON CHEMICALS

We were made in the image of God but Satanic Delusion took advantage of the independence God gave to man and all things. To reinforce Satanic Delusion is to believe in ultimate death, disease, and all suffering as perpetually real, instead of giving them only Cosmic Dream Reality or ignorance-born reality, or imagined reality.

Our imagination of death and disease when awake is different from the delusive imagination of dream and death which is instilled by the Cosmic Delusive force within us. A dreaming man dashing his dream skull on a dream wall thinks he is hurt, but he knows that it was only a dream.

On the other hand, it is also true that if a man in the wakeful state thinks that his skull is delusion and dashes it against a wall it will certainly be broken, but one who beholds Spirit sees neither the skull nor the wall, and so cannot be hurt. Also, if a man sits quietly and imagines that he is dashing his skull against wall, that cannot hurt him either.

Death and disease are real to the one under the influence of the suggestions of the Cosmic Satanic Dream, in understanding matter as delusion, one must positively know that one can only know matter as frozen Cosmic Consciousness when his consciousness and Cosmic Consciousness become one. To believe in final death and the perpetual existence of diseases, i(s) to reinforce the already suggested delusions of death and disease imposed upon man by Cosmic Delusion.

To use too much medicine and depend too much upon material methods for the cure of disease of the body leads to the bad habit or relying upon limited methods of cure instead of making use of the help of the limitless healing power of Cosmic Consciousness. Food and chemicals are only indirectly helpful to the body. Divine force helps the body directly as well as indirectly by directing the food chemicals to operate for the benefit of the body. In other words, we should depend directly upon God and not upon chemicals.

PRE-NATAL AND POST-NATAL CHANGES ARE DIFFERENT EXPERIENCES OF THE SOUL To make Truth win this tug-of-war between Satanic Delusion and Evolution and Reincarnation, every human being must meditate upon the laws of the thoughts and actions which reinforce progressive evolution. Everyone must look upon the pre-natal and post-natal changes as different experiences of the soul. Diseases must be looked upon as broken laws resulting in inharmony of body, mind and soul, producing disturbances of the body and the peace of the soul. These should be taken as danger warnings, not as punishments. Disease are the result of the delusions of one's own wrong actions, which should be uprooted by material and spiritual laws.

-Page Three-

You must realize that the soul cannot be affected by disease. A chloroformed man does not know of an accident or a disease, so by discipline a man should neutralize the attachment of his consciousness to the body. He must consider his body from an impersonal stand point.

The body is the closest friend and relative of the mind. That is why it suffers only through identification, closeness of association and imagination, and for no other cause whatever. Do away with mental sensitiveness. You must speak of all experiences as dream experiences, real to the deep dreamer, unreal to the awakened in wisdom. To say to the mortal dreamer that disease and death do not exist is to confuse and delude him. He must be made to awaken in God through meditation then he will realize that he was only dreaming disease and death.

APOLOGUE
GRANDMOTHER'S BITTER LESSON

There was once a certain boy who lived in a little village with his grandmother. When he was very young, his parent died, so he was left to the mercy and care of an over indulgent grandmother. She was so blind in her attachment to her grandson that whether he was right or wrong, she tried to fulfill his every desire. Besides, to the rich grandmother her grandson was perfect and could do no wrong at any time.

After a while the little boy began to attend the village school. He was so mischievous that in a short time the whole school was astir with the exploits of this naughty little pet. The school teacher wrote to the grandmother in regard to her grandson's detrimental conduct, but she turned a deaf ear to the complaints of the teachers and scolded them for finding fault with her boy, so immaculate was he in her estimation.

Under the protection of the grandmothers approval of every thing he did, the boy grew worse and worse and finally turned from playing pranks and performing other trivial misdemeanors, into a perpetrator of graver offenses. After imitating other boys in the use of profane language, and so forth, the boy started stealing different articles from his school mates. One day he stole a costly fountain pen from a class- mate. He hurriedly got away from the school and raced for the endearing, welcoming, and caressing arms of his prejudiced grandmother. Upon his arrival, the grandmother began to shower him with kisses and embraces.

The boy could scarcely get his grandmother's attention to speak to her so great was the impetuosity of her affection.

At last, when grandmother sobered down and her mumbling torrent of affectionate words ceased, the grandson said; "Grandmother, I tried to tell you, but you would not let me, that I wanted a fountain pen, & so cleverly and unnoticed I picked one from my classmate's pocket."

The Grandmother as usual, gave the remorseful grandson a great big hug and said; "My little sonny Boy, you can do n(o) wrong. It is all right with me whatever you do. The grandson was extremely astonished that he received caresses instead of the expected and well deserved scolding. Encouraged, the boy started stealing books, pens, and other valuables from his classmates.

Matters grew so bad that the village teachers called a special meeting of all teachers, and after a violent discussion, even the most unscrupulous teachers voted to get rid of the spoiled child. The grand mother's intention was all right, but due to her erroneous methods, the boy as he grew older developed into a professional and regular thief. Now grown to manhood, he had become a full-fledged criminal and had joined a crime syndicate, scientifically planning and working out many crimes. The neighbors began to find their cattle and chicken missing, and other neighboring villagers began to lose their silver ware and other valu¬able articles from their homes. There was a great commotion, and volunteers and vigilantes were appointed to apprehend the thief.

The grandson, now an expert thief became bolder and bolder because he was able to elude detection of his clever crimes. As no one can forever hide his crime, and no one can fool all the people all the time, the boy thief ran into a trap laid for him by the outraged village vers. He was finally caught and flogged by the angry villagers and remanded to the jail. There was a hasty hearing and all the rich grand¬mothers attempts to save him failed, and her wicked grandson was sentenced to ten years of rigorous imprisonment for his confessed crime of about forty thefts.

But as the grandson was being led to jail, he made a last request -- that he wanted to whisper a secret in his grandmother's ear. The grandmother, being called in great joy and sorrowful tears, came to her grandson and stooped down and placed her right ear in front of her grandson's mouth. No sooner was this done than the grandson sprang up¬ward like a mastiff and held the right ear of his howling grandmother in between clenched saw-like teeth. After many punches and kicks from the policemen, the grandson at last let go his grandmother, after bitting off a piece of her ear. As the grand mother cursed and wailed, the grand¬son triumphantly, with great satisfaction in his eyes, cried out: Remember if you had scolded me when I stole the first fountain pen, today I would not have to go to jail and serve ten years at hard labor.

The moral is: It is not only bad for you personally to do evil but it is extremely pernicious for you to tolerate evil in your dear ones by sanctioning their evil deeds. Evil actions attract evil consequences, as the grandmothers evil tolerance resulted in her losing half of her ear and losing the affection of her grandson and ruining his entire life.

HEALTH CULTURE SCIENCE OF NUTRITION
DIET AND STRONG TEETH

No one doubts today that diseases of the teeth are preventable or that the preservation of the teeth in later life depends upon their care during childhood and upon the diet throughout life -- beginning even with the prenatal period. If the teeth are to be of good quality and if they are to last through adulthood without decay they must be composed of the proper materials and they must have proper care from the beginning -- and this means the temporary first teeth as well as permanent ones which develop later.

(continued in Next Praeceptum)

SAVORY STRING BEANS
1 lb young beans
1 sweet red pep(p)er
1 large onion
2/4 teaspoons✳ vegetized salt

1 small clove or garlic
2 tablespoons sweet butter
2 egg yolks
1 cup boiled water

cut beans length wise, and onion thinly sliced, minced garlic, minced pep(p)er, salt, butter and hot water. Cover and cook 15 minutes Remove from heat and stir in well beaten egg yolks. Serve.

PEANUT BUTTER ICE CREAM
1 cup peanut butter
2/4 cup orange juice✳
3 1/4 cups irradiated evaporated milk
1 cup cold water.

1 1/2 cup whipping cream
1 cup powdered raw sugar
1/8 teaspoon vegetized salt

Stir water and orange juice into peanut butter. Beat until fluffy and add sugar, salt, evaporated milk. Fold in whipped cream and freeze.

✳See Editor's Notes

Page Five

P R A E C E P T U M   I N S P I R A T I O N

THE LOVE OF GOD PROTECTS YOU

Do not long for human love. This longing in your heart is really the desire for God. His love you will find will be with you through eternity and through all your trials and miseries you will feel His love protecting you. You came with Him, you are still with Him, yet you deny Him now, but when your loved ones are gone He still will be with you. When you hear the voice of God saying that He loves you, then you will be satisfied. He will never let you be the victim of trials and suffering, for His love will be the power that will guard you.

Human love, when it is charged with the Divine, becomes perfect. When you cut off the little brook from the fountain, then it is imperfect. Remember, you are your own judge. Will you doom yourself to suffering and ignorance or will you say: "I shall free myself." If restlessness troubles you, meditate.

The greatest of all temptation is restlessness. When restless ness comes, it causes evil. If you meditate regularly, you will be with God all the time.

P R A E C E P T U M   A F F I R M A T I O N

In my little chamber of quietness,

I am always resting: I never speak

but with the voice of my silence.

Through my silence, eloquently con

verse with me.

YOGODA SAT-SANGA FORTNIGHTLY INSTRUCTIONS

BY

PARAMHANSA YOGANANDA

TEACH US TO DEMAND THY LOVE

Heavenly Father, tear away our ignorance, tear away our veil of delusion. Be Thou the only ambition on the throne of our desires. Be Thou the only love on the throne of our craving. Father, Mother, Beloved Spirit, reveal Thyself unto us. Destroy our indifference. 0, Endless Thrills of intoxication, visit our Souls. Intoxicate our hearts with the wine of Thy love. 0, Love of All Ages, 0, Creation of Our hearts, may the endless dreams of our desires melt in Thy Holy Ocean, and may we find fulfillment and satisfaction in Thee.

Father, twinkle through the stars, vibrate through the atoms, whisper through our thoug(h)ts, and love us through our love. Teach us not only to pray, but also to demand Thy love, for it is our privilege to love Thee. We are a reflection of Thee. Father, wake with us in the dawn, vitalize us in the sunlight, and as we enter the port(a)ls of the evening, receive the love of our hearts' devotion-flowers which bloom in the garden of the Soul.

Come out of the blossoms, come out of the valley, come out through the windows of flowers and the souls of men, come out through our secret silence in the cave of the soul. Come Father, shatter the veils of space and mind and show Thyself to us in all Thy glory. Father, forget us not, though we forget Thee, remember us, though we remember Thee not. Be not indifferent unto us, though we are indifferent unto Thee. Teach us to receive wisdom from Thy lips and power from Thy concentration, and strength from Thy Cosmic Energy.

CONFLICT BETWEEN THE FINITE
AND THE INFINITE
Part II

WE HAVE THE POWER OF FREE CHOICE There are always two forces trying

to get hold of you. Listen to the voice of God first. Never say: "I must do this." Remember, you have free choice. It is also a delusion to think that you like evil ways. No one wants to hurt himself. You love yourself more than anyone else. You will sacrifice for yourself when you will not sacrifice for others. That is why you should do what is of real, lasting benefit to yourself. You must not do anything that brings you sorrow. The law of action gives you free choice, so that it does not become influenced by evil. Evil leaves traces in your consciousness.

Altho (sic) there is evil and good in the world, free choice is our saviour. You can well understand what I am saying. For instance, the animal does not have free choice. Animals know neither good nor evil. They just live by instinct and some intelligence, and they evolve to higher forms. But man has the power of free choice. Nothing can influence him unless he chooses to accept it. Unless you drink poison, you will not die from poison; unless you cultivate hatred, you will not receive hatred in return; unless you (are) jealous, you will not receive the effects of jealousy. Your actions will lead either to good or to evil. Just a mental conception of good will not make you good. Both virtue and vice require activity.

YOU WILL HEAP WHAT YOU SOW Thought is just as had as action. According to Western ethics, you are not considered evil unless your actions are evil, and you are not considered virtuous unless your actions are virtuous, but in India it is considered evil to have evil thoughts. According to the law of action, or karma, we reap what we sow. Remember, the law of action does not mean fatalism. Before you act, you have freedom, but after YOU act, the effect of that action will follow you whether you want it to or not. That is the law of Karma. If you read the wrong book, in spite of the fact that you know that it is not good for you, nevertheless you will reap the results of reading that book. Do you see? You are a free agent, but when you perform a certain act, you will reap the results of that act.

If you do not want to redeem yourself, no one can redeem you. If you choose to live altogether on the material plane, you will have to be material, not spiritual, and no one can help you. You have a freedom of choice. Some day you will say: "I am a free man." Kick evil away from you. Every time something bothers you, meditate.

The way to freedom is through service to others. The way to happiness is through meditation and being in tune with God, Let your heart beat with the love of others, let your mind feel the necessities of others, and let your intuition feel the thoughts of others. Break the barriers of your ego; break selfishness; break the consciousness of the body; forget yourself; do away with this prison house of incarnations; melt your heart in all; be one with all Creation,

EVIL WAS NOT CREATED BY GOD   If you are convinced that temptation is bad because it promises happiness and gives sorrow, then Delusion can't get possession of you. Temptation is alluring. There is no doubt about that. It is alluring because our senses are all turned outward. There is a current flowing from the brain into the eyes, ears, and taste and touch nerves, and as such, sensations flow outward. We always like things that are flowing outward. That is what is appealing to the outward senses.

Remember that temptation is temptation because you have no sense of comparison. The quickest way to destroy temptation is to first say "no" and get out that particular environment and then reason it out later when your wisdom is a prisoner. The best way is to be so merged in the happiness of God that all other happiness will only be secondary to that sublime state.

Why should you let evil wreck you just for a moment of false happiness? Keep your will power free from the clutches of bad habits. Replace evil with good, and then, when you have an abundance of good habits, you will be free and able to fight evil. If you force good onto a child the first chance he gets he will do what he was told not to do. Never force yourself into anything. Be sincere with yourself.

A child must be made to see why a thing is wrong and another's will power must not be forced upon him.

Evil was not created by God. You should help God to establish His kingdom. He can only establish it through your cooperation.

THE LAW OF CAUSE AND EFFECT   Those who deny evil go on doing anything they please, but when one recognizes the law of cause and effect, there is no chance of delusion. God is telling you to do good and evil is influencing you to do wrong. To deny evil is to be filled with delusion.

-Page Two

All your sins and errors are only a covering. God made you as light; darkness cannot exist in you, only you cover up the light. You are a child of God. It is wrong to say that you are a sinner, for you are the ever-burning X-Ray Light of God.

In this life sometimes we are the victims of disease and trouble, but we do not realize that sometime, somewhere we were the cause. Blame yourself for anything that happens to you, but do not worry, as you can remedy matters for yourself. How? By doing good deeds now. To become bored with life is wrong. When you meditate you will see what life really is. "0, aged wine of my heart, I found Thee bottled in my heart, corked with ignorance. As I drink Thee, I look in the bottle of my heart and find Thee untouched."

God will never bore you. Nothing in this world will give you sufficient joy, apart from God, but when you have God, you will find that He is sufficient. God is complete. The love that you are seeking in passion, you will find in God. The power and prosperity that you are seeking in the world, you will find in God, who can please you as nothing else can.

THE VALUE OF GOOD COMPANY: Some people put a little water of practice on seeds, and then the seeds die. Others water the seeds but do not put a hedge around them, and they are soon destroyed. It is very important to put a hedge around, and good company is that hedge. Go(o)d company is a boat that carries you beyond the ocean of misery to the shores of eternal blessedness. We live in an environment with certain people and that environment completely influences us. Greater than will power is your environment, but the greatest of all things is the company you keep. Choose your friends carefully. You can't please everyone. Go(o)d company will stimulate your actions and thoughts in the right direction, and they will germinate, and if the good becomes abundant, evil seeds will be crowded out.

Fear no one. Remember, you are living in a glass cage and everyone is watching you. Try to improve yourself. If anyone criticizes you, try to see your faults and mend your ways. Do not be affected by praise. Do not allow yourself to be flattered. If your love and kindness cannot hold them flattery will have no effect. Flattery is poison to your Soul and poison to the Souls of others.

Your conscience is the whisper of God. It is the voice of God. If you listen to Him, you will be saved from evil and its effects.

Be proud that you are a child of God. He is shining in the high and in the low, in the white and in the dark races. It is better to have the glory of God than the (g)lory of man. To die in God and live forever is the highest ideal.

THE APOLOGUE
KRISHNA, THE EVER-CHANGING, YET CHANGELESS ONE

Many years ago a great artist came to the Court of King Balaram of India. He told the courtiers that he had traveled all over the world, had visited the kings of different countries, and had painted their portraits, for which he received many costly presents. The artist heard that Sri Krishna, the brother of King Balaram, was the embodiment of beauty, so he approached the Court of Balaram to ask permission to paint a portrait of Sri Krishna.

King Balaram was finally persuaded to send for Sri Krishna to ask him to pose for the artist. Krishna willingly complied with his older brother's request and posed for the artist. The artist finished

-Page Three-

66

painting the portrait of Krishna in a few hours, then he brought the painting to King Balaram. Krishna was sitting near his brother. When the King saw the painting, he was astonished and said that there was absolutely no resemblance to Krishna in the portrait painted.

When the artist discovered that he had painted the picture of some one of his own conception and not a likeness of Krishna, he pleaded for another trial. Krishna again consented to a sitting, but again the portrait was a dismal failure. For twelve years the artist, with unceasing patience, tried to reproduce the beauty and spirituality of Krishna in the painting. Finally, he became so discouraged with his efforts that he wanted to end his life. Fortunately, just at this time, Narada, a great devotee, appeared upon the scene and told the artist that he would show him the way to paint a true likeness of Sri Krishna. Furthermore, Narada requested the artist to introduce him as his Guru. The next day the painter followed Narada's instructions.

Narada carried a large empty picture-frame covered with black cloth and he asked Krishna to sit on a small sofa. He then asked the artist to hold the covered frame in front of Krishna. He then asked Krishna to be very attentive, as he was going to paint his portrait instantaneously. Krishna became all attention, and the artist also was eagerly watching to see what Narada would do. Narada then removed the black cloth and revealed a mirror that was inside. The result was that Sri Krishna appeared faithfully registered in the bright mirror, no matter how many times he changed his posture or transfigured himself by Divine power. Then Sri Krishna knew that Narada had shown the artist the correct way of painting him -- Krishna, who is changeless, and Krishna who can change. As Krishna transfigured himself every time the artist painted something, so at last the mirror registered the correct form, no matter how many times Krishna changed.

The moral: A clever psychologist may paint the character of a famous person on the canvas of his mind, but he will fail to paint in his oscillating intelligence the ever-changeable, yet essentially changeless characteristics of God. When, through the help of a Guru-Preceptor, the intellectually wise psychologist learns how to remove the dark cloth of ignorance which covers the mirror of calm intuition, then he will be able to hold in this mirror the proper image of the ever-changing, yet changeless Spirit, or Krishna.

GLOSSARY

The artist represents an intellectual psychologist.
Narada - a proper Guru-Preceptor.
The black cloth -- the dark cloth of ignorance covering the mind.
The mirror is the calm intuition developed by meditation, which can reflect in it all the changeability and unchangeability of God.

HEALTH CULTURE
THE SCIENCE OF NUTRITION

DIET AND STRONG TEETH   The teeth begin to develop as early as the eighth week of prenatal life. It is therefore apparent that anything which influences the development of bones and teeth is very important almost from the time of conception. It is also true that any adverse influence during the pre-natal period will have a profound effect upon the dental history throughout life. "It is well known that diseases as syphilis, measles, scarlet fever, and other exanthemata✳ in the expectant mother are likely to result in defective teeth in the child."

✳ See Editor's notes

-Page Four-

S-6 ✳ P. 142

The sustenance of the unborn baby is received from the mother and for this reason, the mother's diet should supply all of the calcium necessary to build strong bones and teeth. If enough for this purpose is not supplied by the daily intake of food, it is drawn as far as possible from the mother's own body. This explains why so many women who have recently borne children need the attention of the dentist.

It is equally necessary for the development of general vitality in the child, as well as for strong bones and teeth, that the nutrition of the expectant mother should include all of the other essential nutrients found in the protective foods -- dairy products, fresh fruits and fresh vegetables.

SUPPER SALAD
chilled honey dew melons or cantaloupes   cream
cottage or cream cheese   French dressing

GREEN BEANS MEXICAL
2 tablespoons minced onion   2 large tomatoes
2 tablespoons olive oil   1 teaspoon vegetized salt
1 pound green beans, sliced   1 teaspoon raw sugar
Cook onion in olive oil, add diced tomatoes and simmer 10 minutes. Add beans salt and sugar. Cook until tender.

AVOCADO ICE CREAM:
1 cup powdered raw sugar or honey   1 egg white
1 teaspoon vanilla   1 quart milk,
½ cup water   1 pint cream
                                        2 cups avocado pulp
Make syrup of sugar and water by boiling together 4 minutes. Add vanilla, milk and cream. Freeze to mushy stage. Mash avocado pulp and beat well with the white of egg. Combine with partly frozen mixture and finish freezing. Makes one gallon of ice cream.

PRAECEPTUM INSPIRATION
CALMNESS IS THE BREATH OF IMMORTALITY

Retain your calmness. Ordinary life is like a pendulum, all the time swinging back and forth. Then the calm individual remains calm and when he wants to work he swings into action, and as soon as he is through, he swings back to the center of calmness. You must always be calm, like the pendulum that is still, but ready to swing into action whenever necessary.

Activity must be under your control of calmness. If activity controls your calmness, you may get some results in the world but you may not be able to use that success or prosperity. Be calmly active and actively calm, a Prince of Peace sitting on the throne of poise, directing the kingdom of activity. Be calm while you are active and always be ready to be active. Calmness must not act as an opiate to dull your activity.

Calmness is the immortality within you. You are a prodigal son when you worry. You have static on your mind radio. God's song is the song of calmness. Nervousness is static, calmness is the Voice of God in the radio of your Soul. When even death cannot frighten you, then you are a God. Calmness is the God within man. Remember, calmness is the breath of immortality. Nervousness is change and death.

PRAECEPTUM AFFIRMATION

I am Thy prodigal dew drop, quivering on the hollow, trembling leaf of life and death, which floats on Thy shoreless sea. I am Thy truant dew drop, homeward bound at last.

-Page Five-

YOGODA SAT-SANGA FORTNIGHTLY INSTRUCTIONS
BY
PARAMHANSA YOGANANDA

SONGS OF OUR LOVE FOR THEE

Heavenly Father, make our hands become busy doing good to ourselves by serving others. Make our fingers play the cords of our feelings, and play a virgin music of devotion as Thou comest into the temple of our daily silence.

Divine Beloved, keep our hands peacefully busy with only the ar(ch)itects of proper living food cells pass by the gates of our lips to help build Thy temple of health.

Keep our (v)oices enraptured with the songs of our love for Thee. Keep our feet ever busy in serving Thee in the temple of all minds. Keep our eyes busy beholding Thee through the beauty windows of flowers, through the nooks of space, through the portals of Souls.

In Thy One Temple of SILENCE, we are singing unto Thee a chorus of many-voiced religions. Teach us to chant in harmony our love's many expressions unto Thee, that our melody of souls may rouse Thee to break Thy vow of silence and lift us onto Thy lap of Universal Understanding and immortality, that we may hear Thy Song's refrain in all our tender chants to Thee.

Our One Father, we are traveling by many true paths unto Thy one abode of light. Show us the One Highway of Common Realization, where meet all by-paths of theological beliefs.

Make us feel that the diverse religions are branches of Thy One Tree of Truth. Bless us, that we may enjoy the intuition-tested, ripe, luscious fruits of self-knowledge hanging from all the branches of manifold Scriptural teachings.

HOW TO DEVELOP THE VOICE

A violinist knows that before he can become an accomplished player he must be equipped with a good violin bow, good dry violin cords, a good violin box, and last, but not least, the mental skill to produce good music by a harmonious contact of the bow and the (v)iolin. It is also true that a speaker or a singer must first become familiar with the four following factors involved in good singing and speaking before he can even begin his training.

(1) How to use the breath in order to produce harmonious sounds. As the bow properly used against the violin cords produces the right notes, so the breath used over the vocal cords in the right way produces the desired magnetic speech or magnetic songs. (2) The throat must be free from hoarseness caused by over use and must be protected from infection at all times. The proper use and care is very important. (3) The art of relaxing and tensing the vocal cords must be practiced daily. (4) The art of gaining musical skill will come through will power, concentration, and the proper use of the vocal cords.

-Page One-

Just as the violin bow must right for use on the violin, so also the knowledge of proper breathing is very necessary in speaking and singing. Just as the bow going up and down in countless ways over the violin cords produces the music, so also the habit will power concentration modulated breath, playing up and down the vocal cords, produces the correct speech and music.

Practice the following breathing exercise for half and hour before speaking or singing, but do not think of the breath or breathing exercise during the act of speaking or singing. Inspiration must be the principal guiding force in speaking or singing. Inspiration is roused by the habit of being inspired and through concentration.

BREATHING EXERCISE   Sit calmly on a straight chair with spine erect and chin parallel to the ground. Keep mouth closed. Put the thumb of your right hand on the right nostril and very slowly inhale through the left nostril, filling the lungs and expanding the diaphragm simultaneously, counting rapidly one to twenty-five.

Then close the left nostril with the forefinger, hold the breath and count one to six or one to twelve, T her. open the right nostril by removing the thumb, while keeping the left nostril closed the forefinger . Then exhale slowly, counting one to twenty-five rapidly. Practice about twelve times in the morning on an empty stomach, as a matter of daily exercise, and half an hour or one hour before delivering a speech. It is best to eat very little or nothing for at least one or two hours before public speaking or singing. It must be remembered that during the above breathing exercise, the lungs and abdomen must be simultaneously inflated during inhalation and deflated during exhalation. Those who do not practice breathing exercises often, breathe in short breaths and find the breath a hindrance during speaking or singing. Over-indulgence in all foods and especially meats must be strictly avoided in order to stop the accumulation of waste tissues and quick heart action and consequent over-breathing. All public speakers and singers will find long walks, or regular moderate running very healthful in their professions.

TO STRENGTHEN THE LUNGS   Stand erect, extend arms at right angles to the spine. Open palms. Slowly exhale, bring palms together in front. Slowly inhale, tensing all body parts HIGH in pairs, such as both feet, then both calves, and so on from "down up" and extending arms with clenched fists to the first position. Slowly relax all body parts similarly from "up down" and exhale, slowly bringing palms together in front. Repeat at least three times. RELAX AND DROP ARMS. Very important exercise.

TO STRENGTHEN THE CHEST   It is slow but sure suicide to walk, sit, rest, talk, sit at a table, or lie down with a caved-in chest. The lung cells are starved thereby, and maladjustments of the vertebrae occur. It is absolutely necessary always to have the chest a little forward and the shoulder blades a little backward, even when leaning back against a chair for rest. Practice will relieve irksomeness.

Close eyes. Very gently contract both sides of the chest.

Put whole attention there while contracting them. Hold contraction, counting 1 to 30. Then release contraction. REPEAT SIX TIMES. Morning, noon, and night.

Exposing chest to direct sunlight is found to be very beneficial; slowly walk two miles a day. Remain outdoors as much as possible. Eat plenty of raw green vegetables and thoroughly pecan nuts. Clearing throat and nose with mixture of half a teaspoonful of salt in a glass of water early in the morning and at noon, and just before going to bed, has been found very beneficial and refreshing.

THE CARE AND EXERCISE OF THE THROAT The second factor in voice culture lies in the care and exer-

-Page Two-

cise of the throat, the mouth, the lungs, and the diap(h)ragm. All public speakers should refrain from using sour pickles, sour lemons, and sour oranges. It is good to use a little honey after drinking orange juice. Frequent use of honey is very good. The. use of raw ginger and rock candy is very good for the throat. Public speakers who talk for long hours at a time should lubricate their throats with rock candy and a small piece of ginger kept in the mouth, long before the time for the ordeal of speech-making. In fact, to hide a piece of flat rock candy and flat diced ginger between the teeth and the inner cheek during speech-making helps to keep the throat continuously lubricated when it is in constant action. Avoid sore throats through regular good habits and right living. Avoid colds by eating lightly at night and by eating more of fruits and vegetables.

BEST EXERCISE   Put chin on chest, then stretch the muscles of the throat slowly, with the feeling that your chin is tied to the chest. Then slowly force the chin up, holding the tension of the throat while the head goes upward. Then relax quickly and drop the chin on chest. Repeat the above twelve times morning and night.

In public speaking one must not strain the vocal cords by speaking through the throat, or strain the lungs by speaking through the lungs. One must learn to start the breath and the thought waves from the diaphragm and let the breath pass through the lungs and throat into the mouth. The vocal cords must he used in speaking in loud or soft tones not by artificial exertion but by inspiration. Those who have no inspiration and try to impress their audience through loud speech, injure their vocal cords. Deep inspiration should produce loud tones and gentle inspiration should produce soft tones. Inspira¬tion should be the guiding force of the vocal cords. All sounds must be produced through the mouth, inspired by the strength of the abdomen, diaphragm, lungs, and breath trained according to the above-mentioned methods.

THE CURE OF "STAGE-FRIGHT."   Remember, if you, by calmness, can prevent the regular visitation of psychological nervousness, you will never suffer from the more serious and long-continued forms of nervousness, stage-fright is a form of fear which causes nervousness in many people, so that they are never able to do anything naturally. If you are shy and have stage-fright, get your mind quiet and remember that all the power you need is within you, all the power to convince people, all the power to give the direct truth. The particular kind of truth that you want to give is in the Infinite Spirit, which functions through you. Overcome stage-fright: (1) By getting used to talking to groups. (2) By imagining whenever you give a talk that you are addressing an empty hall, or that you are talking to children, or very simple people. Realize that all power to think, to speak, and to act comes from God, and that He is with you now, guiding and inspiring you. As soon as you actually realize that, a flash of illumination will come and fear will leave you. Sometimes the power of God comes like an ocean and surges through your Being in great boundless waves, sweeping away all obstacles. Feel that God talks through you whenever you want to speak.

EXERCISE TO STRENGTHEN THE NERVES   Inhale; hold breath. Contract entire body all at once gently. Hold contraction, counting 1 to 20, with deep attention upon entire body. Then exhale. Release contraction. Repeat 3 times, or any time you feel weak and nervous.

TONIC FOR NERVES   Some of the physical methods of overcoming nervousness as taught in India are, first, a soothing drink made of fresh limes. It is made in this way: To one glass of water add the juice of one-quarter of a fresh lime and about a tablespoonful of sugar, or powdered rock candy. Stir thoroughly, and add a little crushed ice. It is difficult to give exact measurements because of the difference in the size of limes, but it should not taste at all like the ordinary limeade bought at soda fountains. That is far too strong. This drink should be blended so that the sweetness and sourness are equal and you cannot distinguish which you are tasting. Ground rock candy is even better than sugar, but do not use honey. If properly blended, every nerve will feel calm. Sipping two or three glasses of this during nervousness has been found to be extremely beneficial. If you have too much lime or too much sugar, it will not produce the result. The blending must be equal.

PERFECT TECHNIQUE MUST BE ACCOMPANIED BY SOUL INSPIRATION   The daily practice of especially selected graded vocal exercises is highly important in the development of the speaking and singing voice. A great thing in voice culture consists in using concentration to learn the technique of speaking or singing. In a closed room with deep concentration try to very intelligently and inspirationally speak or sing extemporaneously to an invisible audience. Try to apply the technique of correct speaking and singing during your practices before an invisible audience.

The technique of speaking and singing must be practiced without fault or blemish. After that is accomplished, inspiration, concentration, self-confidence, and emotion will guide the technique. In other words, inspiration must be the outstanding power behind the speech of the speaker and the song of the singer. As there is no excuse for a faulty halting speech or a faulty technique in singing, so also, speaking or singing with perfect technique but without Soul inspiration and Soul originality are inexcusable.

SHORT APOLOGUES
THE "MEEK" MAN AND THE BANDIT

One day I was sitting in a public park meditating when a rough-looking man came up to me. He said: "Give me 10 cents. I gave him the money. Then he walked away, but quickly turned around and came a few steps nearer and said: "Give me another 10 cents. I could see that he was thinking that he had met the meekest man on earth.

He kept this up, now asking for 25 cents, then for 50 cents, and finally he said: "Give me a dollar." Suddenly, with all the force and power that I could command, I jumped up and shouted: "GET OUT!" He was so surprised he dropped all the money and ran like a streak of lightning.

I picked up my money and walked away. A policeman was standing near and said: "What did you do to that man? He is a very dangerous character." I said: "Oh, nothing, we just came to a little understanding."

So remember, if you remain calm you can conquer anything, or anyone. Calmness means that God is with you. As soon as you become restless, you will irritate people and they will be angry with you and misery will be dancing in your temple.

Never be afraid of anything. Fear is a form of nervousness. As long as you are not dead, you are alive, so why should you fear? Anyway, when you are dead it is all over and you cannot remember, so why worry?

Always remember, wherever you are, if someone is trying to get you in trouble, say: "I am peace, I am calm," and say it deeply and no matter how people shake you, hold on to that peace. Your nerves will then be calm. You are a child of God and you must never get mad. The more you get mad the longer you will remain a mortal, but if you remain calm, you are a child of God. The minute anyone gets you mad, there is something wrong with you, but this does not mean that you must let them make a door-mat out of you.

-Page 4-

HOW CALMNESS CONQUERED ANGER

Once a man came to me in the hotel where I was staying and in front of all my friends began to insult me. My friends were getting very angry at the injustice done to me and wanted to throw him out, but I remained calm and let him rave, so after he was through he said in great surprise: "Why, I said all kinds of things to you but you didn't get mad?" I replied; "Why, should I become angry? Blame doesn't make me any worse, and praise doesn't make me any better, but I feel very sorry for you, for you only succeeded in revealing your true character. You make a business of criticizing everyone but yourself. You are absolutely a slave to yourself."

Do not allow anyone to take away your peace and happiness. Sometimes little puffs of breath have more power to hurt than big blows.

They destroy your nerves. Keep quiet, rather than argue. Be safe in the fortress of your own peace. The minute anyone wants to fight with you, take a walk. If anyone insults you, just answer with your eyes.

Remember, if you are calm you will open the doors to contact God, and you will say: "My body is well, and my mind is like a telephone, with which I contact God. I have withdrawn my energy and senses and the electricity of life to the brain, and my brain has become the radio of God and the perfect song of God is in my health, and in my soul, and in my mind. "

THE DEVOTED WAITER

Once, when I was in a Pullman car, a certain waiter wanted to serve me all the time. I prayed: "Lord, he has helped me so much I would like to give him something good in return." One day it happened that I did not sit at his table and he felt so badly that he cried and finally he said: "Tell me what it is that you have that draws me so. You have something that I want. Please help me." So, between trains, I taught him the principles of Self-Realization.

You can do wonderful things in changing souls. Healing of body is good, healing of the mind is better, but healing of the Soul is greatest. Your ighest delight will be to change Souls by sending 1 healing energy. Whoever comes to me with a recipient heart, shall never go back the same again. He shall be changed by the divine healing that comes through my hands. It is a wonderful thing to help others.

HEALTH CULTURE
THE SCIENCE OF NUTRITION

DIET AND STRONG TEETH (Continued)　　　In order to have strong, well-formed bones and teeth it is necessary that the conditions of nutrition should be more than adequate -- that is that there should be a plentiful supply of calcium, phosphorus and Vitamin D -- during the time when the teeth are forming (before birth and in childhood). For building excellent bone and teeth structure, the nutrition of the mother and child during these periods is of the greatest importance. In order to preserve the teeth in good condition throughout life it is necessary to maintain a state of good general health. The digestive tract particularly should be kept in a hygienic condition. Of course, it is essential that the mouth and teeth be kept clean and that the body should be supplied with all of the necessary elements for health and vitality.

PRAECEPTUM INSPIRATION
SOURCES OF LIFE ENERGY

Will power and energy are the two things which sustain the body. Take them away and you will die. Will power brings energy from the outer source. Energy is the missing link between the body and the mind. The greater the will, the greater the flow of energy into a body part.

PRAECEPTUM AFFIRMATION

During the dark nights of misfortune, I want the flowers of my appreciation to exhale the scent of gratefulness on Thy Feet of Sacred Silence.

YOGODA SAT-SANGA FORTNIGHTLY INSTRUCTIONS
BY
PARAMHANSA YOGANANDA

SHOW US THAT THOU ART THE PATH THAT WE SHOULD SEEK

Heavenly Father, Thou who are manifest in Jesus and the great Gurus of India and the saints of all religions, bless us. Let the understanding of Jesus and the great ones inspire us to understand Thee. Show us that Thou art the path and the goal, Thou art the desire and ambition which we should seek at all times.

Bring to us the aroma of Thy love, the devotion of Thy Being, the wisdom of Thy Personality. Make us feel that Thou art living on the altar of every cell, in our will power, in every desire, and on the altar of our Souls.

Mighty Being, spread Thy fire over all the earth and over all souls, and dispel the darkness from within us and make us realize that Thy living flame is within and without, and on the altar of our hearts be Thou present evermore.

With all the devotion of our Being, with all the love of our heart, we invoke Thy presence. Those who are real souls, may they find Thee through the secret door of their hearts and through the nook of their minds. Divine Father, the aroma of flowers and all the beauty of the dawn, and all thoughts, we gather together to worship Thee in the temple of silence. Receive our devotion on the Altar of the dawn. Receive our devotion on the altar of the noonday sun. Receive our devotion at the portals of night. Father, be Thou the only love reigning on the throne of our desires.

HOW TO CULTIVATE A GOOD MEMORY

What is memory? Memory is that power by which you recollect your past experiences. For instant, if you have no memory, you have forgotten all your childhood experiences. All the experiences that you have had are reproduced by your mental subconscious faculty so that you may be able to profit by some of them and discard the rest. Memory is something which we all must have. It was given to us by God lest we forget our desirable experiences and fail to learn the lessons they teach.

Why is memory ever asleep? Some people can remember things that others cannot remember. Memory has different grades in different people according to brain capacity. In order to develop your memory, you need education, concentration, meditation, and experiences. Unless you have developed your memory, you are not an educated person. If you had had a certain experience and if you forget it, then it is not yours.

Memory can be developed by recalling all the beautiful things that have happened in our lives. We never become tired of agreeable experiences and good deeds. We should repeat them again and again in our consciousness and replete our lives with better experiences.

SPECIAL EXERCISES   One way to develop your memory is to connect certain things with some brilliant affair, then you won't forget. Memory develops by the association of one thing with another. It is true that most people have a certain amount of memory from birth, but if you limit your memory, you limit your Soul. Memory must be developed. It can be stretched like rubber. It is eternal, elastic, and can record many things if you develop it.

All our faculties have to be cultivated. Some people never give their memory any exercise to develop it. If you practice addition, subtraction, and multiplication mentally, it will help to develop your memory. Try to remember or visualize something. Every day try to recall what you did a week ago that day. That will help a good deal. You must also try to recall what happened in your life much earlier. Try to remember only the constructive things that happened. Another way to develop your memory is to pay strict attention to the thing that you want remember. Why do you remember the greatest sorrows of your life? Because you direct more attention to them. Deep attention is a strong force that develops memory. If you have a poor memory, it usually indicates that you have a "butter-fly" mind. You flit from one thing to another, without giving careful attention to each individual thing. Exercise is very important. You must link one idea with another. Connect certain things with certain other things.

The art of visualization is very important. Look steadily at a certain object, or at some scenery, or in a show window, then see how many of the details you can enumerate. The deeper your impressions, the more details you will be able to remember.

Most people perform life's duties absent-mindedly. That is why they cannot remember much. There is a wide gulf between their actions and their thoughts. You must put great attention upon whatever you wish to remember.

MEMORY HAS NO DISCRIMINATION -- IT IMITATES   You say: We do not remember what we were before we came to this earth. That is because you do not possess the Divine memory. Jesus knew exactly where he came from, where he was going, and so on. This mortal memory is extremely necessary in order to get the best out of experiences. Memory does not discriminate. It takes in anything you will it to take. It imitates. It would be a misuse of memory if you tried to bring back into your consciousness all the evil things that occurred in the past. That would be very bad.

Your memory will do exactly what you tell it to do, so be careful that you do not let it repeat any unpleasant experiences. So many people wa(n)t to give up bad habits but they have repeated them so many times that they have become automatic. Sometimes memory won't let you forget, so you must not feed your memory with the wrong food, or you will suffer from the effect of wrong thoughts and actions. Even the most evil habit if constantly practiced after a while will seem to be all right to you, but it will surely lead to unhappiness in the end. Never repeat anything that is wrong. Give it up quickly. Do not let it remain in your consciousness. I am not telling you to be negative, but you must not be a slave to anything. Remember in your consciousness there are all kinds of records, both good and bad. You must destroy all records that revive memories of unhappiness and evil deeds and unkindness. You must scatter them to the winds.

SOMETIMES YOU MUST LEARN TO FORGET   We must increase the quality of the memory so that, being powerful, we shall remember all the good things that went before. According to many scientists, memory cannot be developed, but we know that it can bo developed by exercise. If you are born a weakling and I insist that you cannot become strong, that is a false statement. There is always something greater if you know where to seek it. Some scientists do not know the art of concentration and memory development, so when they find a weak brain they say;

"According to the laws of heredity, this is going to last to the end of his days." That is foolish.

One great metaphysician said: "Memory gives the power of reproduction." If you can remember some of the experiences of different people in this life, why can't you remember those that have happened in the Soul? Mortal memory reproduces experiences in this life and Divine memory reproduces all the experiences in the Soul.

Memory was given to you to reproduce good things. You must not train it to remember that which is evil. If you remember someone that you hate and every day you are killing him in your mind because you remember what he did, you are misusing your memory. You must not recall such experiences. They are gone and do not now belong to you. By remembering a thing, you live it over again. Develop forgetfulness in such a case.

GOD IS THE ESSENCE OF ALL GOOD THINGS   Remember only the beautiful things that you have felt and seen and experienced. If your five senses only behold the good, then your Soul will be a garden of blossoming qualities, and in the garden of memory there will be no weeds of wrong thoughts, but only blossoms of good qualities. If you can make your garden produce the blossoms of beautiful thoughts, then in that garden of beautiful memories God will visit you. He who loves all good things and remembers all good things will at last remember God, the Essence of all good things. Someday an Invisible Power will come and will smash all the windows of your memory into one big opening through which you may see and remember that you are One with God.

SHORT APOLOGUES
REAL FREEDOM

He who is not controlled by his thoughts and actions is a free person. My Master used to say: "Give me a free man." He feared no one. One day he was sitting in the hermitage and a magistrate came in. He was a mean man. I said to Master: "Please remember that he has authority." Master said: "Is that so?" Master would not even get up to offer him a seat, so I told him to sit down. He sat on the hard bench but seemed very angry and disgusted with everything. Master was sitting in a nice chair.

After a while, the magistrate broke the silence and asked: "What is your philosophy?" Master answered by asking him a question. He said: "What is yours?" The magistrate answered by repeating old orthodox ideas about Truth. He was not speaking, from actual experience, so Master said: "You are not expressing your own opinion. You are merely repeating what others have said about Truth. I want to hear what you have to say and not what others have said."

By this time the magistrate was very angry. Then he said: "I secured first place in the tests and have received a degree. Do you know that?" Master replied: "I never know it until you told me.   After further conversation, the man slumped in his seat and was overpowered by the greatness of Master. He became a devoted disciple.

Master knew the Truth and was not afraid to express it to anyone. When your action is not influenced by anything or anyone, then you are free. That was the case with Jesus. He paid with His life and did not care. That is real freedom. As long as you are influenced by family or national characteristics, or instincts of the past, you are a slave and you do not know it. As long as the slightest desire controls your actions you are not free. Do not be controlled by anything.

-Page Three-

A MAN OF GREATNESS

Many people went to my Master. Some thought he was hard; some thought he did not know anything, and some found God through him.

Those who are great declare their greatness through their actions, not from anything they may say. Whether you understand them or not will be according to the caliber of your own understanding.

One day a man came to see Master and all day long he talked about automobiles. Finally this man came to me and said: "I am so disappointed in him." I said: "You do not know him. He is not the kind of man who the minute you meet him will talk of spiritual matters and try to sell himself. He will join in discussing any subject you choose. He has attained. He can speak on any subject." So I said: "Come along. Let us talk to him." So we went back and talked with Master until morning, forgetting all time.

HE RETURNED GOOD FOR EVIL

An architect friend and student of mine was once blackmailed by a former friend of his who became an enemy, circulating serious lies in regard to his construction work. My friend planned to get even with him, but he remembered that I had said in one of my classes: "Forget the evil that is done you." So one day my student met the man who had ruined him but instead of being mean toward him, he just put his hand on his shoulder and gave him the greatest love. He said: "Do not think of the misunderstanding. Why think of those things? We are all children of God. I have forgiven you long ago." The result was that the man's conscience tortured him for weeks until at last he ran out of his house and went to the house of the architect and said: "I am going to rectify the great wrong I have done you." He went from house to house to vindicate his friend.

AN ELEPHANT WITH A GOOD MEMORY

The power called memory was given by God. Think what a blessing it is. It is given to animals also. Some animals have very good memories. Once I heard a story about an elephant in India. One day he was picking up wood when a little boy pricked him on the snout with a needle, then ran away. A year after this happened the same elephant met the boy again. It was the elephant's chance to reciprocate, so he picked the boy up with his trunk and tossed him to one side. So, animals have a memory too. If they did not have, they could not recognize their offspring.

HEALTH CULTURE
THE SCIENCE OF NUTRITION

DIET AND STRONG TEETH (Continued)   Calcium, phosphorus and vitamin D are the three elements which are especially necessary for building and maintaining strong bones and teeth. They also perform other functions. (See Praecepta 62 and 63, and Inner Culture, Sept. 1935 and Jan. 1936.) Foods having a high calcium content are, watercress, kale, cheese, turnip leaves, milk, tomatoes, cabbage, dandelions, romaine lettuce, okra, spinach, butter, cottage cheese, and lemons.

The best phosphorus foods are egg yolk, milk, cheese, whole grains, dried beans, nuts, radishes, pumpkin, mushrooms, watercress, Brussel sprouts, lettuce, cauliflower, spinach, dried soyabean (sic) meal, leeks, asparagus, and barley.

It is very essential for good health, strong teeth and bones and general well-being of both children and adults that they have an adequate supply of vitamin D. Its lack is considered the most serious

-Page Four-

dietary deficiency. Unlike other vitamins, vitamin D is not found in many human foodstuffs. The best source is sunlight on the bare skin.

It is wise when possible for everyone to take a daily sunbath or to use one of the specially designed lamps for this purpose. The richest known source in food materials is cod liver oil. Vitamin D is now being added to many prepared foods, particularly canned milk and yeast, by a process called irradiation.

BEETS ESPANOL

½ cup minced onion
2 sweet peppers, diced
3 cups diced cooked beets
1 tablespoon butter

2 cups tomato juice
vegetized salt
Smoein seasoning

Cook onion and peppers in butter over low fire. Add tomato juice, beets and seasonings. Cover and simmer for 2 hours. Serves six.

FRENCH VANILLA ICE CREAM

2 cups milk
3 egg yolks
½ cup raw sugar

3 eggs whites, stiffly beaten

½ pint heavy cream, whipped
1 teaspoon vanilla flavoring

Heat milk in double boiler. Beat egg yolks, stir in sugar and then the hot milk. Return to top of double boiler and cook until mixture coats the spoon. Remove from heat and fold in stiffly beaten egg whites. Cool. Add vanilla to custard mixture and fold in whipped cream. Freeze in freezer. Serve with crushed berries or other fruit. Serves six.

PRAECEPTUM INSPIRATION
MEMORY IS DEVELOPED THROUGH MEDITATION

What is meditation? It is becoming one with the Soul; it is when you drop your relation with the muscles and with human limitations and try to remember that you are a Soul. When you begin to relate yourself to the soul, then you will be aware of more of your past experiences, and you will know that you have come down from the bosom of God. In God lies all the memory and experiences of your life. In your contact inside, the forgotten times and powers will come back into your consciousness. Meditation leads you to remember that you are not a mortal, but that you are One with God. During the daytime, when you are not meditating, you remember that you are a mortal, but in meditation the reverse is true. Meditation means dropping the consciousness of the body and remembering who you are and then coming back and ruling the body.

God is speaking through all forces of Nature. He is talking through our brains, through our hands, through our will, through our intelligence and love. They all represent glimpses of the Divine power. The power of feeling and the power to discriminate came from the Spirit Bosom and we are the sparks of the Divine Fire. You are the waves of the sea, so you must remember when you are peaceful, when your conscience is satisfied, then you are in tune with God. Conscience is the voice of God. If we do wrong, something tells us. Through the voice of conscience and reason God speaks to us.

PRAECEPTUM AFFIRMATION
CLOSE YOUR EYES. MENTALLY AFFIRM:

"THOU AND I ARE ONE. I AM THOU, THOU ART I. I AM THY CHILD. I AM FREE. AWAY, AWAY, AWAY, DARKNESS, DISEASE, IGNORANCE; AWAY, AWAY, AWAY."

YOGODA SAT-SANGA FORTNIGHTLY INSTRUCTIONS
BY
PARAMHANSA YOGANANDA
WE ARE PART OF THY CHANGELESS BEING

O Spirit, make us realize Thy presence beneath the waves of appearances. We toss and dance on the waves of Thy Creation. O Spirit, divert our eyes within to see the vastness of Thy glory behind all appearances.

O Beloved immortality, teach us to behold Thy vastness, Thy changelessness behind all things, that we ray perceive ourselves not as part of the change, but as part of Thy changeless Being.

We dropped our tears of light through the eyes of stars at the feet of the blue. Father receive our gathered tears of light to wash Thy feet of immortality. We are Thy children, make us realize that. From the incense vase of our heart we pray unto Thee. We offer unto Thee the fragrance of our love. Thou art ours; may we not become enthralled by passing desires, but may we be awakened to Thy glory, that we may drop this dream of delusion and behold reality; make us immortal stars in the firmament of Thy Being.

Peace unto all people, peace unto all nations, good will unto all religions, peace unto all creatures, peace unto all that lives. Father, Mother, Friend, Beloved God recharge our beings with Thy power, recharge our minds with Thy efficiency, recharge our souls with Thy everlasting wisdom.

Cast away all feelings of the body. Inject every cell with Thy joy and peace of meditation.

WHAT INDIA CAN TEACH US
Part One

All re(li)gious beliefs either originated in India or were influenced by the Scriptures of India. The Indian sages did not seek to identify themselves with religious names and forms. They asked "What is the science that will help us to find God? What is that, knowing which, I shall know all?"

India's civilization is much older than the civilization of Egypt. First came the material life, then the intellectual, and then the period of spiritual investigation. Every nation has to go through these three stages.

THE PANTHEISTIC CONCEPTION OF GOD   From Hindusim we must take the pantheistic conception of God and the practical, scientific methods of approaching God. Hindus say: "You do not have to profess any special religious belief, all you have to know is the method of contacting God." Spiritual Truth cannot be taught by one who has only committed Truth to memory. Truth must be understood and experienced before it can be effectively taught.

At first the belief was that God was many, and then they found that God is one. Some people believe that God is all and others believe that there is God and matter. The pantheistic belief is most correct

79

because it teaches that God is everything. Ocean and waves are the same and sunshine and rays are the same. Pantheism is a teaching of the Yoga philosophy.

THE TRUE MEANING OF SYMBOLS   When you forget the meaning of a symbol, that is idolatry. A symbol should remind you of the thing it stands for. Most people think that the Hindus are idol worshippers. That is not true. They worship only the meaning of a symbol. As you have the cross as a symbol of mercy and forgiveness, so Hindus have little statues with different spiri¬tual meanings. Every time you see a cross and you say: "Father, forgive them, for they know not what they do, " that is not idolatry. To become lost to the idol's meaning is idolatry.

Hindus speak of God, not as an Idol, but as omnipresent. We are all seeking Him through the pathways of ambition. We are all seeking that one thing -- perennial happiness, which is God.

Many peole think that Hinduism is connected with crystal-gazing, but this is not true. In India there were no factories to make those crystal balls which people associate so often with India. Hypnotism is wrong. The snake hypnotizes the bird by animal magnetism, which paralyzes its body. Magnetism is your expending vibration. Hypnosis is when your consciousness is taken away and you do what others tell you to do.

VARIOUS PHILOSOPHIES   From the Hindu philosophy came the Buddhistic philosophy. Buddhists started the first mis¬sionary Movement in India. From Bud(d)ha we get the consciousness of love and devotion and kindness. Buddhism, however, lacks a clear teaching on the consciousness of the ultimate supreme Being. Buddhism teaches negation or cessation. On the other hand, Hinduism teaches that there is something beyond. "From joy we come, in joy we live, and into the SACRED JOY we melt."

Fifteen years of the early life of Jesus must have been spent with the Hindu Saints. His entire teaching is in accord with Vedanta Truths. However, it does not really matter where the Truth came from. What we are all primarily interested in is the Truth itself.

HOW TEACHERS ARE CHOSEN IN INDIA   India is very particular as to the method of teaching Truth to people. In the Western world the method is different. Usually the disciple has to be coaxed to accept the teacher, but in India the disciple seeks the teacher.

Hinduism is thousands of years old. Recent archaeological discoveries have proven that India's civilization is older than Egypt. Therefore, India precedes in almost all forms of development. In the beginning, each nation, like a child, is busy with material develop¬ment, then intellectual development, then spiritual development.

India went through these three stages long ago. That is why India has had a chance to put down all dogmas and understand the Truth. That is why people with different belie(f)s have left the temples and gone into the quiet places where great teachers live the life and who are not elected by a church board. India has gone through that process of religious evolution.

I used to fall on the ground to purify my body in the dust on which these Saints had walked. I met three Souls of exalted character. They had God in their hearts. If you met them you would ask: "Have they a following?" I would answer: "No. They live in a little hut with a few students around them." Americans would think they were odd because they had no following, but I would rather sit with one of those Saints and know that I am in the presence of God than be associated with a great following of those who have no Self-Realization.

-Page Two-

Day after day, as I sat these Saints, all the darkness and gloom of doubt began to vanish and I began to perceive the God that everyone forgot, and that God was real. In that vast shroud of nature, He is sleeping and He does not care whether you call Him or not. You cannot rouse Him except by your love and desire to know Him.

If your heart is ready, if you are desirous of knowing God, and you continuously again and again march toward the spirit, then you will meet the Saints of India and recognize them, otherwise you may meet them and yet not recognize them. If you will follow such a teacher with due reverence and with open eyes, you will save yourself years of wasted time, for no one can lead you to God unless he himself has first found God.

This is the theme of India: The Saints are not found in the temples and churches. The people of India do not go into temples to learn the deeper Truths. They go where there are real teachers. If a Saint lives in the woods it does not matter, as the devotee is seeking Self-Realization, wherever he may find it.

Many times I have upbraided myself for not more completely understanding my Master when I lived with him. I lived and ate with him but I did not fully realize his greatness. So, remember this, if you ever go to India, visit some of those spiritual giants. Keyserling and Brunton met some of them. Keyserling said: "When I was walking by the banks of the Ganges, I felt the invisible vibrations that the Masters had left there in meditation."

THE TRUTH MUST BE RETAINED   Do not admire the dogmatism of any reli(g)ion. I believe that dogmatism is due to material causes. Churches should be the laboratories of spiritual experience. Their dogmas should be burned and the Truth retained. I want to bring to the minds of different religionists that the time has come not to hold on to the belief in dogmas, but let the mind of God freely flow through your hearts. My purpose is not to show the supremacy of any religion, but to reveal Truth where it is.

Self-Realization Fellowship is not a sect but offers a technique by which you can calm the body and the mind. To become a member, it is not necessary to change your religion. What is necessary is to establish a fellowship of all religions and to find out the quickest route that leads to God. We do not try to monopolize Truth. Do you see the beauty of that? If you are the follower of Truth, you are God's child.

We must have nothing but the religion of God -- the religion of Truth. So let us make up our minds to follow the Truth. As Jesus said: "The Truth shall make you free."

THE APOLOGUE

THE SAINT WHO CALLED A KING A BEGGAR

A God-known soul abided in dreams of happiness in a little niche on the breast of a mountain glen. Unctuous prayers in spirals of deep sincerity floated heavenward from the incense-vase of his heart. The All-Knowing Silence breathed joy at the singular touch of those fragrant Soul-pourings. There was a ceaseless exchange ol unspoken invisible missives between the Great Omniscience and this devotee. All the prayers of this devotee were visibly granted by the All-Satisfying Commander of all destinies, yet the great Royal Sly Eluder often played hide and seek with the ever-seeking devotee

-Page Three-

81

One day, as the devotee sat in the chamber of ecstasy, he suddenly demanded: "Beloved of all Souls, grant me some mundane riches, that fulfill my desire to build on the hillside a big carved Cathedral. The Great One intimated to the devotee, through the tableau of a vision, that he should see the King of his State. The devotee emerged from the portals of silence, jerked his muscles into activity, and wended his way to his vision-directed destination.

After several hours of pleasant wanderings through blossomed woodlands and matter-vibrating, noisy city streets, the devotee came to the palace of the King and accosted the gatekeeper about the whereabouts of his Majesty.

"He is offering his prayers in the city Mosque. You can visit him there," curtly replied the palace gatekeeper from behind the bars.

The Saint, after questioning many a passerby, and after many detours, at last reached the Royal Mosque. This monumental Mosque had no special reserved seats like paid-for church pews. Without ceremony or introduction, the devotee squatted down near the King on an empty seat on the alabaster floor. The devotee thought, just as he closed his eyes to pray: "I am at last in the presence of his Rich Highness, who has, in all probability, all his desires crowned with fulfillment and does not have to supplicate for anything from anyone. I am glad I have come for financial aid from one who does not beg."

Even as the Saint was thinking this, his attention suddenly caught the whispered prayers coming from the Royal lips. With rapturous attention, the devotee listened to the Royal prayers. He was expecting a Royal prayer from a Royal Being, but to his amazement he heard the following prayer:

"Heavenly Father, owner of all the glittering planets, arcana paradise, and. earth, please grant me more riches, and make me more powerful than all other kings. Give me more territory, which I may annex to my empire.

Stupefied, disillusioned, utterly bewildered, the Saint, disgusted, said to himself: "Ha! ha! This big beggar is begging for more riches and lands." Unable to control his merriment and loud laughter, and looking straight at the king, he cried out with scorn just as the Mosque services were ending:

"Ha! ha! I am satisfied. I must get away from this place." He then started to walk away from the Mosque. The laughter and loud, derisive outbursts of the Saint had broken up the prayer meeting, and in wrath the King followed him, shouting: "Arrest the Blaspheming Imposter."

The Saint stopped suddenly and looked at the King, then fell into a fit of uncontrollable laughter. Courtiers and city codgers surrounded the angry King who was confronted by the fearless, laughing holy man.

Seeing that threats were of no avail, the King composed himself, and with folded hands knelt down before the Saint and gently said:

"Pray, will you satisfy my great curiosity as to the cause of your laughter and strange antics during the services."

The Saint answered by asking a question: "Do you make the same requests in your prayer every day as you did today? "

"Why yes," the King answered.

The Saint laughingly replied: "I came to you for some financial help for my hermitage."

"Of course I will grant you anything, but why did you laugh and then leave," interrupted the King.

Page Four

This story offers a golden sermon to Souls who vainly seek to quench the thirst of their dreams from the desert of limitations.

This earth may have a few oases momentarily satisfying our Soul thirsts, yet the spring of Nectar lies beneath the rocks of our indifference, which must be continuously hewn by devotion until they allow the celestial flood to flow through us and quench all the buries thirst of incarnations forever and forever.

HEALTH CULTURE
THE SCIENCE OF NUTRITION

HONEY -- ITS NATURE AND USES   Honey is one of the oldest foods known and has been widely used for centuries by all races of men. It is produced in practically all parts of the world and under the most varying climatic conditions from Alaska in the far north to the southern plains, deserts, mountain tops, and valleys.

In ancient times honey was considered so valuable that it was used only in ceremonies and celebrations of the utmost importance.

It was deemed so essential that it was used as an offering to the Gods, and the bee was considered sacred. In India it was thought to bring good luck when dropped on the tongue of a new-born babe.

(To be continued)

TOMATOES AND MUSHROOMS ON TOAST
3 large green peppers cut in narrow strips
small onions, sliced
4 tablespoons butter
3/4 teaspoon celery salt

3/4 lb. mushrooms, skinned and sliced   4
4 large tomatoes, skinned and quartered
¼ teaspoon paprika

Sauté peppers and onions in butter until tender, add sliced mushrooms, quartered tomatoes, celery salt and paprika. Continue cooking for about 15 minutes and serve on buttered whole wheat toast.

PISTACHIO PARFAIT
2/3 cup sweetened condensed milk
½ cup cold water
1 cup whipping cream
1 egg white

¼ cup halved pistachio nuts
few drops green vegetable coloring
1 teaspoon almond extract

Beat together condensed milk, cold water and almond extract, Whip cream to custard-like consistency and fold into mixture. Add few drops green coloring, and nut meats. Fold in stiffly beaten egg white. Freeze to stiff mush in automatic re(f)rigerator. Beat 2 minutes and finish freezing. This may be served with slightly sweetened whipped cream and chopped pistachio nuts if desired.

"Oh, no, thanks," the Saint replied, as he continued his accusation before the whole audience: "Mr. King, when I heard you, during services, pray for more opulence and territory, I was convinced of what you are. You are nothing but a big beggar. Big-King-Beggar; did you get that; you are the biggest beggar I ever met and I do not choose to beg anything from an unconfirmed beggar like you. I am going back to my dream-valley and my Beloved in the temple of ecstasy, and when I meet Him, I am going to scold Him for sending me to a beggar for financial assistance, when He is the richest and only King of the Cosmos, who has everything and does not need to supplicate for anything from anyone."

-Page Five-

P R A EC EP TU M INSPIRATION
INVOKE THE BLESSED LORD OF AUM

Think of the powers that are playing within you! You can be master only when you realise this power. You must be persistent with determined thoughts, so that you may realize that you are a child of God. When you realize that, then you are saved. You must seek wisdom and power and prosperity from God. If you prefer material desires to God, that is only a travesty or an error of judgment. Do not strive for unimportant things and reject God.

God is not something mystical. He is tangible, because all tangible things come out of the Intangible. If you would only realize that! Why walk on the trail of life pursuing material desires and go on suffering. Why do that? Even great and materially successful people will realize the emptiness of their lives in the end, but those who find God in this life are already rich in joy and power.

Peace eternal, joy eternal be the glory of your Being. On the altar of peace and ever-new happiness invoke the Blessed Lord of Aum. Bliss is the altar on which God stays forever. He who is filled with joy shall make the altar for the Lord, within.

P R A E C E P T U M   A F F I R M A T I O N

I behold Thee as the only friend, helping me, encouraging me, through all my friends.

-Page Six-

YOGODA SAT-SANGA FORTNIGHTLY INSTRUCTIONS
BY
Paramhansa Yogananda

MAY WE BEHOLD NOTHING BUT TRUTH

Heavenly Father, awaken within us Thy Consciousness of peace and happiness beyond dreams.
Teach us to find the one highway of inner spiritual law through which we may find Thee. Father, Thou art our Beloved. It is our birthright to seek and to know Thee. Naughty or good, we are Thy children. Reveal Thyself to us.

We offer to Thee our devotion. Bless us with calmness and understanding and right effort, that we may s ee all the rivers of our desires moving to Thy presence within and without. Lead us from worry to divine love. With a burning heart, with a flaming soul, with a burning, mind we lay at Thy feet of Omnipresence all the flowers of our devotion.

Open the stars, open the blue, open the doors of blossoms and call our thoughts and feelings, and Nature and history, and show to us Thy great Presence. Father, Almighty Being, our Beloved God, with every cell of our body, with every thought of our Being, we long for Thee.

Wherever light is, darkness is no more. We closed our eyes and beheld darkness only. Open our eyes, that we may destroy this self-created darkness and behold naught but Thy Light, and may we emancipate ourselves in that Light. Let us behold naught but beauty, naught but good, naught but Truth, naught but Thy eternally immortal Fountain of Bliss.

WHAT INDIA Can TEACH US
Part Two

We are the children of the One God. He, being the source of contentment, the time has come for us to find Him. We must know the technique of Self-Realization before we can know God. Let us seek realization of Self, which is the Teaching of India. You cannot destroy self and you cannot lose your consciousness in God. You can expand. These Teachings will show you how to come into the consciousness.

Truth is marching on and our creeds and dogmas are bowing down to Truth. If you have the hive, you must have the honey also. Self- Realization will supply the honey, in the final analysis, real unity will only come when all the faiths take all truths and put them in the pot of Self-Realization and keep only those that stand the test.

The real purpose of Meditation is to burn your dogmas and build in your heart an everlasting temple of Self-Realization.

A dumb man once ate some honey and he was asked what the taste of honey was like. He could not speak but he made such motions that the other person understood that honey was very sweet.

The mind knows that it cannot know God except by discrimination and devotion, and when it unites itself with the Infinite, then it knows that it knows, but it cannot describe what that contact is like. As a pain is very real to you and yet you cannot make others know what it is like, so it is with the perception of the Infinite. It cannot be described. It is something one cannot explain to others. It must be experienced.

NOTHING EXISTS BUT GOD By the great methods discovered by the Master Minds of India you must rise above the body so to speak. India teaches how to rise above the body - then you can feel your identity with God; then you see that you are in Spirit, spreading over the stars, twinkling through their luminosity; then you see yourself as the ocean of ether and everything floating in you; then you see that you are the end of all; then you see your smile in every face; then you can say: "I work through all hands and think through all minds; my heart throbs through all hearts; my presence I feel in everything; the stars are but the ornaments of my vast body of matter" -- then you are in Spirit.

Body and mind are the two aspects of spirit. The ocean in the storm and the calm ocean are the same thing. Spirit manifest as matter exists, why deny matter? What we see came out of the same Spirit. It is delusion when we see apart from God, because matter is a part of God. When you are tossed on the wave, you forget the vastness of life, but remember, whether the ocean is calm or restless it is still the ocean. When you see the ocean and the wave together, then you will see God and yourself together as One, but that does not mean that you will lose your consciousness of yourself. You know that you are existing and God is existing, and you and He are One. The wave and the ocean are one.

If you are tossed on the wave, you will not see the ocean, but do not forget the ocean. Forget the body. Unite your heart with your family, with your nation, with everything that you see and say: "They are my relatives." In meditation get away from the body and spread your body everywhere and say: "Here I see God in meditation and I know that God can exist without creation and in creation also. " When you realize that, then you know that God alone exists; nothing else exists.

MATTER IS A REFLECTION OF GOD   To deny matter in a blind way, and still go on doing everything for the body, is a contradiction of your own belief. Jesus said: "Take no heed for the body" because He knew that body and matter do not really exist. He had risen above them both.

Space is swallowing matter and one day solids will be changed into liquids, and liquids will be vaporized into electricity and melt into God. Matter exists as a reflection of God. Do not deny matter. Rather say: "Everything is God, which is the truth. Matter could not exist without God. Waves could not exist without the ocean. Creation could not exist without God, but God could exist without Creation.

In India we say: "Matter is not as it appears to us." This absolutely dissolves all criticism. Why? Because science teaches that matter is nothing but frozen electricity. Denial only creates doubt. Just say that when you are in God you will see that this body is only God's dream. All sickness will vanish when you are in God.

Suppose you have a broken bone in your dream and you are crying. All I have to do is to wake you up and then you will know that there is no bone broken. So, when you wake up on God, then you will know that the body does not exist. By contacting God deeply you can express God in health, wealth, and happiness in your body. That you must realize.

-Page Two-

It is when you are in the divine consciousness that you do not realize the existence of medicine or matter, but before you have that God consciousness you must not try to drink poison, thinking that there is no sensation in matter. This form of reasoning is based upon the theory that matter does not exist. Do not deny medicine. Acknowledge what good doctors are doing. But you have the right to say that mind is a greater power than medicine. To live by the power of mind more than by the cover of body and medicine -- that should be your aim. But avoid extremes. You cannot live entirely by mind. Give the body good food and then forget it. There are far greater things to study than food.

However, India teaches you how to live more and more by the power of mind until you can say: "God is living in me." You will see one day, when you tune yourself in with God in meditation, then you will say that, there is no matter, no death, only change. But as long as you do not know that, do not deny the body. Get to that state where you can live more by mind and then you can say that matter does not exist. You must not deny medicine because you eat and food is medicine which builds up the body.

GREATER THAN ALL THINGS IS TO KNOW GOD   You have been given intelligence and you are Souls, and you must realize the necessity of solving the Soul's problems, There is no breath or blood but God's. He is the energy in muscles, in flowers, in grass; everything is God. You must realize that. But when you see creation and God, remember that matter exists as frozen God. How can you realize this? When you see a beautiful sunset say; "It is God who has become that form. It is God who is reason; it is God who is blood; it is God who is love, and everything that exists is God in motion."

Greater than all things is to know God. Awake! Do not delay and you will find, if you have the zeal that India is here with the diamonds of immortality, and as you awaken your desire to know; God, you shall decorate yourself with immortal realization and shall declare your desire for God. Find God first and then ask Him what you should do. You must have this desire for God foremost in your life. You must not have any other desire stronger than the desire for God.No matter how many mistakes you have made, it does not matter as long as you have no other desire before Him.

When you watch through the window of your mind, He will keep looking at you without your knowing. Like someone following you, and when you look, He has gone. You know that He is in the flower and you go to squeeze it, and then He has gone. And He is hidden behind the portals of your mind. You go to the garden, and you seek Him in the mountains and in the sky and in the people about you, and you do not find Him but when you sit in the silence of your soul, and when you follow those whom you feel have Self-Realization, then you will feel Him on the altar of everything.

We are all the children of God, ready to meet Him and worship Him on the altar of our hearts. Let us all, with our united hearts and united minds, offer our devotion to God, who is just behind our love, and just behind the words with which we pray. Let us sing with our Souls to our one God who sits on the united altar of our hearts.

Do not limit yourself to racial prejudice. Do not put on a badge and say: "I am a Hindu," or "I am an American." Say: "I am God' child." We are only for a little while Hindus or Americans, but before we leave the shores of this earth we shall know that we are all God's children.

-Page Three-

I have come to give you the treasures of India, the happiness of India; if you could only feel this, you would throw everything away and say: "Oh what joy, what happiness, what great volumes of happiness. Lord, where is the end. I was a slave and you made me a King."

THE APOLOGUE
HOW A SAINT SATISFIES AN EMPEROR'SLUST FOR MIRACLES

LUST FOR MIRACLES

Long, long ago there lived in India a mighty, cruel emperor. He was violent, tyrannical, inquisitive, and brooked no one who tried to act against his will. Any political servant who worked under him, or any visitor who came to his palace and dared to act against the cruel emperor's will was sure to meet his doom.

The atrocity of the emperor reached its zenith when one day he met a stubborn Saint. This Saint, named Govind Singh, was known far and wide in India due to his performance of many miracles under the direction of the Divine Spirit. Many afflicted Souls received instantaneous physical healing. Also, many Souls steeped in the darkness of ignorance beheld the all-freeing light through the contact of this great Saint.

Every day the stories and testimonials about Saint Govind Sing's healing power flooded all India, until finally they reached the emperor's curious ears. Thus, when Saint Govind Singh reached the presence of the cruel emperor he demanded: " If you are a Saint and people rave so much about your so-called miraculous powers, then I command you to save your neck by demonstrating some miracles in my presence."

But the Saint, being solely guided by divine will did not feel disposed to cheapen his divine powers by uselessly displaying them, so he maintained a stoic silence. Repeatedly, with ever-mounting wrath, the cruel emperor urged the Saint to perform some miracle, but finding no response he at last shouted: "Sirrah! Saint! I brook no one to withstand my will, and be assured that this unsheathed sword of mine will sever your head from your body if you do not satisfy my lust for miracles.

At last, Saint Govind Singh gently but firmly said: "Curious King, then swiftly sever my head, and then, and not before will your lust for miracles be satisfied. This I will do in order to cure your wicked nature. But, just the same, I defy your will; not until you have slain me will you behold a miracle. This supreme sacrifice of my body I will perform in order to heal your ignorance. My miracle will satisfy your curiosity about the presence and miraculous power of God. Be quick! Let your sword sever the head from my immortal body."

The king was beside himself with wrath at the Saint's continued defiance. Unable to control himself, this most atrocious emperor suddenly ran his sword blade through the neck of Saint Govind Singh. The emperor, with his outstretched arm holding the blood-dripping sword, was aghast and almost frozen with fear as he beheld what followed, for Saint Govind Singh, truly kept his word. His severed head began to dance on the marble floor of the king's palace around the king's feet, and without the help of the lungs or any other part of the body, began to talk loudly at the same time writing in blood on the floor: "Cruel emperor, I have given you my head, but not the secret of my religion.

-Page Four-

I can talk and I am alive evermore in spirit, even though you have severed my head."

The above story illustrates that great Masters who are in tune with the Infinite, as Jesus Christ was, will readily give up their lives rather than act contrary to a divine principle. No devotee of God ever plans to do anything against the will of the Divine Father. As God, with His infinite miraculous powers, does not use His miracles to demonstrate His presence by imposing upon the free will of His human children, so also He expects all His devotees to behave like Him. God, by the display of His powers, could easily frighten man into mechanical submission to His will, but his is the farthest from the Divine Father's wish. Instead, He lays before the eyes of His children gifted with wisdom, the whole panorama of the miraculous universe, and He expects them to use their wisdom, love, and free will to seek Him, find Him, and love Him.

Thus it is that true devotee of God never displays divine miracles when challenged by ignorance, as is so beautifully brought forth in the life of Saint Govind Singh. Jesus also refused to give signs to prove His divinity to those who challenged Him with a wrong attitude. He demonstrated His miracles, even resurrection, under divine sanction in a unique divine way, only to increase the faith of those who are real spiritual seekers.

HEALTH CULTURE
THE SCIENCE OF NUTRITION

HONEY -- ITS NATURE AND USES   Besides being a natural sweetening agent, honey contains many ingredients in addition to sugar. Small amounts of the following mineral salts make honey a valuable food; silica, iron, copper, manganese, chlorine, calcium, potassium, sodium, phosphorus, sulphus, aluminum, magnesium. Honey is potentially an alkaline food and its distinctive flavors make it a universal favorite.

Ordinary cane and beet sugars must be broken down into simpler sugars by digestion before they can be assimilated. These simple sugars, dextrose and levulose, occur naturally in honey and honey requires practically no digestion for its sugars are almost wholly available for immediate absorption into the body. Because of its depth of flavor and intense sweetness, honey is more satiating than other sugars and therefore less of it is needed. Its use thus tends to reduce the sugar intake. It is an excellent source of readily available food energy for growing children.

(Continued in Next Praeceptum)

HONEY ICED CHOCOLATE

2 tablespoons cocoa	3 tablespoons honey
½ teaspoon vegetized salt	2 cups scalded milk

Blend cocoa, salt, and honey. Add to scalded milk and simmer for 5 minutes. Pour over chipped ice. Top with honey, meringue or whipped cream. Serves 3. For hot chocolate use 3 cups of scalded milk instead of 2.

HONEY SYRUP

1 cup honey	½ teaspoon vegetized salt
1 cup brown sugar	½ cup water

Allow brown sugar, water and salt to boil 5 minutes. Add honey and simmer slowly for 5 more minutes.

-Page Five-

BAKED HONEY CUSTARD

5 eggs	⅛ teaspoon powdered cinnamon
½ cup honey	½ teaspoon vegetized salt
4 cups scalded milk	

Beat eggs enough to unite yolks and whites, but not enough to make them foamy. Add the other ingredients and bake in a moderate oven. The custard cups or pan should be set in hot water while baking.

PRAECEPTUM INSPIRATION
GOD IS THE POWER BEHIND EVERYTHING

God can be reached, only you do not mean business. When other interests are in your heart, why should God come to you?

Some people think that friendship is the greatest thing, and some think that marriage is the greatest. But remember, God is the power behind friendship, and God is the love behind marriage.

Without Him you can't even love anyone. Why not think of the thing that expresses itself in your love and friendship? Why not think of that great Spirit? If you can be kings and emperors, why be beggars? Find God. You must contact God; nothing else is as important Can you sit for hours lost in God. If you can sit for two or three hours absor(b)ed in a superficial play, why can't you be lost in God for that many hours? You can't do it because your mind is on the body. You are not with God, If you want a lesser thing, you deny your identity as an immortal child.

The Bhagavad Gita, (the Hindu bible) says: "You are your greatest enemy and you are your greatest friend; if you are the enemy of your Soul, your Soul will act as your enemy; if you are your soul's friend, your Soul will be your friend. "

PRAECEPTUM AFFIRMATION

I WILL REMAIN IN HEARTS AS THE UNKNOWN FRIEND, EVER AROUSING ALL IN THEIR FLAMING FEELINGS, AND SILENTLY URGING THEM THROUGH THEIR OWN NOBLE THOUGHTS TO FORSAKE THEIR SLUMBER OF EARTHLINESS. IN THE LIGHT OF WISDOM I WILL DANCE WITH ALL THEIR JOYS IN THE UNSEEN BOWER OF SILENCE.

YOGODA SAT-SANGA FORTNIGHTLY INSTRUCTIONS
BY
PARAMHANSA YOGANANDA

SING UNTO US THY SONG OF INFINITY, O FATHER!

Father, Mother, Friend, Beloved God, no more with words but with the burning flame of our hearts we worship Thee. We demand Thy presence. Destroy our ignorance; drive away our restlessness; come to us in all Thy splendor. Forsake us not, though we forsake Thee; remember us, though we remember Thee not; be with us always; be not indifferent to us, though we are indifferent to Thee. Make us like little children, free from jealousy, free from insincerity; unite our hearts.

Thy glory is fragrant within us. The temple of memories often is filled with doors of desires. Drive them away, for we want to behold Thee alone sitting on the altar of every thought and every consciousness within and about us. Behold Thy consciousness within and about us. Behold Thy consciousness glimmering within us. Make us behold Thy consciousness in everything.
We were blind. We found not a door, but Thou hast opened our eyes and we find doors everywhere, through the hearts of blossoms, and through the hearts of friendship and all lovely experiences.

Thou art present just behind our prayers, just behind the darkness, just behind the thoughts of our devotion, just behind our heart-throbs, just behind our brain. Break Thy vow of silence. Speak to us; no more are we satisfied with the whispers in the moon, in the twinkling of stars, or the song of the nightingale. Sing unto us Thy song of Infinity.

ADVANCED SPIRITUAL TEACHINGS

OUR GOD-GIVEN REASONING POWERS   God has given us independence, power, and reason. Man can find God because he was given reason. To spend your time just playing with life and not finding God, means that the power within you is being wasted.

The great Masters of India found out that reason governs everything, and the reason within us tells us that we cannot live without that reason. God gave us reason that we might find freedom.

Self-Realization Fellowship is teaching you the divine discrimination by which you will be able to distinguish between spiritual truths and theologica(l) beliefs. Learn to develop discrimination. Millions of people do not exercise this power. Discrimination does not mean that you should become biased. When you boil down a reason to a right conclusion, then you must harness that reason to will power and act up to that. Discrimination does not amount to anything unless it is accompanied by activity. To have it is to be awake and very much alive, so that everywhere you go you will be able to perceive correctly. No one will be able to deceive you.

Divine contact will show you immortal ways of expression, so that you, a mortal, may be an immortal and express yourself in the divine way. You get so entangled in life that you forget to us your will power properly. The divine soul is really free like the lark -- free like the sky.

How much do we know about this earth on which we live? If the earth causes a little tremor, our homes and loved ones are destroyed.
If God were to destroy this little cell in which we live where would we be today? We are literally floating on the outside of a ball, which God is directing in its rotation through the heavens. How little we know of this earth! And how dare we forget God, to whom we are indebt
ed for our existence!

HAVE A PURPOSE IN LIFE   Be master of yourself, that you may create
at will what you need. Whenever you need health, you must have it, whenever you need money you must have it.
Do not be lured by your unnecessary "necessities," however. You must use reason, and you must not be influenced by anything but your own good habits and reason. No one should be able to tempt you to do anything that you do not want to do. You must not be a slave to anything. Have you that power?

We are all acting like the little worm in the cocoon, but there are some worms which cut through the cocoon and develop wings and fly. In a few years you will be gone. Why live in uncertainty? If you do not cut through and become a divine butterfly, death is going to overpower you.

So many people scarcely know that they are living. They are a part of the cogwheel of the machine of activity, but they do not know the purpose of life. They eat, live, multiply, and are gone, leading the life of an animal. So many people are living behind the times. Most people think that to have good clothes, fine cars, plenty of money, and so on, is keeping up with the times, but that is far from it.

Do not sacrifice your Soul on the altar of indifference. Do your duty to God, and through God do your duty to your family. Once a man said to me: "I have no time for God." I said: "Wait a minute; suppose God had no time for you. If He had no time for you, you would be dead right now. " You came alone on earth and you will go alone from the shores of this earth. Find God first, then everything will come to you.

Remember the parable of the master and the servants. The master said he was going away for a while, so all the servants took a rest while he was gone, all except one servant who said: "But master might return any moment, so I will go on with my work." The master did return and found all his servants idling their time away except one, so he kept that one and discharged the rest.

So it is with God. You must always be ready to serve Him. Do not idle your time away. Some people do very little. They just eat and sleep and do a little mechanical work. As human beings, you must do more than this; you must accomplish something worthwhile, and you must use discrimination every day. Do not waste your time. Find out what you are and why you are here.

To acquire all the wisdom in the world would be impossible in one life time if you had to get it from hooks, but there is another angle of approach. To have Cosmic Consciousness means to know all things in Nature. Cosmic Consciousness does not mean that you must have an arrogant attitude of superiority, but you really contain all wisdom within yourself, only you must know how to be aware that you have it,

Instead of trifling away your time on small things, it is your highest duty and privilege to spend it on God, Follow the path that leads you to His infinite presence. Life must be lived in a worth-while way. When you came into this world, you cried and everyone else smiled. You must so live your life again that when you leave, everyone will cry, while you will be smiling. Many live like the moth attracted to a flame. They are temporarily attracted to the fire of pleasures, only to burn their wings of happiness, but those who embrace the everlasting fires of wisdom will find the darkness burned forevermore.

IMITATE THE LIFE OF A YOGI   The Yogi is one with others. When he tries to be one with others, he does not take this as a mental concept or just try to be a little courteous or a little helpful to others, but he tries to forget his little self and merges in the selves of others so that he feels his consciousness moving through all. Unselfish sympathy is the bridge which connects each Soul with other souls. Sympathy is the door to all hearts. It must be impersonal and must not exclude one in preference to another. Sympathy must first be practiced with some, purely, perfectly, then extended to all hearts.

The devotee should mentally try to feel the tremor of the leaves. He should feel the wind around his body and in his lungs. He should feel the oxygenic vitality of God in his blood cells. He should feel his consciousness moving with the breeze, entering in the lungs of people, and giving them life. He should mentally feel himself omnipresent with the whole atmosphere around the earth. He should feel the sun's rays as his muscles. He should feel himself cushioned on the earth, offering his services to others who may walk upon him. Be must feel himself in the temple of Souls, in the temple of hearts, in the temple of minds.

INTUITION AWAKENED BY MEDITATION   As you cannot receive the ocean in a cup, so it is impossible to receive the ocean of wisdom in the small cup of intelligence. The small cup of intelligence must be expanded or enlarged into the boundless cup of intuition in order to hold in it infinite Truth. Intuition is that power of Spirit inherited by the Soul, by which it can perceive all things directly without the medium of any other faculty. Man has to use the powers in the eyes, ears, and other senses, and in the mind, in order to know about Truth. When the senses and mind lie about things, the reason builds a wrong conclusion about it. The Spirit, or the Soul, does not require the senses or the mind to perceive substance. It sees into things through the directly-perceiving power of intuition.

To study the scriptures with intellectuality, keeps the Truth locked up in the mind unassimilated and undigested. That is why one must study the Scriptures with self realization, which produces the spiritual brain, the intuitive heart, and teaches you how to absorb spiritual Truth. The best way to study the Scriptures is to feel them in the body, in the mind, in intuition, and in the Soul.

Before studying the Scriptures, the intuition should be awakened by the power of meditation. A restless mind, or a highly intellectual mind, cannot absorb scriptural Truths, which can be perceived only through intuition. Just as sugar cannot be tasted through intellectuality or mental imagination, so the sweetness of spiritual perceptions cannot be received through the intellect.

DEVOTION PLUS WORK   If you work all the time, you will become too mechanical and will sacrifice God to your work, and if you are too discriminating, you may lose God that way, and if you have devotion for God without work, your devotion may turn into emotion. Meditation balances all of these.

Close your eyes to shut out immediate contact with the world and matter. Know that God is in everything. Then, forgetting all matter, feel God in meditation.

The average mind is like a match stick that is soaked with water. Scratch it and it won't light. The mind of concentration is like a dry match. Strike the match and it is immediately aflame with the fire and burning love of God, the flame of happiness.

SHORT APOLOGUES
THE GREATEST MIRACLE -- THE LOVE OF GOD

Once I went to Master and said: "When shall I have God? " He said" "You have Him now." Then said: "You are looking for miracles and if all the universe was given to you, you would become tired of it in a day. But when you have God you will want nothing else." I said: "Yes, I have found God.

"O aged Wine of my Heart, Thou has become sweetened through incarnations. Drinking of Thee, I drink again and again, and my bottle is always filled. I know not the name of this wine, but I do know that it is the wine of happiness - the wine which talks to me, which guides me at all times."

The greatest of all miracles is the love of God. Through His love He is always talking to you. "I fled Him down the day, I fled HIm down the night and through the orchards of the years." You are not seeking God; God is seeking you. You are flying away from God through doubts; you are hiding from Him through material pleasure. If you do not find contentment in God, you will not find contentment anywhere.

Although we are very insignificant, still God is following us. "I take these things away from thee, that thou mayest receive these things from My hands, from Me." God did not take these things away to punish or worry us, but to tell us to come home. It is in Him that we shall find everlasting health, prosperity, and wisdom.

In order that you may wake up and know the laws of the stars and the glory of spiritual happiness, and the mystery of life and death and the hereafter, you must first learn that you can only find these things in God, through God's laws.

Rouse yourself and say: "I have long wandered away. I must find God." Then seek Him, and through the study of the advanced methods in the Fortnightly Praecepta, you will know the history of the stars, the strata of the earth and life, and you will say: "I am the child of God. I was sent here to be entertained by the drama of life, but not to be caught in its meshes. " Mortal ways will never give you freedom.

THE TEST

In Cleveland when I went into a beautiful temple there, I had a great vision. I always had a hobby for temples and large buildings, so God showed me a great temple with a beautiful organ and ten thousand people in the temple and He said: "Do you want this temple without Me?" Then He showed me a vision of a tree with myself and a few disciples seated under it, and He asked: "Or would you prefer this, with Me." I quickly said: "Lord, I would rather be under the tree, with a few disciples and with Thee in our midst. "

"Because Thou art, all things are. All beauties are but the windows through which we behold Thy Infinite beauty. The beauty of the rose and the beauty of the moon are but reflections of Thy beauty."

HEALTH CULTURE
THE SCIENCE OF NUTRITION

HONEY -- ITS NATURE AND USES Honey has many different flavors because bees gather nectar from many kinds of flowers. All honey is good honey but all flavors may not be equally pleasing to all people. Buckwheat and clover are favorites in the Middle West, while orange blossom and sage are preferred in the far West.

-Page Four-

Honey my be bought as liquid, in the comb, and in a solid or granulated form. Granulated honey can be restored to liquid by putting the container in warm water until the honey melts. In order to preserve the true flavor, honey should not be cooked at high temperatures.

It is of the utmost importance to have the right temperature in cooking with honey. A scorched spot or surface will affect the flavor of the entire honey product, especially those containing flour, mixtures containing honey should be baked slowly and evenly, for the exact time stated in the directions. Use a slow or moderate oven for baking with honey. When a cake has shrunk from sides of pan, lightly touch the upper crust and if no dent is made, the cake is done. A honey mixture cooked on top of the stove should be simmered and not boiled.

(To be continued)

SIMPLE HONEY DRESSING

½ cup honey

¼ cup lemon juice

¼ teaspoon vegetized salt

3 tablespoons crushed pineapple.

Stir lemon juice and honey together, add salt and crushed pineapple. Delicious with crisp head lettuce, plain banana salad or cole slaw.

PRAECEPTUM INSPIRATION

THE JOY OF MEDITATION

The most effective way to overcome temptation is to compare it with the joy of meditation. Temptation does not mean just doing something wrong from the material standpoint; it also means to forget your soul by becoming too engrossed in the body and its comforts. That is temptation too.

No matter how many cords are around your feet, no matter how many sins you have committed, remember this, the minute you know in your heart that the happiness which is found in the temple of silence is most tempting, then you will be free. You must have that joy, then you are already released. That can only come through your own determination.

One of the most impressive things my Master used to say to me was: "Learn to behave." I can never thank him enough for that. I find, however, how difficult it is to behave.

With the dawn of divine experience, with the dawn of divine joy, we behold the glimmer of beautiful thoughts and experiences within our hearts. When ignorance comes within our hearts, we are filled with gloom, and in this gloom we behold the goblins of dark thoughts, but when the light of God shines within us, we behold the divine love of God. Within our Souls lie buries the immortal soldiers of God, who are constantly fighting the forces of evil in order to establish within us the kingdom of the Great Deity,

PRAECEPTUM AFFIRMATION

I will behold the person who now considers himself as my enemy to be in truth my divine brother hidden behind the veil of misunderstanding. I will tear aside this veil with the dagger of love so that, seeing my humble, forgiving understanding, he will receive the offering of my good will.

श्रात्मानं विद्धि

REALIZE THY SELF

YOGODA SAT-SANGA

FORTNIGHTLY INSTRUCTIONS

YOUR PRAECEPTUM

No. *148*

Thy Self - realization will
blossom forth from thy
Soulful Study

YOGODA SAT-SANGA FORTNIGHTLY INSTRUCTIONS

BY
PARAMHANSA YOGANANDA

DANCING TO THE BLISS-PIPINGS
Part One

From the pure white sheet of life
I want to erase all dark blots of groan-producing sensations.
On this milk-white sheet of life
God wrote the blameless words and messages of bliss,
But Satan came and took the pen of destiny
And dipped it in the ink of gloom
And splashed the ink of sensitiveness
All over the clean sheet of perception,

I will take the neutralizing acid of intuition
And dissolve the misery-producing blotches of sensations.
O sweet enslaving home of flesh!
In thee dwells the charming venomous snake of sensitivity.
Some day I will destroy this serpent of sensitiveness
And make this flesh the temple of deathless experiences.

From the flesh I will remove all pain-making sensitiveness
And death-producing sensibilities.
I will kill the flesh-frailty, that it no more delude me with
its cries of cold and heat, pain and pleasure
I will make this flesh dumb forever, that it may never
Speak again of its delusions of pain.
But I will resurrect each cell of this fleshly frame
In the life of indestructibility.

Each cell of my body shall dance in the flames without being
        scorched or burned.
And each cell of my body shall dive into the bosom of mortal
fire without being hurt And all these children body-cells,
Pierced a trillion times with points of sharp daggers,
Shall not be scratched.
And these body-cells,
Scorched a thousand times by the scalding, sun,
Shall not thirst for a taste of water,

(To be Continued in Next Praeceptum)

GRADUATED METHODS OF YOGA
Part One

RELEASING THE MOTION-BOUND SOUL TO UNITE IT WITH THE MOTIONLESS INFINITE
BY YOGA, OR METHODS OF SCIENTIFIC UNION   The word "Yoga" is an ancient
word which comes from the Sanskrit root, "yuj," signifying union. Therefore, the
word Yoga in Hindu philosophy is usually used to signify scientific union of
Spirit, and individual Soul by psycho-physical methods of meditation.

     A Yogi can be a worldly man or a man of renunciation, who scientifically
practices the Yoga technique of meditation in order to logically unite with God.

The science of Yoga (or scientific union with God) has been used variously to classify different methods of Yoga:

1. Hatha Yoga   4. Mantra Yoga
2. Raja Yoga   5. Laya Yoga
3. Karma Yoga

1. Hatha Yoga teaches various gymnastics of the body in order to make it fit for meditation and a high experience of ecstasy and to absorb the high voltage of Cosmic energy emanating from God. However, it is not necessary to go through all the various body twisting of Hatha Yoga. The 84 or more body postures advocated by Hatha Yoga are most effectively practiced by children. Men and women, after the age of forty, should not practice the difficult postures of Hatha Yoga, as their bones, muscles and nerves have become unyielding. There are people who wholly condemn Hatha Yoga for the simple reason that some old people who tried to practice the difficult postures hurt their unpliable bones and tendons. In fact no meditation is possible without having some control of the body. Most dietary laws and some postures of Hatha Yoga are very good indeed and can be practiced with benefit to the health.

It must be remembered, however, that Hatha Yoga should not be practiced all through life, keeping the Soul busy only with the discipline of the body, forgetting the real purpose of Yoga, which points out the necessity of uniting Spirit and Soul. The body for the advent of the spiritual growth, and Hatha Yoga methods are not an end in themselves. The body discipline is meant to prepare for spiritual culture, embodying spiritual peace, and not merely to gain good health. Therefore, do not condemn Hatha Yoga altogether, nor be absorbed in some of its methods that only attract public attention. Search deeper.

2. Raja Yoga signifies the Yoga methods which are royal, or the best and most inclusive. It combines the simple methods of body discipline with a very high technique of spiritual realization, as taught throughout the Praecepta. Self-Realization methods teach Raja Yoga techniques of uniting Soul and Spirit, and combined all the good in all other forms of Yoga.

3. Karma Yoga signifies union with God through performing good actions primarily, and meditative actions secondarily.

4. Mantra Yoga consists in uniting soul and Spirit by loud chanting, whispered chanting, or by uttering root words, and by vibrations which create the Cosmos through deep concentration.

5. Laya Yoga signifies complete absorption of mind upon any mental concept or inner astral sounds. It consists of listening to the Cosmic sound of Om (Aum or Amen) emanating from the Universe in the superconscious plane of concentration. Laya signifies melting the mind on some inner concept, or inner experience, or astral sound. Mantra Yoga teaches us to concentrate upon and be merged in the real astral sounds emanating from the various inner creative forces of God in Nature, and not in those astral sounds imitated by the human voice.

First Step: PROSCRIPTIVE RULES -- YAMA "Yama" means the rules which are prohibitive. Things that the devotee should not do.

Second Step: PRESCRIPTIVE RULES -- NIYMA "Niyama" means things that the devotee should do. All religions agree to these two phases or foundations of religious practice. If one meditates a great deal and at the same time does not practice Yama-Niyama it will be like building a large superstructure on a loose foundation.

Such things as stealing, killing, being jealous, and so forth come under Yarn and are things that the devotee should not do. And such things as unselfishness, sharing with all, truthfulness, and so forth, come under Niyama and are things that the devotee should do.

-Page Two-

These are the foundation principles of all religions. Many religionists are contented just to practice Yama-Niyama (proscriptive and prescriptive rules) and that is why they do not progress beyond that. Some say: "I have never done anything wrong and I have done all good things in my life and I am satisfied. " Such a person receives inner satisfaction but he does not progress beyond that.

Patanjali gives the eight-fold path of salvation and that is what all devotees of Yoga, all pursuers of the spiritual path, must use for their spiritual attainment on the solid foundation of Yama-Niyama . Of course, in Nirbikalpa Samadhi one goes beyond Yama-Niyama , but not before that.

Third Step: PRACTICES IN MOTIONLESSNESS OR ASANA   After Yama-Niyama, Patanjali says that the devotee must practice Asana, which means posture -- correct posture, The purpose of posture is to rise above or stop the motions of the body which cause restlessness in the soul. The soul is a part of the calm Infinite, and the body is a part of the restless nature. The soul is often a part of the restless body and forgets its infinite calm nature. Therefore, in order to send those prodigal souls from the land of restlessness to the kingdom of infinite calmness, it is necessary for the soul to remain still. That is why it is necessary to have correct posture.

CONCENTRATE UPON THE ENDS FOR WHICH DIFFERENT TECHNIQUES ARE USED

Patanjali always points to the purpose of spiritual actions and tells the devotees not to become identified with any process of salvation but to use that process of salvation until the necessary end is attained, Patanjali warns the devotee not to be identified with the prooess of salvation so that one forgets the purpose for which that process or technique of salvation was prescribed. Many spiritual devotees remain within the confinement of Asana. They concentrate upon physical gymnastics and the suppleness of the body. They enjoy the freedom of the body which Asana brings and forget to attain the ffeedom of the mind and soul. Therefore, Patanjali does not prescribe lengthy concentration and the practice of various postures, but he says that any natural, normal posture in which the spine is erect and the body is steady and the mind is peaceful and the body is fairly restful, is the correct posture, or asana.

Fourth Step: DISCONNECTING THE MIND FROM THE SENSES BY SWITCHING OF LIFE FORCE FROM THE SENSE TELEPHONES, OR PRANAYAM, OR LIFE CONTROL (NOT BREATH CONTROL)   There are thousands of devotees who identify themselves with the various postures and do not seek further spiritual progress. Patanjali says that posture is necessary for stillness, and stillness is the altar of Spirit. Where motion ceases, Spirit begins to manifest. After a steady posture and a steady mind, Patanjali advises the devotee to practice Pranayama with the object of attaining Pratyahara. Pranayam means switching off of the life force from the five sense-telephones.

Fifth Step: MIND INTERIORIZATION BY PRATYAHARA.   Pratyahara signifies the mind when it is disconnected from the five sense telephones. Various schools of breath control, meditation, chanting, devotional songs, concentration on the prayer wheel, holy rolling, concentration by discrimination, concentration by diversion, and so forth have arisen as off-shoots of the real pranayama of switching off the life force.

Fourth Step -- Continued UNDER PRANAYAMA TECHNIQUE COME ALL OTHER TECHNIQUES OF MEDITATION   There are various unscientific methods of diverting the mind from the senses to God, for example, by chanting, negative silence, prayer, emotional singing, intellectual discriminative meditation, social

-Page Three-

and religious work. But the pranayama life-control technique of Yoga (scientific union) teaches the scientific way of disconnecting the mind from the sensations of touch, sound, sight, smell and taste by switching off the life current (by Pranayama technique) so that it may be united to God. Yoga constitutes all the scientific techniques of uniting soul and God, and Pranayama is the greatest technique of uniting soul and God.

SLEEP, OR UNCONSCIOUS PRANAYAMA The state of sleep is unconscious pranayama, or the unconscious process of switching off the life force from the five telephones.

In sleep one practices the mortal posture or Sabasana. In this posture the body is still, the muscles have stopped working, venus blood is reduced, the heart slows down, and the energy in the heart becomes quiet; therefore, the energy from the five senses is switched off.

Then the mind attains unconscious pratyahara, or unconsciously returns within and concentrates upon unconscious peace. Patanjali's statement of the direct use of pranayama is very significant, since he does not beat about the bush but tells one to adopt that scientific measure by which sensations can be disconnected from the mind. What is attained during sleep, or unconscious switching off of the life current, can be attained consciously by adopting conscious methods of pranayama.

(To be Continued in Next Praeceptum)

T H E A P O L O G U E

THE MAN WHO MISUSED MIRACLES

Part One

Several years ago there lived in Bengal, India, a Mohammedan miracle man named Afzal Khan. If Jesus came on earth today and performed his miracles in the city of New York, it might cause a great deal of excitement, so likewise the above miracle man, Afzal Khan, rocked Bengal by using his miraculous powers.

Unlike Jesus Christ, Afzal Khan used his miraculous powers for attracting the attention of people to garner wealth, fame, and power, While Afzal Khan was still a small boy playing in his native village in India one day, he was met by a great Hindu Yogi (Master). The Master, on meeting the boy Afzal, demanded: "Son, I am very thirsty. Fetch me some water." Little Afzal replied: "Master Saint, I am a Mohammedan. How could you drink water from my hands, you who are a Hindu Yogi?"

The Master, well pleased with the boy's truthfulness in regard to his race, with infinite compassion in his eyes said: "Son, I know that you are a Mohammedan and that I am a Hindu, but we are all children of the same Heavenly Father and as such I do not believe in the false ostracizing and limiting rules of ungodly sectarianism. Go, fetch me some water quickly."

The boy Afzal meekly responded to the wishes of the Master and brought him some water. After quenching his thirst, the Master endearingly looked at the boy and advised him as follows before he left: "Son," he said, "I am well pleased with you and I am aware of some of your deeds of good actions which you brought from the past, and I am going to give you a technique which, if you practice up to the age of thirty will enable you to acquire wonderful miraculous powers which you can use for constructive purposes, but beware never to use them for destructive purposes, as in that case you will come to grief. Remember, also, that you have some bad tendencies brought over from the past and do not sprout them by watering them with fresh evil actions."

The Master then vanished from sight, leaving little Afzal utterly amazed. Afzal strictly followed the instructions of his

-Page Four-

Master and secretly developed his powers, until at the age of 30, true to the prophecy of his Master, he acquired miraculous powers. It is said that a power disembodied Spirit was always invisibly present with him, ready to materialize any of his wishes. Afzal Khan always addressed the Spirit as "Hazrat." Human traits, however, got the best of Afzal Khan and, contrary to the warnings of his Master, he began to misuse his miracles on all occasions.

My earthly father himself told me that Afzal became terrible for whatever he touched and returned apparently remained intact, but after he left, the object touched by Afzal invariably vanished. Afzal made it a point to go to large jewellery shops and touch their jewels, feigning to examine them, and, although he returned them to the jeweller, after he had left the store the touched jewellery vanished.

He used to take hundreds of his curiosity-attracted students to the railroad station and pretend to buy tickets for them all, but after he touched the tickets he would return them to the ticket-seller saying: "I have changed my mind. I won't buy the tickets now." But when he boarded the train with his students he had in his possession all the tickets that he was supposed to have returned to the ticket seller. This created a great uproar of resentment so that government officials sought to arrest him for his evil doings, but they could do nothing, because Afzal always could make anything that he possessed disappear by just saying: "Hazrat, take this away."

My great Master, Swami Sriyukteswarji, himself told me about some of the miracles of Afzal Khan which he witnessed. One day, when I was present with my Master in a boarding house by the Ganges at Serampore, he said to me: "Behold, right on this balcony overlooking the Ganges and the very room you are living in, Afzal Khan, single-handed, without any assistance, in broad daylight performed some miracles before twenty of my friends and myself. While we were on the balcony with Afzal, he looked at me and said: 'Write your name on a piece of brick, or anything that you can find, and throw it in the Ganges as far as you can possibly throw it, and I will bring it back to you."

My Master did as requested and brought a piece of stone and wrote his name on it, and with his powerful hand threw it far into the Ganges. Then Afzal said: "Go and bring a pot of water from the Ganges." Master brought a pot of water and then Afzal asked him to put his hands into the pot and see if he could find anything there." Master did so, but found nothing. However, while Master's hands were still in the pot of water Afzal cried out: "Hazrat, put that stone back in the pot." Immediately Master felt the stone grow in his hand and when he pulled it out of the pot he found his signature still there, even unwashed after being in the water of the Ganges. Master, even though he was young at that time, was very intelligent and told me that this could not have been done by any sleight of hand or any kind of material magic.

(To be Continued in Next Praeceptum)

HEALTH CULTURE

THE SCIENCE OF NUTRITION HONEY -- ITS NATURE AND USES

The only difference between liquid honey and comb honey is the absence of the comb. To obtain liquid honey the combs are uncapped and the honey is forced from the cells by centrifugal motion.

Honey blends very readily with fruit and other ingredients because it is a liquid sweet. When honey is used, it is not necessary

-Page Five-

to stir fruit in order to dissolve sugar crystals because honey penetrates and flavors fruit quickly when lightly drizzled over the top. Honey also combines very easily with dried fruits and nuts for various fillings.

Liquid honey is also very good used as a syrup for sundaes, waffles, etc. If a thinner syrup is desired, dilute the honey with warm milk, whipped cream or honey meringue.

(To be continued)

HONEY SPICE CAKE

1 cup shortening	½ teaspoon vegetized salt
⅓ cup sugar	1½ teaspoons cinnamon
3/4 cup honey	½ teaspoon cloves
2 eggs, separated	½ teaspoon nutmeg
3 cups whole wheat pastry flour	1 cup sour milk
2 teaspoons baking powder	1 teaspoon vanilla
½ teaspoon soda	½ cup nut meats

Cream shortening, add the sugar. Beat in the honey. Add beaten egg yolks. Sift dry ingredients. Add 2 cup to nuts and add the rest alternately with sour milk and vanilla. Fold in beaten whites. Bake in a well-greased loaf pan in a moderate oven (350 degrees) for 45 to 50 minutes.

PRAECEPTUM INSPIRATION
PROTECT YOURSELF IN THE CASTLE OF SINCERITY

The greatest sin against God is insincerity. The greatest sin against man is treachery. You must never hurt anyone either through speech or action, even if you consider nothing but your own protection. You will be the one to suffer. There is nothing greater than sincerity in your dealings with others. Sincerity will conquer your enemies. It will make your friendship based upon the Rock of Ages. Without sincerity, it is easy to make friends, but hard to keep friends; it is only by sincerity that you can keep friends.

If you can protect yourself in the castle of sincerity, you will be the prince of your kingdom and remain on the spiritual path. Do not be afraid of the Truth. Truth will conquer even if you have something against someone who has offended you. Most people forget that sincerity is much more powerful than falsehood. Those who are beneath your consciousness, replete them with your wisdom if they are willing to be enlightened. Always endeavor to move higher in Self- Realization.

It is not what you are thinking, it is how you act; you must harness your actions to your resolutions, pursue your path diligently. Most people wish for good things, but do not deserve good things. Most people want to know God and want to be good, but do not make the effort to know God. Those who make the right and continuous effort are the ones who find God.

PRAECEPTUM AFFIRMATION

BLESSED ARE THOSE WHO SHARE THY GIFTS, FOR THEY WERE GIVEN TO THEM, THAT THEY MIGHT LEARN TO GIVE.

-Page Six-

PUBLISHED BY

Yogoda Sat-Sanga

Self-Realization Fellowship & Shyamacharan Mission

Founder—Paramhansa Yogananda

President—Sister Daya.

Yogoda Math, Dakshineswar, P. O. Ariadah.

Dist : 24, Parganas, West-Bengal, India.

YOGODA SAT-SANGA PRESS

YOGODA SAT-SANGA FORTNIGHTLY INSTRUCTIONS
BY
PARAMHANSA YOGANANDA

(To be Confidentially Reserved FOR MEMBER'S USE ONLY)
DANCING TO THE BLISS-PIPINGS Part Two

Good and bad are as odors,
They shall not disturb the calmness
Of the transmuted immortal cells.
Nor sound vibrations
Burst the ear-drums of these baptized immortal cells.
Nor the cruelest sights
Disturb the vision of the God-entranced body cells.

I will smear the acid of wisdom
Over the eyes and destroy meager mortal sight,
And implant there the penetrating telescopic eye of insight
I will piece the ear-drums with the deafness of ecstasy,
So that the mortal ears no more dance
Like puppets when the strings
Of praise or blalme are pulled.

And then my inner ears,
Free from the noise of maddening material sounds,
Will register the music of the spheres.
And the living tunnel of my nostrils
Will no longer be enthralled by the sirens of fragrances or odors.

I will dislodge the tyrant greed
Sitting on the throne of taste.
I will enthrone there
The king of ever-present self-control.
From the secret cave of sensibility
I will dislodge the grizzly bear of happiness-devouring pain
And there invite the ever-joyous hermits of Bliss Perception,
Free from the delusion of dualities and relativities.
(To be continued in next Praeceptum)

GRADUATED METHODS OF YOGA

Part Two

KRIYA   Lahiri Mahasaya technique, or Kriya, which will soon be given in
the Praecepta, is the greatest form of Pranayama because by continuous effort
of oxygenation (as known to the student) the carbon blood is burned out and
venous blood is gradually made to disappear so that the heart is saved from
pumping venous blood into the lungs. This enables the heart to become quiet, and
when the heart becomes quiet, the energy is switched off from the five senses
and the mind attains a conscious state of Pratyahara, or consciousness of the
within. Those who practice Pranayama, or any other method of breath control,
and forget the purpose for which they are practicing do not attain Pratyahara.

Maharshi Patanjali signifies that the purpose of Pranayama must be Pratyahara, or making the mind return within. Thousands of devotees and students are satisfied with Yama-Niyama, and thousands are satisfied with Asana, and thousands are satisfied with only practicing Pranayama. If results are not forthcoming when practicing Yama-Niyama, the devotee should intensify the practice of Pranayama so that the life force is switched off and the mind becomes free from sensations. If results are not forthcoming when practicing Asana, the devotee should intensify the practice of Pranayama so that the life force is switched off and the mind becomes free from sensations. All devotees must be able to practice Pranayama so thoroughly that they can use it to immediately attain Pratyahara, or interiorization of the mind.

THE REAL SEVEN STEPS IN THE LADDER OF SELF-REALIZATION TO CLIMB TO THE KINGDOM OF GOD - SAMADHI   There can be many theological steps in the understanding of the theoretical phi- losophy of God, but there are only seven distinct steps of Self-Realization which lead to the perception of the Infinite. In following each step, one must not only have some new ideas about God, but one must have a distinct change of consciousness and Self-Realization with each Step, until, when the Seventh Step is finished one will be directly contacting God as Ever-New Bliss

Followers of the path of devotion, meditation, chanting, and praying, must remember that they should so deeply follow their methods that the mind becomes so engrossed within (Pratyahara) that it forgets sensations or restless thoughts. Those practicing any form of meditation, or Pranayama, unless they can quickly interiorize the mind (Pratyahara), they have not stepped on the fifth step of the ladder of Self-Realization. Every step should yield a definite Self-Realization.

First and Second Steps: Yama-Niyama yield self-control and perfect mental equilibrium. Third step: Asana -- mental and physical calmness, so that the Yogi devotee can sit for hours in one position without fatigue or mental restlessness. Fourth Step: Pranayama should yield heart control, feeling cool and warm currents in the spine, pulse control, life-force control, and mind control. The Fifth Step: Pratyahara yields freedom of mind from the sensations, and power of interiorization. The Sixth Step: Dhyana -- the God. The Seventh Step: Dharana gives the mind a chance to conceive the vastness of God by feeling or intuition. The ultimate realization is Samadhi, or complete union with God.

SIXTH STEP Only after mastering Pratyahara, Dhyana, or meditation is possible. Thousands of people think it is easy to meditate but really, meditation is impossible without climbing the steps of Yama- Niyama, Asana, Pranayama, and Pratyahara. Those only who have practiced those can practice Dhyana, because Dhyana means one who has controlled the body and moods and habits and is able to switch off the current from the five senses so that his attention, which is tied to the sensations, is free through Pratyahara to go within and meditate upon God.

The devotee is one who has scientifically attained or understands what meditation means. By Pratyahara, when the mind goes within, then it is possible to concentrate upon God. Otherwise, the mind will be experiencing sensations and the thoughts arising from restlessness. So many spiritual teachers ask their devotees to meditate without explaining that meditation involves the meditator, meditation (with the mind withdrawn from the senses by interiorization, etc, and. the object of meditation. Patanjali says: "Meditate upon God (Iswara) Then he goes on to say
that the average person has no conception of God, so he explains that the symbol of God is "AUM," or "OM," the Cosmic Vibration and the Cosmic Sound.

Patanjali took it for granted that people would know the meaning of Aum, as the definition is given in the Upanishads. The definition of Aum is, as oil continuously flows from a barrel, so does Aum flow continuously from the cask of Spirit. It in a cosmic sound like the sound of a bass voice or gong bell. It is on all-permeating sound. This sound can be heard in the body first and then it has to be heard all over creation and in everything (by Dharana or larger conception). It is the sound coming out of all atomic vibration.

When Patanjali said to concentrate upon Aum, chant Aum, and understand the meaning of Aum, he meant that people should not be taught to just loudly chant Aum, or chant Aum in a whisper, or chant Aum mentally, but they should repeatedly engage the mind upon the Aum that is heard in the body (and emanating from Cosmic Vibration) by certain techniques, as taught in Praecepta Nos. 27 to 30 inclusive and particularly in Praeceptum No. 29, as well as throughout the Seven Steps of Self-Realization. Those who chant Aum loudly, or in a whisper only create a sound of their own through the voice and imagination, and are limited by that sound. But the sound that is going on in the cosmos is unlimited, omnipresent, and omniscient —the Holy Ghost or vibration emanating from the transcendental God, the Father, and containing in it its guiding principle -- Infinite Intelligence.

Patanjali says that in superconscious chanting the devotee keeps his attention riveted to this cosmic sound and tries to understand and feel this sound of Aum as the representative of God in all matter. The Word (Cosmic vibration) was made flesh (all matter, the physical body of God). This Aum is spoken of in the Christian Bible as the Holy Ghost. Within this Holy Ghost is reflected the Christ Consciousness. The consciousness existing beyond all creation is God the Father Consciousness, or Absolute Consciousness. Many people, not understanding the significance of Patanjali's words, go on chanting loudly without understanding why they chant. Of course, it is good to chant loudly if one tries to feel behind his chanting the cosmic presence of the Aum Sound. This Aum Sound is the Cosmic trumpet heard by St. John as described in Revelation, and the "Amen," the faithful witness of the beginning of the creation of God.

Then Patanjali says that by superconscious chanting or inner perception of the Aum Sound and by thinking of the significance of Aum, one begins to identify his consciousness in Aum as heard in the body, and also as Aum as expressed in the universe. When Patanjali says to chant Aum, that means, listen to the Aum Sound that is going on in the temple of meditation. Then, when he says, "Think of its significance," he means, do not limit Aum by a boundary of your own concentration but try to feel Aum beyond the boundaries of the body in all things and in all eternity.

SEVENTH STEP: DHARANA OR CONCEPTION OF AUM NOT ONLY IN THE BODY BUT IN THE UNIVERSE   After Dhyana of meditation comes Dharana, which means conception of the magnanimity of Aum. Dharana means meditation of Aum with an interiorized mind. "Artha bhabanam" (think of the meaning of Aum) and "Dharana" (conception of the Aum Sound as present in the body and the Cosmos) are the same thing, signifying conceiving the perception of Aum not only in the body but in the universe. By doing this, the devotee attains Sabikalpa Samadhi; that is, he deliberately forgets the wave of the body (not unconsciousness by diversion) in order to concentrate upon the ocean of Spirit. In Sabikalpa Samadhi, the devotee concentrates so that his concentration is completely obliterated from outside, but he is extremely super-sensitively conscious of the Spirit within. Sabikalpa Samadhi has many forms.

When the devotee becomes one with the Cosmic Sound of Aum, that is called "Aum Samadhi." When the devotee is one with the Cosmic life in this vibration of Aum, then it is called "Mahaprana," or Cosmic Life Samadhi." In the Astral Samadhi, the devotee is one with the Cosmic light, and then comes the "Ananda Samadhi," or the oneness with the Cosmic Joy in everything. Then comes the Gyana Samadhi, or Wisdom Samadhi, which is to be one with the wisdom in everything. Then comes devotion Samadhi -- to be one with the devotion of all devotees. Then comes Love

Samadhi, or Prema Samadhi, which is to be one with the Cosmic Love in all creatures and in everything, and in God. Then comes Sundara Samadhi, which is beauty Samadhi, when one becomes one with all beauty in Spirit.

In Sabikalpa Samadhi, the devotee is conscious of these various manifestations of God as sound, light, devotion, bliss, beauty, and so on, to the exclusion of the consciousness of the body or the world. After the devotee attains Samadhi, which means oneness with the various manifestations of God, he brings that consciousness of God back to the body, thereby attaining Nirbikalpa Samadhi.

THE ULTIMATE REALIZATION   In Nirbikalpa Samadhi the Soul becomes conscious of the ocean of Spirit with its manifesting waves, the body, the mind, and the Soul at the same time. All these various steps suggested must produce Nirbikalpa Samadhi, and the devotee must not remain confined to one step, but he should climb all the Seven Steps of salvation until he reaches the pinnacle of spiritual Self-Realization in Nirbikalpa Samadhi.

THE APOLOGUE
THE MAN WHO MISUSED MIRACLES
Part Two
Suddenly Afzal was attracted by a wonderful gold chain and antique watch decorating the breast pocked of one of Master's friends. He curiously and smilingly touched it, and after a few minutes his friend cried out: "My watch and chain are gone. " He cried and pleaded: "Please Afzal, return that heirloom of mine which I prize so much. I will give you anything else of mine but give me back my watch and chain. "

For a while Afzal was stoically silent, and then he said: "You have 500 rupees in your iron safe. Bring them back to me and I will tell you where the watch and chain are."

The man was so enraged and grieved at the loss of his prized heirlooms that he forthwith ran home and brought back the money which Afzal Khan had clairvoyantly seen in his iron safe. Then Afzal said: "Go back, stand under the little bridge near your house and say: "Hazrat, give me back my watch and chain."

The grief-strioken man left for the bridge, and as soon as he was there and cried out: "Please, Hazrat, give me my watch and chain, " behold, the heirlooms came tumbling down from a few feet overhead into his right hand. He forthwith went to his home and locked the chain and the watch in the iron safe and came back to witness some more mischief-making miracles of Afzal Khan.

My Master said that when they were on the balcony Afzal said: "Tell me what you want to eat. " So, two or them spoke first. One said: "I want hot milk, " and another said: "I want whiskey." Afzal Khan looked up toward heaven and said: "Hazrat, give me a bottle of whiskey and a bottle of hot milk. "

Immediately two sealed bottles came tumbling down from the sky and landed with a thud without breaking, and when the seals were broken, lo, in one bottle there was hot milk and in the other bottle there was whiskey. After this, Afzal Khan said: "You are all hungry. Why not have a lunch served by Hazrat -- anything you want, and you won't be bothered about washing the dishes. "

And Master continued: "Of the twenty people and myself surrounding Afzal, each one asked him to materialize some out-of-season fruits and intricately-produced delicacies to be served on gold dishes. Many asked for grapes and mangoes, which could not under any circumstances be found in the little village of Serampore, and as soon as I and my twenty friends finished describing the kind of lunch we wanted, there was a great jingling sound of dishes and platters landing on the floor of this very room where you are now staying, and Afzal Khan immediately asked us to follow him into the room, and when we entered, behold! glittering jewel-studded gold dishes had exactly everything that each one of us had ordered.

"We all marvelled as we enjoyed the delicious fruits and hot good food given to us in the twinkling of an eye. This dinner was not materialized by mass hypnotism or by auto-suggestion, for I have been absolutely invulnerable to hypnotic influences from my childhood, I, myself, being blessed by the Great Ones. This was an actual case of materializing food atoms and dishes from etheric energy by an act of highly developed will power.

Even as God materialized all things from His Mind, so also miraculous powers in man can materialize many things, and as we left the room after the hearty lunch, we heard a tremendous noise of dishes thrown around, and when we looked in to see what had happened, behold! there was no trace of those soiled glittering gold dishes or the left-overs from the delicious dinner. We dispersed and lost sight of Afzal Khan for a long time."

(To be continued in Next Praeceptum)

HEALTH CULTURE
THE SCIENCE OF NUTRITION

HONEY -- ITS NATURE AND USES When liquid honey is allowed to stand for some time in a cool place, it crystallizes or "sugars." There are many uses for this granulated honey:

1. CAKE ICING. Warm the honey slightly so that it will spread easily, then add chopped nuts and coconut. A delicious fudge icing may be made by mixing the solid honey with butter and cocoa, 2 parts of honey to 1 part of butter and sufficient cocoa to give the chocolate flavor desired.
2. HARD SAUCE. Blend solid honey with butter.
3. CANDY. Mix solid honey with ground fruit and nuts.

PRAECEPTUM INSPIRATION THE GARDEN OF SOULS

If you have wisdom, people will come to you. There is a lot of difference between being learned and being illiterate. A Saint once said: "I prefer the company of an illiterate man who is humble, to the man who is proud and does not know how spiritually illiterate he is. Still better, I admire one who is intelligent and knows how to act."

When your actions are bad, you are acting like the man who sat on the bough of a tree and started sawing off the bough on which he sat. He forgot that when the bough would be entirely sawed off, he would fall.

Each Soul has blossoms of nobility. You must go into the Garden of Souls and pluck from it a beautiful Soul Flower and transplant it in your own heart. And that you can only do through "Sat-Sanga," which means fellowship.

To love others means to seek happiness in their happiness. God's love alone is pure. When all the world is against you, He is there, and when no one is with you, He is with you always. And when you leave the shores of this earth, He will be with you.

PRAECEPTUM AFFIRMATION

WHETHER I AM AWAKE OR ASLEEP, ALERT OR DREAMING, THY ALL-PROTECTING PRESENCE ENCIRCLES ME.

YOGODA SAT-SANGA FORTNIGHTLY INSTRUCTIONS
BY
PARAMHANSA YOGANANDA

DANCING TO THE BLISS PIPINGS
Part III

All body-cells shall die and lose their mortal
    limitations,
Resurrected in the fire of infinity.
They shall see joy,
They shall hear joy,
They shall taste joy,
They shall smell joy,
And they shall feel the ever-new joy

Dancing to the bliss-pipings of God-Infinite.
The flesh shall die to live forever.
Murder sensibilities and let them walk

As goblins of deathless peace,
Forsaking their ghoulish dance of pain and sensitive
death.
Painful sensations shall change

Into eternal sensations of joy.
The boundaries of sensibility shall be broken

And the kingdom of infinite happiness shall reig(n).
No more the body diving into the sea,
Or swallowed by the sepulcher of volcanoes,
Shall pant for breath, or cry with pain,
All agents of destruction
Shall change into the angels and servitors of eternal
    happiness.
Andd the body shall cry no more with pain,
But with eternal bliss.
For body is the shadow of God --
His shadow in the body immortal.

(To be continued in next Praeceptum)

KRIYA -- THE HIGHER INITIATION
Part One

Words are inadequate to express to you the Self-Realization- producing vitality of this Kriya (Kree-ya) Instruction. Whether you understand the theory or not, if you conscientiously practice this Super-Technique, your all-accomplishing power of concentration will increase, and creative inspiration and ever-new, ever-increasing happiness will be at your command.

He who practices Kriya is a Kriyaban, or a true Brahmin or true twice-born Christian, or a man of Realization. He is born again, as spoken of in the Christian Bible:

"Except ye be born again, ye cannot enter the kingdom of heaven." The physical birth is given by the father; the spiritual birth is given by the Guru (preceptor), the one individual who is able to lead the disciple to God-Consciousness. One may have had many teachers before, but when he finds his Guru, the Guru becomes the only one throughout life. The Guru is the vehicle of God, through whom God teaches and calls the disciple to Himself.

HISTORICAL BASIS   This evolutional technique was given by Supreme Master Babaji; who, despite his present incarnation of unusually long duration, (as proved by records) has retained his youth, and has Christ-like powers. He gave the technique to his disciple, Lahiri Mahasaya. Lahiri Mahasaya gave it to his disciple, Swami Sriyukteswarji. The latter gave it to his disciple, Swami Yogananda, to be brought to Western disciples, in order that they might be equipped to expand the Cup of their Self-Realization in order to hold the Ocean of Omnipresent Christ or Cosmic Consciousness. This technique is to be the foundation and the eternal, continuous base of your own Self-Realization, leading you beyond the Seven Real Steps to Cosmic Consciousness. So you must be true to yourself and us; we are in earnest with you and are resolved to show you that Cosmic Consciousness and Divine power are attainable in one life, if you properly and continuously cooperate in this Divine endeavor.

Your fervent prayer for a new life, full of the abundance and happiness due each sincere soul, is herewith and herein answered. With the proper and persistent practice of these forthcoming principles and techniques, you may expect to attain that Supreme Goal of Self-Realization, that Goal exemplified in the life of Sri Lahiri Mahasaya, who toiled in the world, but remained ever apart from the world.

KRIYA IS INITIATION COSMIC CONSCIOUSNESS   By this Initiation, the consciousness which is in the body, and which is identified with the senses, is transferred to the spine and the brain, and thus transmuted into Super-Consciousness and Cosmic Consciousness. Through the practice of this technique, you will contact Christ and the prophets of this world, and through them you will find your union with God, the Infinite Spirit.

You may have passed through the stage of worshiping idols and following blind beliefs, and you may have worshiped many material things, but at last you must see that, no matter what you worship, the highest truth is within yourself. That is why this great initiation has come, by which you can awaken the spine and create an altar within your spine, and you can then say that God is not in restless things, but in the greatest measure within yourself. Worship God on the altar of the spine, behold Him in the temple of every thought, in every activity. At last, after several eons of worshiping many gods, Self-Realization Fellowship has come to show you that you can find Him in the spine, right within yourself.

If you just imagine that you are in Cosmic Consciousness, that does not make it so; you are in the flesh; but as soon as you disconnect yourself through this Technique, then your mortal thread of the body is cut and your consciousness is centered in the spine. When coolness of the spine comes, all the energy from the senses is sucked into the spine, producing perfect sensory relaxation. It is perfect control of the senses. Just as if you were standing near the switch and some one said: "Put the lights out." You do not lose consciousness, for you have perfect control of the switch. And when you wish to, you may switch the senses back on again. These are the results the practice of Kriya gives.

Jesus said: "Except a man be born of water and of the Spirit, he cannot enter into the kingdom of God." (Water is flesh, and Spirit is the second birth). That is why Brahmins in India are called "twice-born." Dwija (twice-born) means the second birth, when one's consciousness is awakened in the spine. This is the baptism by the Spirit.

CONSCIOUS LIFE   While you are eating, your consciousness is centered upon the little palate; while you are listening, your mind is upon your eardrum; when you are smelling, your mind is

-Page Two-

110

centered upon the nostrils; when you are seeing, your mind is upon the retina; when you are thinking, ordinarily or otherwise, your mind is partially upon the brain, but mostly centered upon the body and senses; when you are feeling, your mind is upon the heart; when you are expressing your will power, your mind is at the point between the eyebrows. (Will Center) and in the muscular movements. Conscious life is marked by restlessness.

In sleep, your consciousness and energy are centered in the vital organs and not in the muscles. Subconsciousness is marked by peace felt unconsciously. In meditation, your consciousness and energy have to be consciously withdrawn from the senses and muscles, to the spine.

The purpose of Kriya is to magnetize the spine by circulating life current lengthwise around it, and thereby withdrawing the life current from the senses and involuntary organs and concentrating it in the spine. This also helps to change the center of consciousness from the body and senses to the spine.

The spine and brain are the insulating altars where Divine energy first descends in the body and goes out to the senses, keeping the Soul busy with material thirds. When, by the practice of the Kriya Technique that will be given in the following Praecepta, consciousness and energy become centralized in the spine, boundless ever-new joy will be felt in the spine.

"PRANA" MEANS LIFE ENERGY   There are two kinds of Prana. (a) the Cosmic Energy, the source of all living things; (b) the specific Prana or Energy pervading each human body.

The Cosmic Energy is the cause of the creation of planets and all living organisms. The Life Energy in the body of all organisms is secretly supplied by the   Cosmic Energy. But the Life Energy loses this contact the more it becomes individualized, selfish, and body-bound, ignoring its Cosmic connection. The Cosmic Energy is finer than electrons or any other vibratory force existing in Nature, and is conscious (but not self-conscious). It is the missing link between Consciousness and matter.

The Spirit vibrating outward first becomes Cosmic Consciousness, then, as it vibrates into grosser states, it becomes Conscious Cosmic Energy, followed by the grossest material vibration or matter. Hence, the connecting link between the human consciousness and the gross body is established by the specific Life Energy.

The Soul vibrates into Consciousness, Consciousness vibrates into Life Energy, which in turn vibrates into the gross human body. Hence, those who do not understand the functions of Life Energy find a great difference between mind and matter, or ignorantly deny the existence of matter. Mind exists, matter exists, but both are vibrations of Spirit. Invisible mind vibrating as Life Energy is converted into gross matter. Matter does not exist as it appears to us; it is nothing but vibrations of Life Energy, which in turn are vibrations of Consciousness.

To be able to understand the functions of Life Energy is to be able to dematerialize the body into its original constituent principles. The Life Energy in general, as present in the human body, is spoken of as "Prana" in Sanskrit; it is conscious Energy; it builds the human body out (of) a spermatozoon. Its seat in the human body is the Medulla Oblongata.

-Page Three-

THE APOLOGUE
THE MAN WHO MISUSED MIRACLES

Part III

Later we read the following summary in the newspapers about the personal confession of Afzal Khan: "This I write to warn all my fellow beings who are in the spiritual path that they must not, under any circumstances, misuse miraculous powers as I have done. This I write from the bitter gall that I have tasted and the misfortune that has befallen me in losing divine grace as a punishment for wrongly using the miraculous powers imparted to me by the grace of God and my Master. Recently,

I had a terrible awakening and that is why I am writing this confession to warn fellow spiritual brothers, who have spiritual powers, to avoid encountering the disasters that overtook me.

Against the advice of my Master, I became so drunk with the spiritual powers given to me that I felt that I could do anything by myself and that there was no one able to prevent me or help me. I was to use my miraculous powers for healing others and helping them achieve prosperity, but instead I used my inner powers to take money away from the rich by an unethical method, and that is why I recently have had some terrible unforgettable experiences.

Once, as I was walking on the outskirts of a city, I met a rather old man walking with a limp and carrying in his hand a glittering object which looked like solid gold. I was attracted by the gleaming metal and wanted to possess it by making it disappear by my spiritual power. With this evil intention, I quickly approached the old man, who kept his head bowed. At first I thought that I had seen him before, but then the greed for gold blinded me and I forgot myself and paid no more attention to the thought as to whether I knew him or not.

The old man, with his head still bowed, and with half-closed eyes, asked: 'Who are you?' 'I am Afzal Khan, the great yogi,' I replied. Then forthwith this old man requested: 'Please heal my limping,' and to that I replied: 'Well, well, I will see to that, but tell me, what have you in your hand?' Then the old man quickly said: 'Why, that is a ball of solid gold.'

Upon hearing this, I became blind with greed again and said: 'May I touch it, please?' The old man said: 'Of course,' and handed the ball over to me, and after touching it I returned it to him. In a few minutes, While the old man was still conversing with me, he found that his ball of gold had disappeared. Then he cried and entreated: 'Please don't take the piece of gold, the only material possession I have in the world. I implore you to return it to me, and please heal me.'

Scornfully I refused his request, but as I was about to walk away the old man caught hold of my hand and we stood face to face. Looking straight into my eyes, in a stentorian voice he cried: 'Do you recognize these eyes and this voice?' For a moment I stood speechless, for I saw that this superficial-looking old man was none other than my Master who had given me the miraculous powers and whom I had met in the village in my early boyhood.

When my Master saw that I recognized him, in a very stern voice he rebuked me: 'So, this is why I gave you the powers, is it? At last you apply your miracles to practice dishonesty on me, so now I shall take away your spiritual powers. Your Hazrat is leaving you now and you will cease to be a terror to the people of Bengal and all India. Shame on you! Repent.'

-Page Four-

THE SCIENCE OF NUTRITION

HONEY -- ITS NATURE AND USES   In replacing sugar with honey in a cake or cookie recipe, the amount of liquid should be reduced one-fifth for each cup of honey used. To be absolutely sure of the correct amount of liquid to use, remove 3 tablespoons and 1 teaspoon of the liquid for each cup of honey used.

In some cases where certain ingredients like chocolate, dates, raisins, nuts and mixed fruits are used, the honey cake mix will use as much liquid as the same type of sugar cake owing to the absorption qualities of the fruits or chocolate.

Less honey than sugar is required for sweetening fresh and dried fruits. Drizzling, is the simplest way to use honey. Cold honey pours in a heavy stream but warm honey drizzles easily from a sharp pointed pitcher or glass. Place the honey jar or pitcher in warm -- not hot -- water for about 10 minutes, before using. It will then be of the right consistency to drizzle in tiny threads and can thus be controlled without getting the food too sweet.

(To be concluded)

BROWN SAUCE

2 tablespoons butter
1 small sliced onion
3 tablespoons whole wheat flour

vegex or savita
1 cup vegetable stock
1 teaspoon lemon juice

Cook onion in butter until yellow. Stir in flour and add stock slowly. Bring to boiling point, stirring constantly, add seasonings, remove onion.

HONEY GINGERBREAD

2 cup cream
1 egg well beaten
1 cup brown sugar
1 cup milk
1 teaspoon baking soda
2 ½ cups whole wheat pastry

1 teaspoon ginger
½ cup honey
¼ teaspoon allspice
1 teaspoon baking powder
½ teaspoon vegetized salt
1 teaspoon cinnamon

Sift flour, measure, and sift again with baking powder, baking soda, salt and spices. Combine cream, sugar and egg. Combine milk and honey. Add cream mixture and milk mixture alternately to dry ingredients. Mix thoroughly. Pour into well-oiled shallow pan. Bake in moderate oven 30 minutes.

PRAECEPTUM INSPIRATION KNOW GOD'S TRUTHS

As sunshine is given to everyone, but nevertheless some people live in utter darkness, so God's wisdom is scattered all over, but some remain in ignorance. They look at the world through the dark glasses of their own ignorance and live mostly in the darkness of their own thoughts, but there are some who constantly live in the sunshine of wis¬dom, who refuse to bring the darkness into their lives; they are the ones who are happy.

Develop your mental powers. When you increase your perception and feeling, when the all-seeing eye is open, and when the all-absorbing power is felt, then you will automatically absorb Truth from the book of Nature. Absorb Truth within from the depth of silence. No matter how many mistakes you make, if you have the desire to know God's Truths, you will find them. He will lift the clouds and talk to you; you will hear His voice in the babble of the brook and gurgling of the river.

PRAECEPTUM AFFIRMATION

I am Thy Babe of Eternity rocking in the cradle of Thy Omnipresent Bosom.

YOGODA SAT-SANGA FORTNIGHTLY INSTRUCTIONS
BY
PARAMHANSA YOGANANDA

DANCING TO THE BLISS-PIPINGS

Part IV

And when death shall come and make me deaf
I will listen to the
voice of my Beloved.
When death shall come and congeal my smell
I shall breathe the fragrance of His presence.
And when death shall congeal my tongue,
I shall drink His Ambrosia,
And when death shall obliterate my sight,
I shall see His Omniscient Light
Enthroned in everything.
And when death shall freeze my blood and sense of touch,
I shall embrace the warmth of His omnipresent feet everywhere.
When my eyes will not see earthly things any longer,
The light of my vision shall penetrate into the heart
Of all things and photograph their mysteries.
When my ears shall hear no longer,
I shall hear the whisperings of all things past, present, and future.
When I shall smell no longer,
I shall be like the Hound of Heaven,
Tracing the scent of all secret things.
When I shall taste no longer,
I shall remember all things that I tasted
Through all the mouths
that ever lived now, or will Live hereafter.
When I shall feel no longer with this body,
I shall feel with my Cosmic Body,
The secret touch of all things, here and afar --
The bubbles on the surface of all seas,
Or the feelings of the bubbles of universes
Floating on the sea of space.

(Conclusion)

KRIYA -- THE HIGHER INITIATION
Part Two

THE SPIRITUAL BENEFIT OF PRACTICING KRIYA   The Kriya technique will
bring you to the source of inspiration and will give to you answers, clear the
brain and stimulate it, strengthen the medulla, and ope with Spiritual Eye, as
well as greatly magnetize the body.

By this method, the blood becomes so oxygenated that that gradually dependence
upon mortal breath becomes less and less. In this way the student of Self-
Realizaton lives more by Word of God, or Cosmic Energy, and less by the bread of
life, or breath and solid and liquid foods. When the current is sent through and
around the spine, the higher perception of God in the spine and brain is felt.
The spinal cells then become the whole body.

These are the Control of Prana exercises and not ordinary breathing' exercises. The Kriya exercises have been practiced by numberless students with the greatest benefit to their spiritual and moral growth.

Your Souls are seeking that which is tangible, and in this Kriya Technique you will get a mathematical result. Results will be according to how much you practice. To those who are sincere and want to go ahead, I recommend this Truth. Whenever you find stagnation, practice Kriya exercises and you will see how you will be helped.

Twenty-four hours of ordinary silence will not produce as much spiritual benefit as one hour of deep meditation, and this Kriya technique produces more results than 24 hours of meditation. I can vouch that this is one of⁜ the greatest techniques that my Master taught.

Every time you practice correctly you may be sure that your entire system is changing and your brain power and mind receptivity are expanding, and then you will be able to say that the Masters of India have given you everything. Through this practice, the time limitation in evolution is overcome and the receptive power of the spine and brain is increased, so that you will know, see, and feel all from within. This the super-method by which the evolution of body, mind, and soul can be quickened. This is how the attainment of wisdom and Self-Realization, which usually takes numberless years and numerous incarnations of natural evolution is possible in one lifetime. Therefore, by deep devotion and Kriya practice you may acquire Cosmic Consciousness in one lifetime, which otherwise would take several irksome human incarnations to achieve.

SCIENTIFIC BASIS OF THE TECHNIQUE OF KRIYA   Every day science is inventing or discovering some new method or mechanism for increasing the material comforts of man, as evidenced by the scientific magazines and treatises. If scientists had journeyed to a temple, locked the doors, and prayed to God for the invention of radio, airplanes, television, and so forth, they would not have found them. Scientists only discover the hidden truths by using concentration, systematic activity, and experimentation within the laws of Nature, emanating from God. So must religious followers do, in order to attain the bliss of Self-Realizaton.

If you want to be different and reap the richest harvest of complete Truth in this short span of life, you must faithfully make these practical instructions a part of your life. Do not put off studying these Truths until tomorrow. That "tomorrow" will be ever- receding, while your bad habits will swallow your precious opportune days of Immortal Achievements. By adapting these Truths to your life, you will more clearly understand the teaching that you have embraced. In brief, kindly bear in mind that procrastination and subsequent postponement of effort will only lead to stagnation and retardation in the climb up the Seven Steps to Self-Realization.

This fundamental method, the Kriya Technique, which will be fully described in a later Praeceptum teaches how to awaken the Life Force by magnetizing the spine, and teaches how to transmute this Life Force into radiant, all-encompassing Spiritual Force, which in turn hastens the physical and mental regeneration and rejuvenation of the advanced student of Self-Realizaton. This is accomplished by diverting the Life Force from the senses and concentrating it upon the Soul. Specifically, the Kriya Technique will transfer your attention from the sensations of sight, smell, sound, taste, and touch, to the spine and brain, where God reigns in all His glory. Thus the spine is the Altar of God. Any distraction of sensations and their resultant

-Page Two-

thoughts only bars God-contact by diverting the Life Force from the spine to the senses. Therefore, when you are conscious only of spinal perceptions, then you will be One with God.

QUICKENING SOUL EVOLUTION   The natural or evolutionary progress of the human body, mind, and soul keeps pace with the revolutions of the earth around the sun. (Of course, this natural progress is retarded if disease, accidents, undue despondency, or ignorance, or sense attachment and slavery be permitted to invade the body, mind, and soul). Just as the earth's complete revolution around the sun produces one year's effects upon a human being, so the Yogis of India discovered that the time of human evolution could be quickened greatly by revolving the Life Force (the earthly physical (energy) around the elliptical path of the spinal column and its six centers, upward from the coccyx to the point between the eyebrows, and downward from that point to the coccyx, with the Soul as the central sun.

KRIYA QUICKENS EVOLUTION The solar year through outside influences of rays and vibrations quickens the mind and soul to a certain state in a year's time. The Yogis found that the same result could be brought about by internal methods for energizing and spiritualizing the spine, which is extremely sensitive. This quickening of evolution can be accomplished only if Kriya is practised correctly, if the body is kept free from diseases and accidents, and the mind is kept free from disbelief and error.

The Great Ones of India found that it takes eight years of solar evolution and right living to produce a certain kind of mentality. And so, every eight years, according to solar evolution, you change, mentally and physically. According to that calculation, one million years would be required for one to attain Cosmic Consciousness.

Eight years of food and solar energy can produce a specific refined brain but the Saints of India said: "Well, we will find away to attain Cosmic Consciousness in one life!" They discovered that any effect from the body to the brain is a slow process, but any effect from the brain to the body is immediate. They found a process of sending the Life Force around the spine, thereby quickening evolution.

The spine with its six centers (apart from the seventh center in the head) make twelve points, corresponding to the Signs of the Zodiac. By revolving the Life Force even once around the spine effects a change in the brain and body which is only possible by one year of diseaseless existence, careful eating and solar energy.) The passing of this current once around the spine corresponds to 365 days of sunlight So, any current revolving around the spine once will give you one year of solar evolution.

WHAT IS COSMIC CONSCIOUSNESS Cosmic Consciousness, or Spirit, or Brahma, or the Absolute are one and the same thing. When Creation was not, Spirit was. Creation has beginning and end; the categories of time, space, relativity, dimension, and cause and effect apply to it, whereas Spirit is beyond all categories of time, space, relativity, dimension, and cause and effect apply to it, whereas Spirit is beyond all categories, is beginningless, and unconditioned. All the conditions of existence are contained in Him. Spirit, or the Absolute, is self-born. Spirit is ever-conscious, His attention is equally distributed everywhere, His whole attention is fully concentrated everywhere. We, being made in His image, have the latent power to concentrate and feel our existence everywhere, through the cosmic or all-pervading consciousness. Our human consciousness is the Cosmic Consciousness bottled up in the phial of flesh, corked with ignorance and in isolation floating in the ocean of Spirit, yet cannot contact Him, just as salt water corked in a bottle and floating in the sea cannot contact the sea.

-Page Three-

116

Cosmic Consciousness is the consciousness that is spread all over the universe and everything in it. Human consciousness is limited by the human body and its environment. To attain Cosmic Consciousness means to expand the consciousness of the cells in your body. Through spreading your human consciousness by the faithful practice of Kriya Technique, which is to appear in a later Praeceptum, you will attain Cosmic Consciousness.

(To be Continued in Next Praeceptum)

THE APOLOGUE
THE MAN WHO MISUSED MIRACLES
(Part IV - Continued from Praeceptum No. 150)

'For a little while I thought I still had my spiritual powers, but when I called Hazrat, he did not appear to my sight as he used to, when he was invisible to others! Then and there I realized my terrible blasphemy in using divine powers to deceive and injure people instead of using them to help people, with divine permission. I realized that even divine powers should be used only with divine permission and that exclusively to help people.

I burst into tears and fell at the feet of my Master, and holding them tightly to my bosom I prayed and begged and implored; 'Master mine, thank you for curing my state of delusion. I promise you that I am going to the Himalayas to worship God alone and renounce the world, and I shall try to atone for my evil deeds.

Somehow my Master felt my sincerity and his heart melted, so he lifted me up and looked at me with infinite compassion and said: 'Son, I believe in your sincerity and am glad that now you behold your error. I forgive you. And for your real repentance and your desire to meditate upon God I will do one thing for you. Though I have taken away most of your spiritual power, I again grant you the power that whenever and wherever you wish for food and clothing for your personal use, you will receive them immediately through Hazrat. This I do that it may help you to maintain yourself while you devote yourself to meditation upon God in the solitude of the Himalayas.'

'Saying this, my Master vanished from sight and I was left to myself and my tears. Now, this should warn all my spiritual brothers who are advanced and possess inner powers, that they should never wrongly use them or use them even to do good without divine permission. For God Himself, though He helps all the world, He does not render His help in a spectacular, egotistical way, but in a hidden, indirect way. That is why I am warning all my spiritual brothers, that they be not tempted to misuse their spiritual powers, as by so doing they will lose the blessing and grace of God. Those who misuse God-given powers are of course disloyal to God and thereby betray His trust. God is the only bestower of spiritual powers and that is why a great spiritual offense casts the Soul into the mire of divine separation, misery, and ignorance. Adieu, world! I am going to my Beloved.'"

The above story should be a great lesson to all those students who may have developed great will force and personality and spiritual magnetism through the deep and continuous study of the Weekly Praecepta. It should teach them that they should not in any way employ their high-powered will in wishing evil, even to their enemies. The above story illustrates that evil acts like a boomerang and comes back to its initiator. Therefore, you must be careful never to harbor even a revengeful thought in your mind, for mental bombs in the ether explode and hurt oneself as well as those against whom they are used. All objects in the world represent the materialized thought force of human beings and God.

-Page Four-

The above story further illustrates that seeds of evil must never be allowed to grow on the fertile powerful soil of the mind, Evil thoughts lead to evil actions, and vice versa. Allow to grow in the mind only that which is good.
(Conclusion)

HEALTH CULTURE
THE SCIENCE OF NUTRITION

HONEY -- ITS NATURE AND USES   Honey that is slightly diluted is more convenient to use for sweetening cereals, candying sweet potatoes or parsnips, or baked apples and in making fruit drinks. 1/3 cup of water to 1 cup honey gives density of maple syrup, 1/5 cup of water to 1 cup honey gives density of corn or cane syrup. 2 tablespoons of water to 1 cup honey gives density of molasses.

For general use the maple syrup density (1 cup water to 3 cups honey) is most satisfactory. The honey should be blended with hot water and kept in covered container in a cold place. Honey is easy to measure if the cup or spoon is first used for measuring shortening or greased with oil.

Keep liquid honey in a warm dry place where the temperature is 75° F. or over, or in a cold place where the temperature is below 50° F. Freezing does not injure the color or flavor but may hasten granulation. Do not put comb honey in the refrigerator. It is better kept at room temperature.

CANTALOUPE AND GRAPE SALAD It is wise to make good use of cantaloupes while they are in season for they contain several valuable properties. They are alkaline in reaction and contain vitamins A, B, C, D, and G. Also they produce about half the calories as the same amount of potatoes.

1 cup cantaloupe cubes or balls   1/4 cup American cheese, diced
1 cup seedless grapes   Dressing

Mix ingredients, chill and serve on crisp lettuce with favorite dressing. Garnish with strips of cheese.

SPINACH LOAF

1 cup steamed spinach,   1 cup cottage cheese
    chopped fine.   1/2 cup toasted whole wheat
1 egg, well beaten   crumbs
1/2 teaspoon celery salt   2 tablespoons melted butter

Mix and bake 20 minutes in a buttered dish. Serve with tomato or any desired sauce,

PINEAPPLE MILK SHERBET

1 can crushed pineapple   1/4 cup powdered raw sugar
1/4 cup orange juice   1 Large can evaporated milk
1 teaspoon grated orange rind   few grains

Mix pineapple (juice and pulp), orange juice, rind and sugar. Stir until sugar is dissolved and add undiluted evaporated milk and salt. Freeze in automatic refrigerator stirring twice during first hour of freezing. Serves six.

-Page Five-

THE DIFFERENCE BETWEEN SOUL AND SPIRIT

As the sun reflects itself in water, it seems to be the sun in the water; in this way the One Spirit reflects in many Souls, or rather, this One Spirit is reflected in us as Souls. When you break the waves of the water, holding the image, the reflected image goes back to the sun; in the same way, when we are emancipated from the body, we go back to Spirit.

If we are made in the image of God, why do we not reflect Him? We are in God; surrounded by God; God is within us, yet why do we not feel Him? There are several reasons. One is, because our attention is directed to the limitations of flesh and earthly things with which we have identified ourselves.

Is Spirit knowable? When we speak of Spirit as the Creative Principle, or Truth, that does not get us anywhere. Spirit, in order to be real, must be real to us in a definite way. To describe Spirit negatively, saying that He is neither mind, nor intelligence, conception nor cognition, sense perception nor thoughts, sky nor earth, ego nor chittwa (feelings), does not describe Him. By the negative method it is impossible to explain Him. Ho is beyond conception, but that does not prove that He is not in conception, for if He is not in it too, He would not be omnipresent.

Spirit as ever-new Bliss, Absolute Consciousness (the Absolute Consciousness which knows only the present tense and is not suppressed or eclipsed by the past or future tenses; He is and He knows that He is) and Immortality (or changelessness; death is change, Immortality is changelessness), we can conceive of the relation in which He may stand to us. By searching through all the motives of our actions, we find that we too are seeking Eternal, Ever-New B(liss), Immortality, and Everlasting Consciousness. We are seeking everlasting Bliss, and along with it are automatically seeking immortality and Self-awareness, for, without these we not possess Eternal Bliss.

PRAECEPTUM AFFIRMATION

I will be as attentive to Thee as a mother is to her child. I will perform my duties diligently and with my attention riveted upon Thee. I will love Thee as the worldly man loves possessions. With the first love of true lovers, I will love Thee.

"OM"

-Page Six-

YOGODA SAT-SANGA FORTNIGHTLY INSTRUCTIONS
(By Paramhansa Yogananda) KRIYA -- THE HIGHER INITIATION
Part III

THE FUNCTION OF BREATH IS TO BURN CARBON   The magnetization of the
spine is accomplishedshed by neutralizing the process of inhalation and
exhalation, which convinces the Soul that the bodily functions are not the
absolute conditions upon which life exists. By a continuous regularity of
inhalation and exhalation, the following results are obtained: During, the
inhalation period, extra oxygen is charged into the body through the lungs and
it oxidizes or burns the carbon or impurities in the dark venous blood. During
the exhalation period, a large amount of carbon dioxide (poisonous material) is
expelled from the lungs. Consequently, when the carbon is burned out, the heart
has very little broken-down tissue to send into the lungs for purification, in
other words, if decayed tissues are oxidized by continuous breathing then
breathing gradually becomes less necessary. In addition, this process not only
explodes carbon but it changes oxygen into its equivalent atomic energy. This
atomic energy is distilled into Life Energy (intelligent electricity).

IN TIME KRIYA TECHNIQUE BURNS OUT ALL CARBON FROM BLOOD Furthermore,
bodily carbon production is lessened to a greater extent when muscular and limb
activity cease during the inactivity of the body in meditation (silence).

        By continuous regulated breathing, as prescribed in the Kriya Technique
in the following Praecepta, the entire carbon content of the body can be burned
out. Carbon accumulates in the body due to the activity of the lungs, diaphragm,
and heart., even though the body is held very still during meditation. The
continuous, regulated breathing when practicing the Technique of Kriya burns
out and removes the last residue of carbon. When that is accomplished, then the
dark, impure, venous blood ceases to flow in the body and no poisonous blood is
pumped into the lungs for purification. Hence, the burning of all bodily carbon
by this practice will give rest to the heart and lungs.

THE PURPOSE OF BURNING CARBON IS TO QUIET HEART. THE PURPOSE OF QUIETING
HEART IS TO CONTROL FIVE TELEPHONES OF THE NERVOUS As soon as the heart and
the lungs, with all muscular activities in the body, become quiet, breathing
will be less necessary and the energy from the five sense- telephones of sight,
hearing, taste, and touch will be consciously switched off and diverted to the
spine (as unconsciously and partially experienced during sleep).

SWITCHING OFF LIFE FORCE FROM FIVE NERVE TELEPHONES AIDS SCIENTIFIC
CONCENTRATION   Sleep is an unconscious state of concentration, as your
thoughts are dormant during that time. This is scientifically accomplished by
the still¬ness of muscular activity and the subsequent decrease in the activity
of the heart and integral organs, enabling the Life Force to be switched off
from the five sense-telephones. Thus, the heart is the switchboard of the senses.
When it partially or completely slows down, energy is automatically switched
off from the five sense-telephones, making it impossible for sensations of
sight, sound, taste, touch, and smell to enter the brain and divert attention by
the rousing of past and present memory thoughts.

SLEEP VS. CONSCIOUS TECHNIQUE OF SWITCHING OFF NERVE CURRENTS This theory
merely states, if in sleep every night, you unconsciously disconnect your
attention from the senses by switching off nerve currents from the five sense-
telephones, then why can't you do it consciously? This can be accomplished by
continuous, regulated breathing, which stills the entire activity of the mind
and organs during the time when the body is quiet.

(1)

REST OF HEART PRODUCES LONGEVITY   This process rests the heart and prolongs longevity, by the heart-switchboard diverting the nerve current from the five senses.

A MIND FREE AT WILL FROM SENSATIONS CAN EFFECTIVELY CONCENTRATE UPON GOD OR ANYTHING ELSE In conclusion, by practicing the Technique of Kriya even a few times, you can burn out the carbon, quiet the internal organs,.still the heart, and thus consciously switch off the Life Current from the five sense-telephones anytime, anywhere, at will and thus free the mind from distractions and impart to it the ability to whole-heartedly concentrate upon anything, or upon God. Whereas sleep, or unconscious quietness, leads you to subconsciousness and its attending peace, the Kriya Technique consciously leads you to an ever-increasing, ever-new joyous state of awareness.

BY ORDINARY LIVING, AN INDIVIDUAL BRAIN CAN BE PERFECTED IN ONE MILLION YEARS FIT TO EXPRESS COSMIC CONSCIOUSNESS   If a man eats right, lives right, and is free from disease -- and accidents, the solar and chemical energy of his body enables him to produce a new brain and a new mind every eight years. The Saints found out that if it were possible for a man to live in health without disease or old age, then by solar and chemical energy he could develop, in one million years, a brain that could express Cosmic Consciousness, or the entire knowledge of this Universe.

LOST PEOPLE REALLY LIVE ONLY FIVE YEARS   The average man lives sixty years. Half of that span is spent in sleep and idleness which reduces it to thirty years, and of this he spends fifteen years in making money. That cuts down the longevity of modern man to fifteen years. Five years he talks about others. Now he is down to ten years. Five years of that, he easily spends in absent-minded pursuits. Hence, he hardly lives even the five remaining years, for he does not pass that time in Cosmic Consciousness.

HOW TO UTILIZE 30 YEARS TO EXPRESS COSMIC CONSCIOUSNESS   Therefore, the problem arises: "How can we express Cosmic Consciousness in the thirty-year span of our sixty years? (Thirty years being easily spent in foolishness and sleep.)

THE DISCOVERY OF THE SAINTS OF INDIA -- ONE MILLION YEARS TO PERFECT BRAIN Our saints in India, found that the human brain and mind change every eight ears. If you live a healthy life, in eight years you will find a certain amount of change in the body and mind. First at 8 years of age, then at 16, 24, 32, and so on. This is provided you remain in good health. The saints calculated that at this rate of development it takes one million years of healthy life and brain evolution before your brain can comprehend Cosmic Consciousness. Can you know the meaning of all the words in the dictionary? No. And yet the whole four Vedas (big Hindu Bibles) were memorized by the saints of India and handed down from mouth to mouth for generations. They were never written for the benefit of others, but were relayed orally. Cosmic Consciousness means expressly all the knowledge in this universe with your human brain. If the saints of India could do this, why not learn their technique in order to be super-efficient like them?

THE WAY TO QUICKEN BRAIN EVOLUTION   Every human brain is the result of certain heredity. So, accordingly, our saints said: "Why adopt the chemical evolution way of salvation? Why wait for the body and brain to change every eight years? Why not

(2)

121

change the brain cells by the proper method? It isn't what ideas you pump into the brain, but what degree of knowledge the brain can be made to hold, by increasing its caliber. How can you increase the capacity of your brain?

The saints found out that if you know a higher method you can express Cosmic Consciousness in a shorter time. For instance, if some one outs a piece of your flesh off, a fraction of an inch at a time, it will take a long time to kill you, but if you are pricked in the medulla you will die instantly. So our saints found out also that any development that starts with the brain can quicken human evolution.

IS IT POSSIBLE TO KNOW TRUTH IN ONE SHORT LIFETIME?　　　It takes a million years to know the truth about the world and its history. Then, has the human brain time to know all this truth -- the truth of the stars and the strata of the earth and planets? How in the short span of human life can we know all the history of life, the heavens, and so forth?

Cosmic consciousness means the knowledge of all that there is in the united kingdom of God, on the pages of heaven, earth, Nature, and human life. How are you going to receive that knowledge within one lifetime? Through the faithful practice of Kriya Technique.

(To be continued in Next Praeceptum)

THE APOLOGUE

THE PRINGE WHO BECAME A BEGGAR

In India it often happens that young men from various walks of life forsake their families and material prosperity to go in search of a Master who can teach them the ways of renunciation and finding God in the temple of meditation, but even in India it is a rare occurrence if a prince leaves his material kingdom in search of the Kingdom of God.

Before Jesus Christ graced this earth, there lived in India a great King, whose spiritual queen had a vision clearly indicating that a great divine Soul was soon to become a member of her household.
Strange to say, but true to the vision, the queen gave birth to a son, whom they named Siddhartha. Later, he was called Gautama, the Buddha, or the "Enlightened One."

Prince Gautama, from his early childhood, was surrounded in his golden palace and gardens with every imaginable luxury and comfort. As the astrologers had predicted in the horoscope of Prince Gautama that he was to leave the kingdom and lead the life of a renunciate, his father took extreme precautions to protect his princely son from the sight of any misery or suffering, or the contact of Saints -- anything which might arouse in him the consciousness of dispassion and desirelessness for worldly objects.

When Prince Gautama became a young man, he felt the inner urge to see the world, so one day he induced his principal attendant to secretly escort him out of the palace on a sight-seeing tour of the kingdom ruled by his father. Once out of the palace, the prince felt a tremendous freedom and joy at the sight of thousands of people saluting him and throwing garlands of flowers at him in token of their reverence for him as the future heir to the throne of India. Very soon, however, the prince began to notice the difference between his marble palace and the rickety homes filled with squalor and dirt. Having been surrounded from his childhood with a spotlessly rich environment, he had become accustomed to thinking that the whole world was like his surroundings. The result was that he became sick at heart upon realiz-

(3)

ing that he was so well provided for while others were wallowing in worries and want.

As the princely chariot moved along, through the cheering crowd, the Prince suddenly saw a deformed, crippled man. He at once thought of his own beaming face and healthy body, and staring at the sorry figure of the crippled man he exclaimed to his attendant: "Pray, good Charioteer, tell me, can my body become crippled or deformed or diseased?"

"O yes, Prince," answered the Charioteer, "the physical body is vulnerable to disease and suffering, one never knows what is going to happen to us.

At this astounding revelation, the Prince became still more sorrowful and inwardly disturbed, and in his Soul he felt the first disillusionment for the temporal material things which encompassed his life.

As the Prince moved along in his golden chariot, he was astonished at seeing a very old man with hoary hair and wrinkled face begging for alms. The Prince stopped his chariot and accosted the old man: "Dear friend, has your body always been like this?"

"O no," the old man replied, "my body was just as beaming and healthy as yours in my younger days. Do not pity my old body, for your body will also become like mine when you grow old."

The Prince gave some alms to the old man but inwardly shuddered at the thought of his own beautiful body sometime becoming shriveled and shrunk. He almost felt that the net of old age was already creeping upon him from all sides. Then to further add to his distress, as the chariot rolled the prince finally encountered four men carrying a dead man on a bed, as is the custom in India. The Prince commanded that the chariot stop before the lifeless form of the man, then, in great bewilderment and agony, he asked his Charioteer: "Pray, tell me, is this the end of all human life? Will my beautiful body be congealed by death?" The Charioteer hung his head and sadly whispered: "Yes, my Master, all life is subject to death and even you cannot become an exception in that event."

(To be continued in Next Praeceptum)

HEALTH CULTURE
THE SCIENCE OF NUTRITION

TOMATOES   Tomatoes are among the most valuable foods grown. They are very rich in iron, calcium, potassium and other minerals besides the four most important vitamins, A, B, C, and G. Like the citrus fruits, tomatoes are alkaline in reaction and next to the citrus fruits, they are the richest source of vitamin C. For some unknown reason, cooking does not destroy this vitamin in tomatoes as it does in other fruits and vegetables. Therefore, canned tomatoes and tomato juice are almost as valuable as fresh tomatoes.

Weight for weight, tomatoes do not yield as much vitamin C as oranges and grapefruit, but tomatoes and tomato juice are usually so much cheaper than citrus fruits that more can be consumed. One medium sized fresh tomato should supply the daily vitamin C need of an adult.

Fresh tomatoes should be served as soon as sliced.

HONEY POPCORN BALLS

3/4 cup honey
3/4 cup raw sugar
1/2 cup water

1 teaspoon vegetized salt
3 quarts popcorn

(4)

Cook sugar, salt and water (stir until sugar is dissolved) to to very brittle stage (300 degrees). Add honey slowly stirring until blended, cook again until thermometer registers 240 degrees (about one minute). Pour over popcorn and form into balls. Wrap in heavy waxed paper.

CREAM OP ONION AND POTATO SOUP

1 cup water	2 cups evaporated milk
1 cup chopped onion	1 teaspoon vegetized salt
1 1/2 cups diced potato	1 tablespoon chopped parsley
2 tablespoons butter	2 tablespoons flour

Add water to onion and potato and cook until tender. Put through sieve. Melt butter, add flour and mix to a smooth paste; stir in milk, and cook until thickened. Combine with puree and simmer 5 minutes, serve with parsley sprinkled or top. Makes 3 3/4 cups of soup.

PRAECEPTUM INSPIRATION
PRANAYAM, OR CONTROL OF LIFE FORCE

Calmness of the heart, eyes and breath is the sign that you have control of your Life Force. Control of this life force means getting control of the force which binds you to the world. Without that training you can never go into deep silence. It is useless to tell students to remain silent without their knowing first the methods by which they can control this Life Force. Holding the breath for a little while is all right because you oxygenate the system and purify your blood, but that is not control ever your breath. Pranayama does not mean just holding the breath in the lungs; it means control of the heart. If you can control the heart, you can switch off the energy. Slowing down the heart is Pranayama. If you know how to do this, then you can practice deep silence and Kriya. Without that, you cannot know God. You must have control over your breath and life.

When you can withdraw the energy from the senses, then you can place your mind upon God, and you are then ready for the practice of Kriya. Control of Life Force produces a conscious state of deep silence. In sleep you experience complete silence. Why? Because the energy is withdrawn from the eyes and all the senses.

PRAECEPTUM AFFIRMATION

I SOAR IN THE PLANE OF FANCY ABOVE, BENEATH, ON THE LEFT, ON THE RIGHT, WITHIN AND WITHOUT, EVERYWHERE, TO FIND THAT I HAVE BEEN IN EVERY NOOK OF MY SPACE-HOME, IN THE SACRED PRESENCE OF MY FATHER.

(5)

YOGODA SAT-SANGA FORTNIGHTLY INSTRUCTIONS
BY
PARAMHANSA YOGANANDA
TEACH US TO HEAR THY VOICE

Heavenly Father, walk through our feet, work through our hands, that we may perform Thy everlasting good. Behold through our eyes what we should behold. Use our speech to speak Thy inspirations and shower Thy kindness from the fountain of words.

Father, let Thy fragrance ooze from our hearts and draw Souls to Thy temple. Father, throb in our hearts, that our hearts may throb with all, in every one. Work through our minds that our minds may bring others to Thy peace. Be forever altared on our peace, be forever altared on our joy.

O Fountain of Flame, ignite all darkness within us. Let Thy Light be established forever within us, about us -- everywhere. O Infinite Energy, Infinite Wisdom, electrify us with. Thy spiritual vibration.

Father, no more forgetfulness; no more shall we walk the pathway of life, torn and bleeding with sorrow. We have been Thy prodigal children. Show us the highway that leads to Thee. Give us bursting devotion of the heart, and in the echo of devotion teach us to hear Thy voice.

PEACE,   JOY,   PEACE.

KRIYA -- THE HIGHER INITIATION
Part IV

Kriya is mathematical in its results. All who practice it correctly and regularly will learn this for themselves. By practicing Kriya correctly fourteen times, morning and evening, while in good health, the spine, brain, and mind become completely changed. To bring about an equivalent change through natural progressive evolution requires one year. Consequently, by practicing Kriya fourteen times in the morning and fourteen times in the evening, two years of natural evolution can be achieved in one day. This is the scientific way of changing material body consciousness into Cosmic Spirit Consciousness.

PREPARATORY EXERCISES it has been found most invigorating and most effective, although not absolutely essential, to condition the body with a few preparatory exercises prior to the practice of the Technique of Kriya.

Exercise A: Stand erect, shoulders back, chest out, chin up, hands down to the sides; now exhale slowly, drop head on chest and bend forward t the waist with hands touching the floor. Then inhale slowly, straightening the body, raising the arms upward over the head, and bending the body backward with head and hands as far back as you can stretch. Hold breath. Then exhale slowly, repeating the exercise. Practice this exercise three times.

Exercise B: the Walking Exercise: Stand erect, shoulders back, chest out, chin up while standing in a position reasonably near an open window, in bare feet. Now raise the hands and feet up and down in alternate succession, as in ordinary walking, but remaining in one place. Practice this exercise for five minutes.

Exercise C: Now practice Exercise B, the Walking Exercise, at a faster gait, the ordinary running gait, for three minutes or longer. This will strengthen your entire system.

PRAYER TO PRECEDE THE PRACTICE OF KRIYA "O Spirit, Saints of all religions, Supreme Master Babaji, Great Master Lahiri Mahasaya, Master Swami Sriyukteswarji, and Swami YOGANANDA Paramhansa, Preceptor Guru, I bow to you all. May your love and wisdom manifest through me forever and ever. Free my spiritual path from all difficulties and lead me to the shores of eternal wisdom and bliss. Heavenly Father, may Thy love shine forever on the santuary of my soul, and may I be able to awaken Thy love in all hearts.

SPECIAL PREPARATION FOR KRIYA   1. Precede the following exercises by first moistening the interior of the throat with a very small portion of olive oil or unsalted butter which has been melted. The butter or oil should not be swallowed quickly, but sipped slowly. It is extremely important to observe this rule, as the throat must be kept well moistened with oil.

2. Face East or North. Choose a straight, armless chair, over which a woolen blanket has been placed, running down under the feet.

3. Correct posture: Spine erect; shoulder blades together; palms upward, resting at the junction of the thighs and abdomen; chest out; abdomen in; chin parallel to the floor; eyes half open or closed, with the eyeballs turned upward and the gaze fixed at the point between the eyebrows without strain; relax the whole body, keeping the spine straight. The correct posture is extremely important and it will be almost altogether ineffectual to perform this exercise with a bent spine.

4. With spine erect, relax all muscles and limbs. During the practice of this Lesson, the spine often bends forward unconsciously through bad habits. Straighten it as often as it bends in order to gain the desired results.

There should be no deviation from any of the instructions given in this Initiation. There are few rules. Obey them strictly.

PRELIMINARY EXPERIMENTS

1. Clench each fist lightly, so as to form a small hollow between the fingers and palm; place the closed fists, one placed next to the other at the mouth, as in diagram No. 1. Slowly draw in the cool air through the mouth and through this "fist-made" tube, noticing particularly the cool, refreshing sensation ascending within the closed fists. Then shift the closed fists to a position just below the mouth, and slowly exhale the warm breath out over the fists, observing carefully the sensation of trickling warmth descending over out-side of the hands. Be most fastidious in observing these two sensations, as they must be closely observed in the practice of this Initiation instruction.

1. Hollow fist

-Page Two-

2. Imagine that the spinal column a mere hollow tube extending from the base
of the spine or Coccyx beyond the top of the
spine at the ne(ck) (Cervical Center) to the
point between the eyebrows or spiritual (Third)
Eye. It is through this imaginary tube that
the cool current and Life Force ascends, while
the warm trickling current and Life Force
descends over the outside of this tube, forming
an imaginary circuit or cycle, as in diagram
FIG. 2.

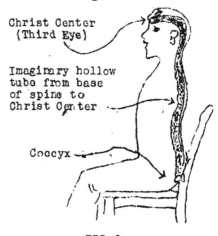

Christ Center
(Third Eye)

Imaginary hollow
tube from base
of spine to
Christ Center

Coccyx

FIG. 2

     Kriya Technique is divided into three
important Parts, namely: Kriya Proper, Part I;
Maha Mudra, Part II; Yoti Mudra, Part III. In
Praeceptum No. 154 will be given Kriya Proper,
Part I. Maha Mudra and Yoti Mudra will follow
in the first Praecepta of Step Seven.

     These Instructions are designed to
create in the home a private experimental
laboratory where the Member may weigh, test,
and apply each new Technique upon himself or herself, logically understand the
true Laws of Yoga, and scientifically attain the pinnacle of Self- Realization.
As a child learning first to walk must walk slowly and then learn to run, so it
is with Kriya. No fear about the practice of Kriya should be entertained because
of this advice, for Kriya is the highest Technique given by the spiritual
specialist, Master of India, for permanently destroying all physical, mental,
and spiritual ills.

     (To be Continued in Praeceptum No. 154)

THE APOLOGUE
THE PRINCE WHO BECAME A BEGGAR Part II

     Prince Gautama from that time on found the slumbering divine memory
of past incarnations awakened within him and he inwardly resolved to leave his
princely surroundings and go in quest of Truth and a Master who would solve
for him the enigma of life. Whenever the prince returned to his palace, he was
always moody and remained aloof from his beautiful wife and courtiers and
friends. The King, his father, upon inquiry, discovered the reason for all the
moodiness of the Prince and immediately doubled the guard in his palace, giving
strict orders never to let the Prince out again into the ugly world.

     Matters progressed in this manner for some time until one night Divine
Love possessed the Prince and he beheld that its intoxication was greater than
even his conjugal love, or his love for his new-born baby. So, one night, as he
sat on his bed and gazed into the beautiful face of his queen and the little
baby, by the glimmering, dim light from the oil-lamp in his palatial room, he
reasoned as follows:

     "I love my wife because God gave her to me and put the desire in my
heart to love her. I love my baby because God gave me the life and love and
intelligence to love him. That is why I should love God more than my family, for
I could not love them without borrowing life and the power of love from God."

Feeling this divine impulse and the call of God, who tests His devotees as to whether they love Him more than His gifts of family and wealth and relatives and friends, Prince Gautama cautiously sprang from his bed and went to the room of his charioteer and wakened him and commanded him to equip the chariot for a trip beyond the garden walls of the palace. The charioteer remonstrated, but to no avail, so he reluctantly prepared the chariot for the journey, but the question then arose as to how the palace gates could be opened, which were guarded by watchful sentries who were under strict orders not to let the Prince out on any account.

It has been said that when the devotee is ready, God responds in mysterious ways, so it happened that when the chariot was ready, the sentries at the gate, according to the Divine wish, were suddenly overtaken with an intoxicating sleep. The charioteer marveled at this but quickly opened the palace gates and Prince Gautama's golden chariot raced out from behind the imprisoning walls of the palace.

Farther and farther the chariot went, until the golden palace vanished out of sight. Finally, arriving near a woodland space, Prince Gautama demanded that the chariot be stepped. The Prince then alighted and one by one parted with his crown jewels and his princely costumes and asked the charioteer to exchange his plain clothes for the Prince's rich attire.

After making this change of attire, which transformed him from a prince to an ordinary man, Gautama, amidst the sobs and the tears of the charioteer and his own thought of a vanished palace and a beautiful wife and son, briskly walked away, barefooted, over the rough road and into the jungles to an unknown world.

Eventually, Prince Gautama went to the city of Benares and there met some Anchorites, who believed only in physical penances. As a result, the Prince at first practiced many austerities and tortured his flesh with physical methods of fasting and discipline, but from this practice he found no peace within and his spirit remained hungry and unappeased, until at last he went to Buddhagaya and sat under a banyan tree, remaining there for seven years without food or drink, with great determination making the following resolution:

"Beneath this banyan bough,
I take this solemn vow;
Let derma, skin and bones dissolve,
But until the mystery of life I solve,
From beneath this tree,
I shall never be free."

The banyan tree to this day still exists in India amidst the glamorous surroundings of many wonderful temples and stone images of Gautama, the Buddha. And the palace was named Buddhagaya because here Prince Gautama found his ultimate Realization.

(To be Continued in Praeceptum No. 154)

HEALTH CULTURE
THE SCIENCE OF NUTRITION

MINERAL SALTS   The body requires sixteen mineral elements, and if any one is missing from the diet, the chemical balance of the body will be upset and a deficiency in some part of the body will result. The mineral salts are found in all natural, unrefined foods, especially fresh fruits and fresh vegetables and they help in the process of digestion, assimilation, and secretion. These mineral elements, along with the foods which supply them, will be discussed in detail later. The following six mineral elements are particularly helpful in the alkalinizing process; potassium, sodium, calcium, magnesium, iron and manganese. We shall consider them first. (To be continued)

PRAECEPTUM INSPIRATION
HUMAN WILL VERSUS DIVINE WILL

Human will, however powerful, is limited by the circumference of the body and the boundaries of the human physical Universe. Man's will can initiate successful activities in the body, or the earth, or in finding the mysteries of the distant stars, but the Divine Will has no boundaries; it varies in all bodies in all things.

God said: "Let there be light, and there was light." God's will works in everything. By deep meditation and by wisdom-guided, unflinching never-discouraged determination, when we can revolve our volition around all our noble desires with success, then that will become Divine Will.

Man's will can ordinarily work within the boundaries of his own little circle of family, heredity, world conditions, destiny, and pre-natal and post-natal karma, or cause and effect-governed-karmas; but super-dynamic volition can change the course of destiny, wake the dead, put the mountain in the sea, and change the course of the solar or stellar systems.

We must remember that God did not make us his inert instruments but instruments endowed with free choice. God's will is not guided by whims or temptation. His will is guided by wisdom. So, also, God made us in His image, made us His children, so that we, like true children, might guide our will with wisdom even as He does. To teach people not to use their will is ridiculous, denial of the Divine Father's wish, and is an utter impossibility.

The man of volition says: "I will use my dynamic volition until success or until death." He refuses to stop even if he dies; he believes in continuing his determined activity in some other reincarnations in order to seek fulfillment if death cuts him off.

PRAECEPTUM AFFIRMATION

Adieu, heart throbs, emotions, thoughts, and memories. I am flying home in the plane of Silence. I go to feel my heart throb in Him.

—Page

YOGODA SAT-SANGA FORTNIGHTLY INSTRUCTIONS
BY
PARAMHANSA YOGANANDA

MAKE OUR SOULS THY TEMPLE

Come Spirit; come with glory of the dawn, come with the vitality of the sun, come through the portals of our silence. Receive the love of our Souls. Father, Thou art just behind the breeze, just behind the echo of our voices, just behind the words with which we pray, just behind the moon and the sun. O Spirit Beautiful, open the window of Nature and the window of our minds, that we may behold Thee in all Thy glory -- in the apparel of all beautiful thoughts.

Come Thou, On Father. Thou art just behind the love with which we love all. Reveal the vast kingdom of Thy Presence. Come Thou, O Spirit, reveal Thyself. Take us away from our wanderings in the wilderness of matter. Reveal Thyself, teach our hearts to pray, teach our Souls to feel that all doors may open and Thy presence may be revealed.

Peace, Joy, Peace.

KRIYA YOGA -- THE HIGHER INITIATION

Part V

This is the first part of the Kriya Technique (Kriya Proper). In Praeceptum 153 we mentioned that Kriya Technique is separated into three main divisions, namely, Kriya Proper, Maha Mudra, and Yoti Mudra. This lesson deals entirely with the Technique of Kriya Proper. The other Technique will appear in Step SEVEN.

The purpose of Kriya Technique is to magnetize the spine by circulating life force, or current, lengthwise, up inside and down outside, and thereby withdrawing the life current from the senses and involuntary organs and concentrating it in the spine. The extra oxygen which you take in when practicing this Technique explodes into life- force. When the current moves in the spine, there is a dynamo formed and that dynamo disconnects the energy from the senses and withdraws it into the spine. This Technique also helps to change the center of consciousness from the body and senses (the limited territory of matter) to the spine (the altar of God, or the unlimited sphere of Cosmic Consciousness.)

After practicing Kriya and resting fox a short time, one is able to do creative work in connection with literature, art, or science. Then intuition develops of itself, without effort, because one's consciousness is then transferred from the senses to the spine and brain. Self-Realization can come only through the development of one's intuition. While practicing Kriya, feel the inspiration of God in the spine.

Remember that, through the continuous practice of Kriya Technique you will attain union with God, the Infinite Spirit.

Solemnly dedicate a temple in your own room, perhaps a corner screened off, or even a ventilated closet, to the divine specialty of meditation. Spiritualize it, sanctify it by devoting it exclusively to the practice of the Technique of Meditation, or Kriya. Consider yourself the minister, the spiritual disciplinarian, of your temple to correct yourself and to teach the audience (consisting of your diverse, untrained thoughts and feelings), so that you may be an ideal example and thereby be of real service to your fellow beings.

TECHNIQUE OF KRIYA PROPER

THE SPINE -- A HOLLOW TUBE   1. With half-opened or entirely closed eyes fixed at the will carter, or Spiritual Eye (the point between the eyebrows, concentrate upon the whole spinal column, and imagine it to be a hollow tube running from the point between the eyebrows to the coccyx, (see Praeceptum 153, Figure No. 2).

INHALATION, ASCENDING-- "AW" 2. Inhale, feeling the breath gently, not jerkingly, pass through the inside of this imaginary hollow spinal canal, with the sound of "aw," made deep in the expanded throat -- See Figure 3 for expanding of throat -- while thinking and feeling a cool breath and life current starting from the coccyx at the terminal of the spine and moving upward until it reaches the top of the tube imagined as running up to the point between the eyebrows as in Figure 2.

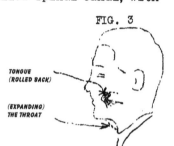

FIG. 3

TONGUE (ROLLED BACK)

(EXPANDING) THE THROAT

The duration of inhalation with the thought of drawing the breath and life current upward must be ten to fifteen counts.

EXHALATION, DESCENDING -- "EE"   3. When the life current and breath have reached the top of the spinal tube, (the point between the eyebrows), slowly exhale, imagining and feeling that you are sending the breath and warm life current over the forehead, through the cerebrum, and on down the back of the spinal column to the coccyx, making the sound of "EE" (high in the expanded throat). While exhaling, the life current and breath must be felt as a fine thread-like tepid (slightly warm) stream slowly, soothingly going over the spine downward to the coccyx. As you exhale, imagining the life current to flow downward over the back of the spine, be sure to make the sound "EE" with the breath.

THE CORRECT PRACTICE OF KRIYA   Remember, there are two indications of the correct practice of Kriya.

1. During inhalation, the upward flowing breath and life current should produce a cool, joyous, refreshing sensation throughout the entire length of the imaginary hollow space in the spinal column, from the coccyx to the point between the eyebrows, and should be accompanied through out by the deep sound of "AW" made by the expanded throat.

2. During exhalation, the downward-flowing breath and life current should be felt as a very slightly tepid, fine, thread-like, soothing sensation, accompanied by the sound of "EE" made high in the expanded throat.

WHEN AND HOW TO PRACTICE   Practice this Kriya Technique fourteen consecutive times every morning before breakfast and every evening before dinner, or three hours after dinner, or before going to bed. Permission to increase the length of practice of Kriya must be secured from the Preceptor-Guru, or the spiritual adviser at the Self-Realization Fellowship Headquarters, and only after several months of faithful practice, reporting on the state of your health, mind, and realization. Never practice on a full stomach, but always at the time specified above. ──

THE PROCESS OF MAGNETIZATION   When you inhale and exhale continuously, you quickly convert the oxygen into life force, especially recharging the lungs and blood. Focusing the vision and the will power at the point between the eyebrows, and imagining the circulation of the current and breath going up and down the spine, will create a positive and a negative pole and will bring about the actual circulation of this current. When you will to move your forefinger, you can do so by sending energy there by will. So, also, will and imagination transmute the oxygen of breath into energy and reinforce it with the energy of the spine and then make the energy revolve around the spine.

REST AFTER KRIYA PRACTICE   Immediately after practicing the Technique of Kriya Proper, you should rest in the same posture for several minutes (the longer the period, the better the result) to feel the life current going up and down lengthwise around the spine. In this way you will begin to feel the magnetization of the spine and have a breathless state (without any exertion) with the consciousness of the contact of the contact of the Cosmic Joy and Bliss.

(To be continued in Praeceptum 155)

THE APOLOGUE
TEE PRINCE WHO BECAME A BEGGAR Part III

Seven years of fasting and extraordinary communion had kept Prince Gautama barely alive, but his body grew very thin, almost like a skeleton. One night, seven years later, as Gautama sat in meditation, some fairies, beautiful women, danced around him through the instrumentality of Satan or Mara, tempting him to give up his love for God and enjoy the frivolities of material life. But Prince Gautama, as he sat in lotus posture, with great determination touched the earth and said: "Mara, Cosmic Delusion, I have conquered thee; tempt me no more." And, as if by magic, all the tempting fairies materialized and subconscious visions of hidden material desires vanished as if by magic and he found within himself an ocean of peace and an ocean of wisdom.

From that time on, Gautama called himself the "Buddha," or the One." The next morning, another princess visited him and gave him a rice preparation to eat and told him that it was not necessary for him to fast so long and weaken his body in order to attain self-realization. She told him that self-realization could be attained through concentration, deep meditation, and continuous inner love for God, without torturing the body, which is a temple of God.

Prince Gautama learned through this princess, who acted as the Divine Instrument, that he could attain spiritual realization only through the spirit within and never through mere physical discipline of the body, so at last, feeling great strength of body and spirit, Prince Gautama Buddha, garbed as a mendicant, went all over India showing thousands of people the way of complete renunciation. His message spread like wildfire and at last his forsaken queen left the luxuries of the gold palace, put on the garb of a beggar, and embraced the discipleship of her husband, who was a Prince, but chose to be a beggar. It was a message of love for all human beings and mercy even for animals, it spread through most parts of India and all parts of China and Japan.

Gautama Buddha especially emphasized the doctrine of mercy, not only for human beings, but for all animals. So keenly did he feel the presence of universal life in all animals that, as he was passing through the palace of a feudal prince in India, he saw that the people were about to sacrifice a little lamb before the temple palace presided over by the local king. Painfully shocked, Gautama Buddha walked straight up to the king and begged him to spare the life of the little lamb and in

-Page Three-

its stead he offered himself as a sacrifice. Feeling the sincerity and deep love of Gautama Buddha, the feudal king, and all the subjects of his kingdom finally became Buddha's followers.

In different periods of world civilization, different great teachers have emphasized the different needs of human beings. When there is a lack of wisdom, a great teacher appears on earth preaching wisdom. When there is a lack of love, another great teacher appears on the earth bearing a message of love. Jesus Christ bore the message of devotion and wisdom to the world. Buddha bore the message of mercy for all animals and all beings.

Many followers of Buddha misunderstood his doctrine and later degenerated his teachings into a nihilistic doctrine of Nirvana, or extinction, and not God-communion, as the end of life. This is the reason that most followers in India ceased to follow Buddha and instead followed Swami Shankara, who established the doctrine that Nirvana and freedom from reincarnation was not only the goal of life but also a positive attainment of ever-existing, ever-conscious, ever-new Bliss-God.

(Conclusion)
HEALTH CULTURE
THE SCIENCE OF NUTRITION
MINERAL SALTS (Continued)

POTASSIUM -- Potassium is one of the most essential elements in an alkalinizing diet. It is stimulating and energizing and helps to stir up the circulation. Potassium has a laxative action; it speeds up the healing of cuts and injuries; it promotes restful sleep; and it normalizes skin function. "It is very active in the liver, spleen, brain, and nervous system, and in the formation of red blood corpuscles." (No citation) Foods containing a high percentage of potassium are: tomatoes, lettuce, celery, rhubarb, turnips, dandelions, cabbage, watercress, Romaine lettuce, chard, cucumbers, cauliflower, beets, eggplant, radishes, parsnips, green lima beans, parsley, figs, prunes, and almonds.

PRAECEPTUM INSPIRATION
ESTABLISH YOUR IDENTITY WITH GOD

As long as you are blindly attached to anything or anyone, you are hindering your progress. God gives you possessions so that you may share them with others, just as He has shared then with you. God is all that really belongs to you.

When it makes you happy to see others happy, to see others possess the good things of life, then you are developing Cosmic Consciousness. Remember you are doing good to yourself by this procedure; not the little yourself, but the big yourself. If this law were always followed, there would be neither poverty, nor suffering, nor sorrow, and each one would be interested in the other person's happiness.

The contact of God is filled with treasures and power; to establish this contact, do not beg from God, but establish your identity with Him. You cannot think without God; you cannot do anything without God, so do not forget that behind your thoughts is the power of God.

Feel your oneness with God first and say: "I and my Father are One; Thou art my Father; what Thou has, I have. Father, guide me to the right thing which I should do."

AFFIRMATION
No dream hath dreamt, no tongue hath told,
Can ever tell, of that -- my beloved music.
But behind the curtains of everything --
I FEEL the lost-and-found
Beloved Music of my Soul!

-Page Four-

YOGODA SAT-SANGA FORTNIGHTLY INSTRUCTIONS
BY
PARAMHANSA YOGANANDA

MANIFEST THYSELF IN THE STRENGTH
OF THY LIGHT

Eternal Light, pour down through our thoughts, through our feelings, and through our emotions. Eternal Love, pour down through our love and make us feel Thy presence. Eternal Power, pour down through our wisdom and inflame us with Thy consciousness. Purify the dross in us and banish disease and poverty from the world evermore. Banish ignorance from the shores of our Souls. Lead us from ignorance to light, from ignorance to wisdom, from sorrow to bliss, from insincerity to sincerity.

The Spirit of the dawn, the Spirit of the Infinite Light abide with us and saturate our Souls with infinite consciousness, and may His glory pour into our Beings. May His presence be felt on every altar of feeling; may His presence be felt on every altar of consciousness. May the glory of the Infinite be with us. On the day of the Sun, may the sunlight of wisdom burst forth from behind the darkness of our minds, and may that great outpouring of light, that great outpouring of peace and happiness, that great outpouring of joy, abide with us.

O Living Christ, present in the body of Jesus and in all of us, manifest Thyself in the trueness of Thy glory, in the strength of Thy light, and in the power of Thy wisdom. Come into the cradle of our consciousness, that we may worship Thee in the light of wisdom and in understanding and truth.

KRIYA -- HIGHER INITIATION
Part VI

CONTROL OF COSMIC ENERGY   The will center becomes the positive pole and the coccygeal plexus becomes the negative pole. The current thus created becomes a magnet of energy which draws more energy from the nervous system and from the Cosmic source. By this method, the adept is enabled to project this energy from the medulla into Cosmic Energy. It is then that this energy in the body loses its limitations and becomes identified with Cosmic Energy. This is what is meant by Pranayama, or control of life force in spine and heart and nervous system, which results in breathlessness and the calming down of heart and lungs, insuring their longevity. Breathlessness is deathlessness. It is then that the life force, which (is) dependent upon oxygen, loses its breath-slavery and moves spirit ward.

Many people think that control of life force means control of breath. That is wrong. The real meaning of Pranayama, according to Patanjali, the founder of Yoga philosophy is the gradual unforced cessation of breathing, the discontinuance of inhalation and exhalation by burning up the carbon in the body by oxygenation through breath.

Trying to control the life force by holding the breath in the lungs is extremely unscientific and harmful. Holding the breath for a long time in the lungs causes pressure on the heart, lungs, diaphragm, and arteries, and therefore should be strictly avoided.

FROM MATTER TO SPIRIT   While inhaling and exhaling, imagine that the breath during inhalation is going upward from the coccyx to the point between the eyebrows; during exhalation, imagine that it is moving downward over the back of the spinal column. The breath really does not circulate around the whole length of the spine, but the increased life force derived from the transmuted breath is directed by will power and visualization to circulate lengthwise, within and without, through the inner and over the outer side of the spinal column continuously during the practice of Kriya. This converts the entire spine into a magnet, which draws all the bodily current away from the senses and nerves, The five telephones of the senses -- touch, taste, smell, hearing, and sight -- are thus disconnected and the attention freed from the invasion of the lenses.

This is also the greatest psycho-physical method for actually reversing the searchlights of the life force, consciousness, and the senses from matter to Spirit.

DURATION OF EXERCISE   Drawing up and feeling a cool current and the breath within the spinal column, feeling a cool current from the coccyx to the point between the eyebrows, and spraying the current and breath as tepid over the back of the spinal column from the point between the eyebrows down to the coccyx counting 10 to 15 for upward inhalation and the same for downward exhalation is equal to one complete Kriya Exercise. This Exercise (Kriya) should be performed fourteen times in immediate succession, morning and evening. The repetition. of Kriya fourteen times equals one year's natural evolution in development of body, mind, and soul. The life current quickly spiritualizes the spine and brain, which in turn spiritualize the whole body. Hindu Yogis state that this current actually changes the atomic composition of the body cells.

By this method of continuous, regulated breathing and the unswerving thought of a cold current ascending in the spinal column and a warm current descending over the spiral column, the spiral column is magnetized and its cells are super-sensitized. The awakened life force, by mental direction, revolves around the spine, converting it into a dynamo. This dynamic energy withdraws the energy from the five sense- telephones, producing a state of superconscious ecstasy.

THE ALTAR OF THE SPINE   If you conscientiously practice this Kriya Technique, you will never forsake this Path. Your joy in the spinal sensation and realization will be boundless. Every magnetization of the spine through the circulation of the cool and warm current, when properly effected, gives unending realization of actual sensation in the spine. This joy will stand supreme in comparison to all material joys. You will find this super-happiness more tempting than temptation of instincts and emotions. This Technique of Kriya will change your Soul consciousness from the identification with the momentarily joy-giving bodily sensations to the Altar of the Spine, where reigns the ever-new, ever-lasting joy of Super-Consciousness.

When you get accustomed to the coolness and warmth in this practice, there will be nothing in the world that you will like better, and your brain will be clear and calm because your entire consciousness will be centralized in the spine. There is nothing in the world to equal this sensation. But you must practice. God never responds unless you know the law. That is where His favorite haunt is -- in the spine.

-Page Two-

In these days of unbalanced living and imperfect material civilization, when the working hours are longer, due to more attention being given to acquiring material things, you must adjust your time according to your vocation.

In order to increase the number of times that you practice Kriya Technique, you must first apply to your Guru-Preceptor, Paramhansa Yogananda , or his approved representative, for permission. After you have progressed sufficiently and received permission to increase the number of times, you may develop so that you are ready to practice this Technique 108 tines in slow succession. Then automtically the current will go of itself, and the joy experienced will be indescribable.

TO SUM UP KRIYA PROPER   The sound of "aw," with the ascending breath inside the spinal column, must positively be made, as well as the "ee" sound, with the descending breath over the vertebrae. The sounds are not pronounced except with the breath, deep in the expanded throat; that is, they are not pronounced with the mouth.

The cool breath and life current sensation must be felt ascending from the coccyx to the spiritual Eye.

The inhalation must cover the count of one to twelve.

The warm breath and life current sensation must be felt descending over the vertebrae, during exhalation. The duration of the exhalation must be one to twelve.

The inhalation and exhalation must be of equal duration and and slowly performed.

The sound of "aw" and "ee", with inhalation and exhalation, respectively, is one complete magnetization of the spine.

Practice this magnetization of the spine slowly, without a break, one after another, until you have practiced fourteen times.

This is not an ordinary breathing exercise and is partially ineffective if the cool and the warm sensations are not realized and felt. Continue until you can feel.

Practice this vital technique of magnetizing the spine fourteen times in the early morning, before breakfast, and twenty times before retiring, about three hours after dinner; that is, practice the above on a partially empty stomach and only when in good physical condition.

This Technique is the foundation of the Seven Steps to Self-Realization and must be practiced daily.

FOLLOW GOD'S LAWS   Those who sincerely and conscientiously practice this Technique will be held to the work by their own Self-Realization. Remember, "where there is a will, there is a way." Remember also that your first and most important engagement is with God, for you cannot keep your engagements with the world without first borrowing the powers from God.

If God draws your life away, then you will have to cancel all your engagements with your family, friends, country, and world, without explanation, No duty is greater than your duty to find and know God, as no duties can be performed without using the God-given powers of life.

The greatest of all sins is to forget God, your own Eternal Being. To forget Him is to punish yourself with the supreme sin of ignorance, which is the cause of all physical, financial, mental, and spiritual miseries.

Keep the exercises strictly confidential. Do not misuse them, and do not entertain any fear. Do not practice when ill, and do not tell your experiences to anyone, as they will not understand. You must follow the laws in order to contact God.

(End of Sixth Step.)

-Page Three-

I DISCOVER THE SUN OF COSMIC CONSCIOUSNESS

I sat on a mound with eyes closed, watching the inky darkness that enveloped me. There was nothing within me but darkness, but I seemed to seek something unknown, yet familiar. I opened my eyes and the gay world of splendor, richly decorated with the measureless sheet of twinkling moonbeams, sublime stars teeming with mysteries unspoken, myriads of flowers, green velvet grass, chains of shining peaks, light- bejeweled waves of the heaving seas, and the mighty power of cities, mocked me and called me "a dreamer." The voice of the proud world seemed to laugh and say: "Foolish dreamer! Why shut your eyes and banish my beauty from your sight and live in empty darkness?"

I silently said within myself: "Audacious Intruder, thy beauty would forever remain unappreciated without the invisible inmates of my dark mental chamber." Even as I thought this, I felt the thrilling call of some mysterious charm within. I closed the doors of my eyes. Then again I was confronted with the same abysmal darkness. I watched with steady vision, looking and seeking in all directions. Sometimes bewildered, I felt that I caught glimpses of opaque thought, which became half visible in that deep mystic chamber.

I steadily watched in the dim but growing light of my concentration. The gloom became softer and revealed its hidden glory. I found that I could see there without my eyes; see each glimmering thought, like dream-lightning, flash and disappear or come bursting like star- shells, with revealing showers of light, and vanish in the mental sky. I could count each flash, each outburst, and could recognize their intensity, their duration, and their meaningful splendors.

I found that I could hear there without my ears, the muffled chafing roars of loud powerful thoughts, softer sweet suggestions of conscience, and the quiet voice of reason. I heard distinctly all they said, as I had never heard before.

Thus, for the first time, I felt the presence of these living inner invisible blood relatives, their warmth and their indifference, toward me. These, my own, long had lived so near in this dark chamber, planning, organizing, molding my destiny, yet unassuming, unnoticed, unseen, unheeded.

What charm you cast around, what stupendous work you do, Invisible Friends! Are you afraid to plainly appear in the crude scorching gaze of human minds? Do you fear to be hurt by the twilight of pale unthinking mentalities, or choked by the gross vibrations of noisy matter?

Yet how stealthily you go out of the dark chamber to build the huge sky-scrapers, the mighty bridges, and all daring material achievements, then slip away, unknown, unthanked, unhonored, unsought. The coursing train in the nightly gloom, the whirling air-plane, the floating steel village with small cabins, the triumphs of art, the Parthenon and Taj Mahal, all man-made miracles, all remind me of you only and your powers, O Mighty Thoughts!

But when I see the sparkling lake welcoming me to quench my thirst, and the dark clouds bursting with eagerness to pour its rivers of rain to fill our life-giving green paddy fields and nectar fruit trees, and the moon's light switched on at the approach of darkness, and the changing round of the seasons, and the hall of the world beautifully carpeted with soft green grass, and the sunlight-painted clouds on the canvas of the sky -- all these matchless scenic pictures -- I begin to question whose is the Cosmic Hand that works so wisely-powerful everywhere. I wonder whose all-pervading voice commands the sun, moon, planets, earth, Nature, the seasons, all blind forces, the ebbing and flowing seas, man, life, and death, and who receives their obedience.

-Page Four-

Is there an infinite chamber of mystery in which one Limitless Luminous Mind hides and secretly reaches forth to decorate the Universe with endless charms?

Down the Window of Memory I looked. I recalled the early hours of my childhood, when the sun of my consciousness first began gradually to appear. As it slowly rose out of the darkness of the unconscious mind, it dimly lighted only one part of my little mental horizon that lay encompassing my mother, playthings, and a few multi-colored candies.

Later, as my consciousness grew brighter, I found that a great part of my mental horizon became illumined. I saw in it many other things -- my friends, relatives, neighbors, my country -- these were revealed and included. Now, as I look within, on the mental sky, the sun of my consciousness seems to be shining brighter than ever in its supreme power. It no longer lights one direction, or only a portion of my mental horizon, or only a few friends, or one nation, but all nations, nay, all creatures and Nature, all planets, all stars, all shining electrons, all universes, all space. I did not know that out of the inky darkness of my mind I would discover the Sun of Cosmic Consciousness.

HEALTH CULTURE
MINERAL SALTS (continued)

Sodium.   There are only about three ounces of sodium in the average body, but it has a very important function to perform. Even though the amount required seems small, most people are low in their sodium intake.

One of the functions of sodium is to hold calcium in solution and it is therefore valuable as a solvent for hard deposits in the body. Calcium is very hard, and if it occurs in too great quantities in the body, stones may form, the joints may stiffen, or the walls of the blood vessels may harden. Plenty of sodium will prevent the calcium from hardening and doing any damage.

Sodium is a powerful alkalinizer and helps with the secretion and excretion of carbonic oxide. Because it is so highly alkaline, it neutralizes all acid chemicals. Since most people eat an abundance of acid-forming foods it is highly important for them to get enough of the alkaline elements to keep a chemical balance in the body. Sodium also has a very soothing effect. (To be continued)

PRAECEPTUM INSPIRATION
KNOW THAT YOU ARE IMMORTAL

Why is meditation the only way to God? Because the only way that He can be known is by following His laws of righteousness and by deep contemplation upon Him until you become one with Him. God is no respecter of persons. He will look in your heart and see whether you have utilized the power that He has given you and whether you know Him or not. Why waste time? Meditation is the only way to know God.

Remember, if you forget God, it wil not be God who will punish you, but you will create your own misery. If you know God, He will reveal to you that this life is only a drama and that you are immortal, that you were never sick, that you were never dead, and you were never unhappy. It was all a dream. There is no other way to find God except through meditation practiced in the way the Masters teach it.

PRAECEPTUM AFFIRMATION

IN THY BLESSED LIGHT I SHALL REMAIN AWAKE FOREVER, WATCHING THY PRECIOUS, OMNIPRESENT FACE WITH EVER VIGILANT EYES, THROUGH ALL THE EONS OF ETERNITY.

YOGODA SAT-SANGA FORTNIGHTLY INSTRUCTIONS

By PARAMHANSA YOGANANDA

SIXTH STEP: PRAECEPTA SUMMARIES

INTRODUCTION   The following Praecepta Summaries of the Sixth Step are presented to you in the form of quick general reviews of the Praecepta, in order to refresh your memory in regard to the most vital points presented, and to fix more firmly in your mind, not only the vital points, but also the relationship between theory and practice of technique, and the importance of one to the other. Reviews are of vast importance, for each time you review a Praeceptum, you will discover something that had escaped you in your previous study of the Praeceptum, or something that had not sufficiently impressed you before. It is through repetition that we learn the most.

Moreover, you will be greatly enlightened by the many new explanatory notes, all of which will be of extreme importance to you in the Intermediary Examination of the Super-Advanced Adept Step which is to follow the installments of Praeceptum No. 155. It has been our sincere purpose to present the authentic "why" of all the principles as expounded by the Masters of India, and, therefore, the summaries which constitute Praeceptum No. 155 will be necessarily continued in a series of installments in order to thoroughly and comprehensively cover the fundamental principles, especially in preparation for the examination.

INSPIRATION OF THE SIXTH STEP   In the Sixth Step, you, the Super-Advanced Adept, must bear in mind the importance of the following salient features:

The knowledge of the Inner Laws of the Cosmos should now have become part of your own realization through the understanding gained in your expanding intuition in meditation. You are making conscious effort to tune in with Divine Will. The nature of Prana is made known to you, and you are now ready to learn control of this Divine Energy. You know that the altar of God in the body is in the spine. You are ready to taste of His Bliss beyond anything you have yet known. You are on the threshold of awareness of eternity.

Greater than ever before is the need of purity of living and one-pointed determination and never-ceasing vigilance. The Kingdom of God is within you, and the Portals are open wide to the expansion of all your being in full consciousness of Its Glory. There is no end, no limit, to its Bliss. Press on -- and on!

FIRST INSTALLMENT

SUMMARY OF PRAECEPTUM NO. 131   "Open the windows of minds and hearts, open the windows of our souls, and show us Thy face hiding behind all windows of Nature and human minds."

Evolutional (sic) reincarnation starts from crystals to the human sphere of existence. The true image of Spirit, that is, individualized Spirit or immortal soul, survives the physical body and gathers to itself another body through which to work out the effects or traces of former desires and actions which lodged in the subtle bodies accompanying the soul in its passage. Matter suppresses the Spirit as Spirit tries to reform or raise matter by evolutional coaxing and expansion.

Reincarnation represents the retrograde stages through which the Spirit returns to Itself from the many to the One (Itself). Reincarnation cannot be intellectually understood, but must be realized; that is, one must become conscious of this process within one's self, through meditation and through becoming aware of the source of desire, which is the root of action -- the wheel of cause and effect. Reincarnation is scientific and is an accepted doctrine of many religions, representing more than half of the human race. One very definite reference to reincar-

tion in the Christian Bible is found in Revelations (sic) 3: 12: " Him that
overcometh will I make a pillar in the Temple of my God, and he shall go no more
out; " meaning that he who overcomes bodily desires will not have go out in
pursuit of the fulfillment of desires. Rev. 2: 7 also refers to reincarnation.
TThe Hindu Scripture, Bhagavad Gita, says, "I, the Spirit, reincarnate myself
again and again in order to uplift the oppressors and redeem the virtuous."

Great souls may reincarnate of their free will in order to help other
souls to freedom. Forced reincarnation, through desire and action, is man's
punishment to himself. You must learn to reverse the search-lights of the senses
so that you can be free to live as a Master, and not have to undergo compulsory
reincarnation.

Thoughts, like words, send out vibrations; that is, they direct energy.
These vibrational waves of energy go on and on, and eventually like a boomerang
they return to the sender. Watch your thoughts. Make God alone your goal.

Each day's diet should supply all of the elements necessary to
growth and health in the right proportions. No one food contains all the
nutrients and requirements, therefore a mixed diet is necessary.

SSUMMARY OF PRAECEPTUM NO. 132   "Forget us not, though we forget Thee;
remember us, though we remember Thee not. Unite our hearts into one great altar
wherein Thy Omnipresence may rest evermore."

Before the individualized spirit in man, or soul, can mingle and become
one with the ocean of Spirit, it must break its imprisoning walls. The
illustration of the 3 jars of salt water, each within the other, floating in the
ocean, very clearly demonstrates this point.

Man has three bodies, as follows:

MAN:

1. Physical body
     a.   16 chemical elements
2. Astral body
     a.   19 elements:
            Mind, ego Chittwa, Intelligence 10 senses 5 pranas
3. Spiritual or idea body
     a.   35 elements:
            Seed ideas corresponding to the 16 elements
            of the physical body and 19 elements of the astral body.

Within the idea body the soul is encased, but corked with ignorance. The
physical body is like another garment. Although the physical body is discarded
in death, the astral body carries the unfulfilled desires, their traces, and
discordant vibrations, which must be worked out or dissolved in other
embodiments. The astral senses are the real organs. The physical senses are the
physical instruments, the mode of expression. Thus you see that the 10 physical
senses are replicas of the 10 astral senses. The astral body must take on another
physical body in order to work out the tendencies of action and desire. Desire
directs energy. Unfulfilled desires form a momentum of energy directed toward
fulfillment. Since the astral body lacks instruments of expression, it must be
""reborn" in another physical body to work out these tendencies. Material
desires thus create an outgoing force which carries the smothered soul on and on
through many reincarnations of experience and suffering. This force must be
reversed toward God in order to free the soul which has forgotten its
birthright and identified itself with the body. This consciousness of the soul in
connection with

the "body is termed "Ego". Man must use his free choice to calm the storm of delusion by the magi(c) wand of will, and must allow his desire-tossed soul-wave to rest back on the bosom of ever-blessed Spirit.

As God said to the discon(ten)ted man in the story, do not build the mansion of your happiness upon the treacherous quicksands of earthly existence. Direct all your desire and will toward God, tune your will with Divine Will, and be free in Infinite Bliss, ever-perfect, ever-new, ever-satisfying.

SUMMARY OF PRAECEPTUM NO. 133   "O Tremendous Love, hiding behind the dusk of evening and behind the gloom of night, hiding behind the mighty dawn, come out, receive our Soul's devotion."

The scientist is right in declaring that all animal bodies are interrelated. Nevertheless, he has never been able to find the "missing link" between animal and man. Because man has animal characteristics it is assumed that he has evolved from the animal. This is not correct. Man is a special creation. All minerals, plants, and animal bodies are made of intelligence and electrons. Spirit is the intelligence in all matter, always conscious, but not self--conscious until it becomes individualized in man. Through progressive experience, through the various kingdoms, mineral, vegetable, animal for further advancement it reincarnates in specially created human bodies. This began with Adam and Eve, the first man and woman. Animal characteristics are soul-memories, or instincts, which cling to the disembodied soul or astral body after death and which must be worked out in the material school of life. Adam and Eve although empowered to immaculately create after their own kind, awakened the sex instincts in the Tree of Life, the soul-memory, or knowledge of good and evil. Thus, by indulging in the sense of touch, and ignoring the warning of God, they lost the power of immaculately creating, and had to create their own kind in the human way.

Action through ignorance, desire, selfish craving, and instinctive reaction to self-created environment, forms a vicious circle, which carries the beclouded soul on and on through thousands of reincarnations, until it becomes conscious of this process, and self-consciously reverses it. Actions performed in a full understanding and without material desire, bring the process to an end and turn the soul toward its Infinite home, God. Even the highest earthly desire of the soul is limiting in comparison to the Eternal Kingdom of the Cosmos. Desirelessness does not mean to be without ambition and negligent. That would result in stagnation. You must be divinely ambitious to do God's will, and to perform all duties for Him, without selfish attachment and craving. You need not go to the forest, for earthly desires can follow you there. You can live in the world, but not of it, unattached, using all for God in understanding of His Will.

In regard to an adequate diet, it should be remembered that the lack of some essential element is not always immediately evident, and the ill effects may not be readily or promptly recognized. However, "Any diet lacking in any essential cannot be continued for any length of time without producing abnormality and often irreparable defects. The deterioration is not only visible but affects the Inner and vial organs, so that the entire organism suffers." (No citation)

SUMMARY OP PRAECEPTUM NO. 134 "O Light of Lighta; O Nectar of Nectara, Joy of all Joys, permeate us within and without; dispel the gloom and inharmony in our bodies, minds, and souls."

At physical death, the physically disembodied soul seeks its own vibratory level; that is, those of like qualities are in groups together. All souls cannot go everywhere in space. The virtuous souls have greater freedom and need not have reincarnation forced upon them. Those with deep realization may come or go from earth as they wish.

The usual understanding of the term "disembodied soul" is a soul that has lost the physical body. Metaphysically defined, the term should mean soul liberated from the three bodies.

All human relationships are but chemicals of life to purify and convert human love into Divine Love. Immortal Divine Love is trying to awaken the all-perfect Divine Love in souls through various processes of divine, conjugal, parental, friendly, brotherly, sisterly, fatherly, and motherly love. Divine Lose is clothed by veils of selfishness, physical attachment, emotional excitement, mechanical family relations, and sex madness. If human love fails to purify in one soul, it will keep on seeking in this span of life and beyond until it finds the expression of all perfections of Divine Love. When perfect pure love and unconditional friendship are expressed between two souls, that love will be registered as One Divine Love. After finding Divine Love in one, you will suddenly find that your heart will feel the same Divine Love for all the members of your family and for anyone and everything in your world.

The story of Byasa teaches the moral that all true lovers of God must so meditate upon God and be in such ecstatic joyous communion with with Him that God will be considered responsible for all actions. Of course, before this divine union is attained, it is wrong to say that God is performing all your actions, some of Which may be evil. Your human will often misguides the energy until your will becomes attuned with Divine Will. In the state of Divine Oneness you may say: "I and my Father are."

SUMMARY OF PRAECEPTUM NO. 135 "Insult not my death with your tears, ye who are left on this desolate shore to moan and deplore. It is I who pity you."

Just as electricity does not die with the breaking of the bulb into which it flows, so is death of the body the switching off of the nerve current from the entire body bulb. Death is a state of passive involuntary relaxation.

According to the quality of the subtle body, disembodied souls exist in different vibratory regions of pranic or life energy. Even as, after a day of worries, you are apt to have bad dreams or nightmares, so after death if you have lived in fear and worry and evil activities, your soul will not be at rest and will have nightmares in the astral world.

It is a dangerous practice to contact any but advanced disembodied souls. Highly developed souls can be invoked consciously, but they respond only to love and the high vibrations of those who practice the breathless silence. Study carefully the technique on page 4 of this Praeceptum. Each detail is important.

"The Wishing Tree" illustrates that our desire and will power (are) the magic wishing tree for each of us. It is wise to keep our attention on only constructive and desirable good things, for the law works for either good or evil, according to your thought and attention.

Prolonged weariness, a tired feeling upon waking in the morning, and frequent colds, are some of the conditions which indicate too much acid in the system.

SUMMARY OF PRAECEPTUM NO. 136   "0 Lord, purify our consciousness with Thy living luminosity." Every action mentally or physically performed, consciously or unconsciously, has an specific effect on the life of man. This law of action, or cause and effect, is termed ""Karma." Your present body and mind, environment and experiences, and the cumulative effect, represent the germination of the seeds of pact desirous action.

Present human action arises from the impulse of this accumulation, the effect in its turn becoming cause, and thus the accumulation continues, until the Self is deeply hidden and there is little or no true freedom of action.

The Springs of Action are:
        Impartial reason of man.
        Acquired habits of present life.
        Impulses acquired in previous states of existence.
        Influence of present environment.

        Independent actions can arise only when the mind frees itself from the clutch of habits, desires, and influences of every kind, and be comes aware of its own process. Knowledge of the law gives freedom. Right action performed through understanding and without desire for specific result, frees one. Also you can, by understanding the law and acting within the law, build good karma consciously. You are the architect of your destiny. Nothing rules you unless you let it rule. Souls re-embody to work out the seed tendencies. Souls freed of parasitical karma realize their unity with their God-source.

        You have no right to judge another person unless you are yourself without fault. Inquire deeply to become aware of your own shortcomings so that you may intelligently improve yourself.

        In general, the foods containing a predominance of acid-forming elements are meats, fish, eggs, and the grain products such as breakfast cereals, bread, etc. These should be used in the diet in a ratio of only 20%.

THE PLAN OF PRAECEPTUM NO. 156   The sectional review; of the twenty five Praecepta, constituting the Sixth or Super-Advanced Adept Step, will be continued for easy and convenient study in succeeding installments of Praeceptum No. 156 in order to complete the comprehensive program of review. Always remember that conscientious perseverance in review and practice sharpens the perception and understanding.

        The Second Installment of Praeceptum No. 156 will follow this installment in the next mailing.

YOGODA SAT-SANGA FORTNIGHTLY INSTRUCTIONS
BY
PARAMHANSA YOGANANDA

SIXTH STEP
PRAECEPTA SUMMARIES
SECOND INSTALMENT

SUMMARY OF PRAECEPTUM NO. 137   "In the wall-less temple we worship Thee with the love of our Inner Being. Burn away our grossness, our weaknesses, our disease, and our ignorance."

You yourself must destroy the undesirable things you have created. You must understand the cause of your present condition, of either health or prosperity, and put forth definite effort to destroy any undesirable tendencies. Your present state is determined by seed tendencies of past lives, and your comprehensive will-efforts of this life. When in meditation, the vital power is felt, then that ray of vital sense must be switched to the brain and held there to scorch out the lurking seeds of failure or disease.

No matter how great a failure one may seem to be, one should remember that there are always success tendencies buried somewhere in the subconscious mind, and it is possible to rouse them by repeated judicious initiative effort. A yogi may not possess much, but through his ability to focus his mind he learns to create at will whatever he needs at any given time. Of course, yogis do not entertain personal desire, except that God's love shall reign on the shrine of their souls, and that they may kindle His love in the hearts of others.

Blind selfishness is the root cause of unbalanced prosperity. Rich people who acquire success and ignore the agonies of others who fail, do much to upset the balance.

If you will try to classify yourself according to the health types as given in this Praeceptum, it will help you to decide what steps to take to correct your condition. Remember in fighting karma you have the good forces of all lives plus God on your side. The story of "The Culprit and the Judge" shows the common fault of most people -- that of showing partiality to themselves. Watch yourself carefully for this tendency. It is not compatible with the injunction to love your neighbor as yourself. In Christ Consciousness all others are as yourself, and you could not show such partiality.

SUMMARY OF PRAECEPTUM No. 138   "Father, electrify cur health with Thy perfection, electrify our souls with Thy wisdom, electrify our minds with Thy Power."

In order to intelligently comprehend methods of rejuvenation, one should have some understanding what a human body really is. This body, which looks so compact and solid, is in reality a bundle of forces whirling together in ultra-rapid motion. All the tiny cells are grouped together by a chemical force. This biological force arranges the cells to form the various tissues of the body. These cellular molecules are in turn made of whirling atoms, protons, and electrons. These are in their turn made of condensed semi-intelligent vital sparks of vital force. Below the surface of the vital sparks lie the waves of sensation, then of thought, feeling, and will force. Hidden below all the layers of waves is the ego.

Each wave is a manifestation of a vaster wave or force behind it. The vital force is a manifestation of the vast force of all forms of subconsciousness, superconsciousness, Christ Consciousness, and Cosmic Consciousness. Therefore, their body as a solid substance occupies a very small space, but since the body on the internal side is condensed Cosmic Consciousness, it is vast and omnipresent.

The nature of matter is change, constant motion. From birth on, the body is undergoing constant decay and renewal. The body being motion, it cannot live without motion. It has to be stirred with life externally by food, liquids, oxygen, sunlight, and internally with vitality derived from Cosmic Consciousness.

It would be entirely possible to keep the body flooded with vitality from the inner source of Cosmic Consciousness. God's omnipresent electric energy is flowing into your body all the time, but you must become conscious of the process and know the law and depend upon it instead of upon the limited physical source.

Death is only a temporary cessation of the body state until the inner notions of the vital forces of ego, soul, and karma, can reappear as materialized motion in a new body. The mind is king of the body. The body as a manifestation of Spirit is the ever-youthful Spirit. If a soul is powerful enough, it can re-change an old body into new, instead of discarding it in death.

Through meditation bring peace and harmony into every cell of your body.

Study the list of alkalinizing foods on page 6 of this Praeceptum, and be sure to include a goodly proportion in your daily diet.

SUMMARY OF PRAECEPTUM NO. 139   "I Am the Silent Joy of Life moving Through all Beings."

During the season of youth, you should be raking life beautiful, instead of sowing the seeds of disease as so many do, but it is never too late to begin to correct mistakes. Man can retain youth but he must know how to connect his will power with God's energy in his body. Infinite powers are at his command, but he must observe certain details, as:

1. Take care of bodily health by observance of correct diet and exercise.
2. Keep the mind busy with creative interests.
3. Connect the body, mind, and will together to evolve energy as per techniques given in this Praeceptum.

4. If you are conscious of a discordant condition in the body, direct God's electric energy through your thought and will power to the seat of disturbance. The Life Force is the all-healing soul X-Ray.

5. The highest form of rejuvenation is to unite the human consciousness and Cosmic Consciousness through meditation. Just as soon as the body is understood to be, not isolated from Spirit, but a number of rising, falling waves of vibrating currents in the ocean of Cosmic Consciousness, then the perpetual rejuvenation of the Spirit can be implanted in the body if so desired.

Food is nothing but condensed atomic energy. The action of the chemical, vital, and mental forces upon the stomach and intestines changes food into energy. Learn to depend more and more upon the limitless supply of the inner finer sources of body energy.

study the two techniques given on page 4 of this Praeceptum, and practice sending energy through your hands. You can use this both for healing yourself and for healing others.

If you seek the Kingdom of God first, and love Him above everything else, Divine Harmony will perfect all things in your life fulfilling all your good desires. It is better to cut off everything in your life that shuts you off from God than to have all earthly possessions without God. All love is from the Fountain of Love, God.

SUMMARY OF PRAECEPTUM NO. 140 "I will reason, I will create, I will do everything, but Father, guide my creative ability to the right thing that I should do."

Every human being is a physical being, a mental being, and a spiritual being. The need of each must be supplied. In order to discriminate as to the real need of each, we must understand the real purpose of life. Then we must know how to withdraw attention and energy from objects of distraction, and concentrate upon the fulfilling of our definite needs.

Prosperity plays a very important part in our consciousness, but we must know in what lies real prosperity. Bodily health is conducive to increased mental efficiency. Mental efficiency nourishes intelligence, whereby we may release the power to create at will what we need. Every though(t) is a tube, a channel, through which the divine light is passing. So, physical and mental efficiency helps to clear the path of understanding, so that our hearts maybe opened to the Divine Flood of God's Light and Love. True prosperity, therefore, lies in the possession of health, the power of mental efficiency by which you can create at will the things you need, wisdom through understanding and happiness. Real success means the having of all things at our command which are necessary for our entire existence.

Every line of business is an art for dispelling certain human miseries. Choose a vocation in which you are physically and mentally fitted, one in which you fasten a deep interest, so that better than it has ever been done before.

There is no saint, no Savant, who does not use money in his work. It is the manner in which you use money that is of importance. It is better to be able to buy your food and physical necessities that to depend upon charity from others. Some one labors for it. Money is a medium of exchange. Therefore, "render unto Caesar the things that are Caesar's. " Money in itself does not possess intelligence. You must direct it with your intelligence to bring happiness and blessings in its path. Only as wealth gives happiness is it of value.

The more you improve yourself, the more you can be a friend to man. God has given you independence to shut out His power or to let it in. First you must make up your mind and then have your will power so balanced that you will stick to a thing to completion. You can remedy your mistakes because reason and will have been given to you. You have more power than troubles. There is no such thing as "fate". You make your own destiny. Claim your divinity. Unite yourself with God, and receive your blessings direct from the hand of God.

SUMMARY OF PRAECEPTUM NO. 141   "Teach me to dive again and again with the armor of Self-Realization. Decorated with the pearls of Thy power, I shall enter into the mansion of Thy Understanding."

Spirit is ever-existing, ever-conscious ever-new Joy. In order to make Himself appreciate His Almighty Bliss, through Himself as many, Spirit differentiated Himself into the Knower, Knowing, and Known. This triune division of spirit was accomplished by the law of relativity or cosmic Delusion. This consciousness of the many holds the appearance of finiteness as separate from the Infinite. The many were to find Bliss by self-seeking, independent effort.

Cosmic Delusion, called "Satanic", or repulsed force from Spirit holds the essential qualities of spirit; hence its independent creative power of choice. The individualized Spirits, or souls, thus evolved out of spirit, instead of being conscious of themselves as living waves of the Cosmic Sea of Life, essentially immortal, were deluded by this Satanic force to believe themselves isolated, having origin and decay. They were further deluded into a feeling of attachment to their passing states of existence. The lack of comprehension of their true nature and the finite attachment is the real cause of all suffering.

This Satanic force, in transforming the Infinite into the finite evolved the law of propagation by cellular division and Sex creation to keep everything vibrating away from the Infinite. Self-defense and its cruelties, and the desire to kill in order to eat, were suggested to man by the cosmic law of delusion; (Jesus said: "Turn the other cheek"). Thus Satanic Delusion took advantage of its independence to pull all things away from God Until humanity awakens, it is under the influence of this Cosmic Satanic Dream.

This Infinite Cosmic Dream of finitude does not affect Spirit, but it does affect the individualized souls. The power of the Infinite wants the individualized points of consciousness to enjoy Its Bliss consciously, and is constantly trying to call back everything to merge into this Bliss consciousness. This process is called "the law of evolution and reincarnation." All substances are constantly changing into finer substances; as inorganic into organic, mineral into vegetable, vegetable into animal, animal into man. In man is the power of comprehension of his Divine Nature, by which he may release himself from Cosmic Delusion. He must awaken in God through meditation and cease to reinforce Satanic Delusion by belief in death, disease, and suffering. Awake in Joy.

The third Instalment of Praeceptum Number 156 will follow this instalment in the next mailing.

YOGODA SAT-SANGA FORTNIGHTLY INSTRUCTIONS BY
PARAMHANSA YOGANANDA

SIXTH STEP PRAECEPTA SUMMARIES
THIRD INSTALMENT

SUMMARY OF PRAECEPTUM No. 142 "Teach us to receive wisdom from Thy lips, power from Thy concentration, and strength from Thy Cosmic Energy." Man's God-like quality is free choice. He always has the power to accept or refuse, to act for either food or evil. Before he acts he has freedom, but after he acts, the effect of the action will follow him. That is the law of karma. Just a mental conception of good will not make one good. Both virtue and vice require activity. So choice must be made. Team(p)tation has power because of:

1. Lack of comparative understanding.
2. Its appeal to the outward flowing current of the senses.

The best way to destroy temptation is to be so merged in the happiness of God that all other happiness will be only secondary to that sublime state. Get out of the environment to give your wisdom a chance to guide you. Why should you let evil wreck you for just a moment of false happiness. When you meditate you will see what life really is, and will find completion of love and happiness therein.

Keep good company. Good company stimulates your actions and thoughts in the right direction. It is a hedge around your good habits.

The portrait painting of Krishna shows how we are inclined to see or paint others according to the conception in our minds. So do we color our conception of the "Changeless One." We must learn to remove the dark cloth of ignorance which covers the mirror of calm intuition, then we shall be able to perceive the ever-changing, yet changeless, true reflection of Spirit.

The sustenance of the unborn baby is received from the mother. If there is an insufficient intake of calcium necessary to the forming of teeth, the supply is drawn to a great extent from the mother's own body. The teeth begin to develop as early as the eighth week of pre-natal life.

SUMMARY OF PRAECEPTUM NO. 143   "Keep our voices enraptured with the songs of our love for Thee. Keep our feet ever busy in serving Thee in the temple of all minds."

Just as, in order to produce good violin music, a player must be equipped with a good violin box, cords, box, mastery of technique and mental skill, so is it necessary in good singing and speaking for one to have both mastery of technique and inspiration. The daily practice of specially selected, graded vocal exercises is highly important in development of the speaking and singing voice. Inspiration must be the principal guiding force in speaking or singing.

Necessary to the mastery of good technique are:

1.   Breath control.
2.   Strengthening of the lungs.
3.   Strengthening of the chest.
4.   Care and exercise of the throat.
5.   Toning and calming of the nerves.
6.   Banishment of stage fright.

The technique of speaking and singing must be practiced until mastered without fault or blemish so that it becomes of natural use; then it must be forgotten, and inspiration must be the outstanding guide and power behind speech and song. Speech and song without soul originality is but mechanical and cannot touch the hearts of the hearers. Technique should be acquired to harmoniously open the channel to the perfect expression of soul inspiration.

Practice regularly the exercises given in this Lesson for the purpose of gaining mastery of technique. Even if public speaking is not your goal, a good speaking voice will help you immeasurably in your daily contact with people by stimulating self-confidence and concentration. Faulty, halting speech is inexcusable.

SUMMARY OF PRAECEPTUM NO. 144 "Mighty Being, dispel the darkness from within us and make us realize that Thy living flame is within and without, and on the altar of our hearts be Thou present evermore."

All our faculties have to be cultivated, and the memory is no exception. It is that power by which you recollect your past experiences. It has different grades according to brain capacity. Unless you have a developed memory you are not an educated person. Memory must be developed. It is eternal, elastic, and can record many things if you develop it. If you limit your memory you limit your soul.

Memory was given to us so that we may:
1.   Learn the lessons taught by experience, and thus profit by them.
2.   Discriminate between good and bad, and eliminate the bad.
3.   Lead the soul through the garden of beautiful and divine memories, so that it will at last remember God, the Essence of all good things.

Factors important to the development of good memory are:
1.   Association of events or ideas.
2.   The art of visualization.
3.   Deep attention.
4.   Deep impression through feeling.
5.   Repetition.
6.   Meditation.

Since memory is mechanical and an imitator, you must never repeat anything wrong. Do not let anything wrong remain in the consciousness, Take the attention immediately away from things you do not want to remember. Destroy all records of evil, and recall only the good and beautiful. Meditation leads you to remember that you are One with God. Meditation means dropping the body consciousness and remembering who you are and then coming back and ruling the body. If you can make your garden produce the blossoms of beautiful thoughts, then in the flowering of beautiful memories you will at last remember God.

-Page Two-

SUMMARY OF PRAECEPTUM NO. 145   Peace unto all people, peace unto all nations, good-will unto all religions, peace unto all creatures, peace unto all that lives."

"What is that, knowing which, I shall know all?" Indian sages, instead of identifying themselves with dogmatic beliefs, go straight to the heart of spiritual investigation by approaching God or Truth through practical scientific methods. Truth must be understood, experienced in one's own Being. One who has not so experienced Truth cannot teach Truth to others. Only he can lead you to God who has himself experienced God and who lives the life in that consciousness of Truth.

In India, those people with an intense desire to know God, have left the temples and sought the great teachers who live the life in quiet places. The disciple seeks the teacher. If your heart is ready, and if you are desirous of knowing God, and direct all the effort of your heart and mind toward realization of the Spirit, then you will meet the Saints and recognize them; otherwise you may meet them and yet not recognize them.

Churches should be laboratories of spiritual experience. Dogmas should be burned and Truth retained. Religionists should realize that the time has come to discard belief in dogmas, and to let the mind of God flow freely through your hearts. Bliss is the altar on which God flow freely through your hearts. Bliss is the altar on which God stays forever. Those who find God in this life are already rich in joy and power.

The pantheistic conception of God is a teaching of Yoga philosophy. It teaches that God is everything, and in everything, and so can be known by Self-realization.

Meet your Beloved in the temple of ecstasy. Be who has everything. Knowing Him, you do not need to supplicate for any thing from anyone.

SUMMARY OF PRAECEPTUM NO. 146   "Wherever light is, darkness is no more. Open our eyes that we may behold naught but Thy Light, and may we emancipate ourselves in that light."

Delusion means, seeing apart from God. Delusion might be defined as "dual-vision." For, when one sees in unity with God, one knows that all is God, that God exists in all, that without God nothing exists. So-called natter is God in motion. God is Love, the eternal divine magnetism of energy and substance holding the universe in order; holding all forever within Itself.

India teaches you how to become conscious of your identity with God, how to overcome delusion, or dual-vision, and know your Sonship with God the Father. In this lies the vital quality of India's message.

God lays before the eyes of His children the whole panorama of the miraculous universe, but he does not display miracles when challenged by ignorance. Neither do His true devotees give signs to prove His Divinity. True devotees, such as Jesus, will readily give up their lives rather that act contrary to a divine principle.

Qualities of Honey:

1. Readily available source of food energy, because the the simple sugars, dextrose and levulose, occur

naturally and are ready for immediate absorption into the body.

2. Contains valuable mineral salts.

5. An alkaline food.

SUMMARY OF PRAECEPT(UM) NO. 147   "Make us like little children, free from jealousy, free from insincerity, unite our hearts. "

God gave us reason that we might find freedom. The reason within us tells us that we cannot live without that reason. Independence, power of reason, discrimination accompanied by will-power directed into activity; this balanced by meditation and vitalized by devotion lead to freedom.

You really contain all wisdom within yourself, only you must know how to become aware that you have it. To acquire all the wisdom in the world in one lifetime, from books, would be impossible. But there is another angle of approach. Intuition is that power of spirit, inherited by the soul, by which it can perceive all things directly without any other faculty. To have conscious knowledge of all things in Nature, unselfish sympathy with all hearts, to see and feel yourself omnipresent in all and behind all, is Cosmic Consciousness. A Yogi does not take this as a mental concept, but really merges his little self in the selves of others so that he feels his consciousness moving through all.

Have a purpose in life. Do not sacrifice your soul on the altar of indifference. Cut through the cocoon of ignorance; develop wings and fly. You must neither be content to be an unreasoning part of the cogwheel of the machine of activity, nor yet become lost in devotion without activity. Devotion without work may turn into mere emotion. Meditation balances all. Find out what you are and why you are here. Make the search for God your purpose in life.

SUMMARY OF PRAECEPTUM NO. 148   "Harness your actions to your resolutions. Protect yourself in the castle of Sincerity."

The devotee should never become identified with the process of salvation, but use the process to its purpose of promoting spiritual growth. For instance, Hatha Yoga is a method of preparing the body for the advent of spiritual growth. One should not remain within its confines but go on to the attainment of freedom of mind and soul, as well as of body.

Raja Yoga is the royal road, as it combines the best and most inclusive of other methods. Self-Realization methods teach Raja Yoga techniques of uniting soul and Spirit, and combines all the good in all other forms of Yoga.

The foundational principles of all religions consists of "Yama" and "Niyama,", namely, the things the devotee should not do and the things the devotee should do. However, the mere practice of the "shalts" and "shalt nots" gives a certain satisfaction, but does not lead to further progress, unless other steps follow.

The third important step is "Asana," or posture. The purpose of correct posture is to rise above, or stop the motions of the body which cause restlessness in the soul. Stillness is the altar of Spirit. Where motion ceases, Spirit begins to manifest.

The Fourth Step is called "Pranayama," or the switching of the life force from the senses, with the object of attaining Pratyahara. Pratyahara signifies the mind when it is disconnected from the five sense-telephones. Yoga constitutes all the scientific techniques of uniting soul and God; and Pranayama is the greatest technique of uniting soul and God. Harness your actions to your resolutions. Those who make the right and continuous effort are the ones who find God.

-Page Four-

आत्मानं बिद्धि

REALIZE THY SELF

YOGODA SAT-SANGA

FORTNIGHTLY INSTRUCTIONS

YOUR PRAECEPTUM

No. 156/4

Thy Self - realization will
blossom forth from thy
Soulful Study

YOGODA SAT-SANGA FORTNIGHTLY
INSTRUCTIONS BY
PARAMHANSA YOGANANDA
SIXTH STEP
PRAECEPTA SUMMARIES

FOURTH INSTALLMENT

SUMMARY OF PRAECEPTUM NO. 149   "Whether I am awake or asleep, alert or dreaming, Thy all-protecting presence encircles me."

Without the attainment of the Fifth Step on the ladder of Consciousness further progress is impossible. The interiorization of the mind, the state called "Pratyahara," is an essential condition which yields freedom of the mind and the power to use this interiorized mind. If you follow the meaning and result of each separate step, you will see why this is so. Each step should yield a definite step of consciousness, as:

1 and 2. Self-control and perfect equilibrium (Practice of Yama-Nyama).

3. Mental and physical calmness. (Asana).

4. Heart control, life-force control, mind control. (Pranayama).

5. Freedom of mind from sensations, and power of interiorization. (Pratyahara).

6. The power to use the interiorized mind to concentrate and meditate upon God.(Dhyana).

7. The power to conceive the vastness of God by feeling or intuition. (Dharana).

The ultimate realization is Samadhi or complete union with God. Thus you may understand that true meditation is possible only after mastering Pratyahara.

Meditate upon God. Since the average person has no conception of God, how can he meditate upon God. Patanjali explains that the symbol of God is "Aum" or "Om," the Cosmic Vibration and the Cosmic Sound. It is an all-permeating sound, oozing out of all atomic vibration. It is unlimited, omnipresent, omniscient, the Holy Ghost, containing in it its guiding principle -- the Christ Intelligence.

Lahiri Mahasaya technique, or Kriya, is the greatest form of Pranayama because through its practice the heart becomes quiet, the energy is switched off from the five senses, and the mind attains a conscious state of Pratyahara. The ultimate purpose for which these techniques are practiced should never be forgotten. Nirbikalpa Samadhi is the ultimate realization wherein the soul is completely conscious and aware of the ocean of Spirit with its manifesting waves, the body, mind, and the soul at the same time. The devotee should not remain confined to one step, but climb to the pinnacle of spiritual Self-Realization.

SUMMARY OF PRAECEPTUM NO. 150   "Except ye be born again, ye cannot enter the Kingdom of Heaven." The transmutation of the consciousness which is in the body and which is identified with the senses, through the spine into superconsciousness and Cosmic Consciousness, is the "second birth," or rebirth into spiritual consciousness.

In meditation your consciousness and energy have to be consciously withdrawn from the senses and muscles to the spine. The practice of Kriya magnetizes the spine by circulating life current lengthwise around it, thereby withdrawing the life current from the sense and involuntary organs and concentrating it in the spine. The spine and brain are the insulating altars where Divine energy first descends into the body and goes out to the senses, keeping the soul busy with material things. Therefore, the Kriya technique is the foundation and the eternal continuous base of your own Self-Realization, leading your consciousness through the spine to Cosmic Consciousness.

"Prana" means Life Energy. Prana is of two kinds, the cosmic energy, or source of all living things, and the specific prana pervading each human body. The life energy vibrating outward becomes individualized, selfish, and body-bound, forgetting its cosmic connection. This cosmic energy is conscious but not self-conscious, and must be consciously directed and connected with its infinite source.

In the human body, the seat of this life energy, or Prana, is in the Medulla Oblongata, when through proper practice, you increase your perception and feeling, when the all-seeing eye is open, and when the all-absorbing power is felt, you will absorb Truth not only through the limited power of the senses, but through the unlimited power of your perception and intuition. "Body is the shadow of God -- His shadow in the body immortal."

SUMMARY OF PRAECEPTUM NO. 151   "When I shall feel no longer with this body, I shall feel with my Cosmic body, the secret touch of all things, here and afar."

Your souls are seeking that which is tangible, and in Kriya practice you will get mathematical results according to how much you practice. These are Control of Prana exercises. Every time you practice correctly, your entire system is changing, your brain power and mind receptivity are expanding. By magnetizing the spine, it teaches how to transmute the life force into radiant, all-encompassing Spiritual Force, which in turn hastens physical and mental regeneration and rejuvenation. The Kriya technique will transfer your attention from the sensations of sight, smell, sound, taste, and touch, to the spine and brain. The Saints of India discovered that any effect from body to brain is a slow process, but an effect from the brain to the body is immediate, and that therefore a process of sending the life force around the spine, thus magnetizing the spine and brain, produces immediate effect and quickens evolution. As in science, so in religion, hidden truths are discovered by using concentration, systematic activity, and experimentation with in the laws of Nature emanating from God.

In order to reap the rich harvest of complete Truth, you must faithfully make these practical instructions a part of your life NOW. Procrastination and postponement of effort lead to stagnation and retardation in the climb up the Seven Steps of Self-Realization.

The solar year through outside influences of rays and vibrations quickens the mind and soul to a certain state in a year's time.

The Great Ones of India found that it takes eight years of solar evolution and right living to produce a certain kind of mentality. By revolving the life force even once around the spine effects a change in the brain and body which is only possible by one year of diseaseless existence, careful eating, and solar energy. The passing of this current, once around the spine will therefore give you one year of solar evolution. Just as the earth's complete revolution around the sun

-Page Two-

produces one year's effect upon a human being, so the time of human evolution can be quickened by revolving the life force (the earthly physical energy) around the elliptical path of the spiral column and its six centers, upward from the coccyx to the point between the eyebrows and downward from that point to the coccyx, with the soul as the central sun, and the spine with its six centers (apart from the seventh center in the head) making 12 points, corresponding to the Signs of the Zodiac.

SUMMARY OF PRAECEPTUM NO. 152   "Bless us with Thy consciousness; Make Thy Joy our joy, make Thy Love our love, that with Thy Love we may love all others as ours."

By the process of breathing, the accumulation of carbon in the blood is burned and the impurities expelled from the lungs. In addition, this process not only explodes carbon, but changes oxygen into its equivalent in atomic energy, which in turn is distilled into energy.

By continuous regulated breathing, as prescribed in the Kriya technique, the entire carbon content of the body can be burned out.
When that is accomplished, then there is no more dark impure venous blood to flow in the body, and no poisonous blood is pumped into the lungs for purification. Hence this practice will give rest to the heart and lungs.
The purpose in burning carbon is to quiet the heart.

The purpose in quieting the heart is to control the five sense telephones and divert the energy from them to the spine. The condition of sleep produces unconscious quietness and its attending peace. The Kriya technique leads to an ever-increasing ever-new joyous state of awareness.

The Saints found out that if it were possible for a man to live in health without disease or old age, then by solar and chemical energy he could develop in one million years a brain that could express Cosmic Consciousness, or the entire knowledge of this Universe.

The Saints also learned that, by the proper method, this evolutional process can be speeded up, by changing the brain cells through magnetization. This can be accomplished by the use of Kriya technique even to the extent of attaining Cosmic Consciousness in one lifetime.

Tomatoes are an extremely valuable food because:

Tomatoes are an extremely valuable food because:

1.   They are rich in iron, calcium, potassium, and other minerals.

2.   Contain vitamins A, B, C, and G.

3.   Alkaline in reaction.

SUMMARY OF PRAECEPTUM NO. 153   "O Fountain of Flame, ignite all darkness within us. Let Thy Light be established forever within us, about us -- everywhere."
The Kriya technique is the scientific mathematical way of changing the material body consciousness into Cosmic Consciousness.
The practice of Kriya 14 times is equivalent to one year of natural progressive evolution. There are few rules to follow, but these few should be strictly observed without deviation.

-Page Three-

Helpful but not essential are the preparatory exercises A and B of this Lesson.

Always precede the practice of Kriya by special prayer. This helps you to tune in with the great liberated Souls Who will help you in your efforts.
Essential preparation:

1. Moisten throat with olive oil or melted butter.

2. Face east or north in straight armless chair over which a woolen blanket has been placed, running down under the feet.

3. Correct posture.

4. Maintain correct posture by constant vigilance, relaxing all muscles.

5. Experiment with the cool and warm currents of air through closed fists, as described in this Lesson, in order to get the "feeling" of it, which you are later to imagine passing around the spine.

The man of volition says: "I will pursue my dynamic volition until success or death." In this spirit, practice your techniques, letting nothing interfere. Thus will your will merge with Divine Will and become wisdom-guided and limitless.

SUMMARY OF PRAECEPTUM NO. 154   "O Spirit Beautiful, open the window of Nature and the window of our minds, that we may behold Thee in all Thy Glory." The contact of God is filled with treasures and power. This technique of Kriya helps to change the center of consciousness from the body and senses to the spine, the altar of God. You will find that you will be able to do creative work with ease in any line to which you apply yourself. Intuition will develop effortlessly.

Give great care to the study of the technique. Every detail must be observed. Practice each part until you are certain that you are doing it correctly. Refer constantly to your notes to be sure   that you have omitted no point.

First observe the rules in preparation, then begin Kriya Proper, visualizing the spinal column as a hollow tube running from the coccyx to the point between the eyebrows. Inhale as directed, slowly, evenly, with the throat expanded properly to make the sound of "aw" -- (study Diagram.) Imagine cool current passing up and inside the spine, to point between the eyebrows; then pass the current in a spray sensation up and over the brain, to trickle warmly and thinly on down the back of the spinal column, while making the sound of "ee," while exhaling slowly.

When you are sure that you have the technique correct, then practice it 14 times in succession, keeping the current passing rhythmically and evenly around the spine. Imagine the cool current going up the spine, and the warm current coming down over the spine. Practice 14 times in the morning and 14 times in the evening. Do not increase the number of times without special permission from Guru Preceptor. Always practice on an empty stomach, before breakfast, and either before dinner or at least 3 hours after dinner, before retiring.
Rest several minutes in the same posture after you have finished practicing.

-Page Four-

Gautama Buddha especially emphasized the doctrine of mercy, and love for all beings.

SUMMARY OF PRAECEPTUM NO. 155   "O living Christ, present in the body of Jesus and in all of us, manifest Thyself in the trueness of Thy Glory, in the strength of Thy Light, and in the power of Thy Wisdom."

During the exercise of Kriya, the entire spine is converted into a magnet, which draws all the bodily current away from the senses and nerves. The will center (point between the eyebrows) becomes the positive pole, and the coccygeal plexus becomes the negative pole. The current created by continuous inhalation and exhalation becomes a magnet of energy which draws more energy from the nervous system and from the Cosmic source. Also, by burning up the carbon in the body, there comes a gradual enforced cessation of breathing. This is the greatest psycho-physical method for actually reversing the searchlights of the life force, consciousness, and the senses, from matter to Spirit. Hindu yogis state that this current actually changes the atomic composition of the body cells.

Study with extreme care the summing up of the essential points to be observed in the practice of Kriya proper. This technique is the foundation of the Seven Steps to Self-Realization. Let nothing interfere with your practice. "Where there is a will, there is a way." So, some day, you too may break through the darkness and perceive the Sun of Cosmic Consciousness.

FINIS OF SUMMARIES   This concludes the Summaries of Praecepta constituting the SIXTH STEP in the study of SELF-REALIZATION. It is our earnest, sincere, and humble request that you devote yourself through conscientious concentration and attention to the complete and harmonious assimilation of these Summaries. These vital, comprehensive facts will be most advantageous to you in answering the questions which are to be given in the SIXTH INTERMEDIARY EXAMINATION.

By testing the intellectual progress and under standing through a group of general questions and answers, we can determine the status of spiritual perception, or Self-Realization, which is directly affected by the mental comprehension, and thus ascertain the most effective method to he used in each Member's case.

The Examination papers and particulars will be mailed to you at the next mailing date, and sufficient time will be allowed to permit you to receive the examination, answer the questions, and return your answers to us, retaining a duplicate for your own personal file. This all precedes the beginning of the Praecepta of the climaxing SEVENTH STEP.

-Page Five-

PUBLISHED BY

YogodaSat-Sanga

Self-Realization Fellowship & Shyamacharan Mission
Founder—Paramhansa Yogananda
President—Sister Daya.

Yogoda Math, Dakshineswar, P. O. Ariadah.
Dist : 24, Parganas, West-Bengal, India.

YOGODA SAT-SANGA PRESS

आत्मानं विद्धि

REALIZE THY SELF

YOGODA SAT-SANGA

FORTNIGHTLY INSTRUCTIONS

YOUR PRAECEPTUM

No......16......

YOGODA SAT-SANGA FORNIGHTLY INSTRUCTIONS
BY
PARAMHANSA YOGANANDA
SIXTH INTERMEDIARY EXAMINATION

INTRODUCTION   The Praecepta can be made very valuable to you if you read and study their contents faithfully and seriously. You can refer to the subject matter over and over again.

The Praecepta are always at hand, like the Dictionary and the Bible, or Geeta, ever ready to be consulted, but the education and enlightenment that you receive from studying these Instructions will be entirely governed by the amount of time and close application that you put upon the work. thing that is the easiest to obtain in this life is seldom valuable. We know from reading the lives of great men and women that they became great in their particular vocations and in the building of their character only thru (sic) the most rigid study and sacrifice, but the result obtained was worth far more than the efforts that were put forth, and that is usually the case.

Perhaps you will think that you have little time to give to the Instructions, but all of us have 24 hours a day to give to something. You will find upon reflection that you really waste much time upon trifling duties and entertainment, time which you could use to much better advantage in the study of life principles contained in the Praecepta. Indeed, there is no comparison between the two methods. One leads to nothing but temporary artificial satisfaction; the other leads to Self-Realization, peace, and permanent happiness. We implore you to use your time to the very best advantage. The study and practice of these Instructions will not only help you in this life but will also prepare you for the life that is to come.

PURPOSE   In order to further help you In your development resulting from the study of these Instructions, we have decided to give you between Steps a thorough examination on the Instructions, in order to determine just how much benefit you are receiving from your study of these valuable principles. We wish you to obtain full value from every standpoint.

This examination will indicate your degree of progress and your readiness for the Seventh Step which is to follow. It will also indicate your present needs, whereby we shall learn the most effective way to help you. We shall be able to discover your weak points and your strong points, and in that we be able to guide you correctly in your future studies.

EXAMINATION INSTRUCTIONS   Please answer the questions briefly, clearly, and concisely. Answer each question in as few words as possible; (5 to not more than 20 words.) Read the Summaries of the Sixth Step as given in the 4 parts of Praeceptum No. 156 for a concise review before answering the questions.

Then do not refer to the Praecepta unless absolutely necessary. The more you answer from memory, the more it will show what you really have learned and assimilated. Also draw on your personal experiences in describing and answering many of the questions. Write only your answers and send to us. Give the Praeceptum number and the number of the answer. For instance, Praeceptum 131, Answer 1. Do not send us the questions that we have sent to you.

We have set a time-limit of two weeks for you to answer the questions and return them to us, and to allow us time for making corrections. The Seventh Step will follow after 2 weeks devoted to the

Examination. (If you are a very busy man or woman and have only a very limited time to write, answer these questions to yourself and refer to the Praecepta to ascertain the correctness of your answers. Then let us know of your approximate examination percentage. On your true, conscientious testimony we shall give you credit, but positively write the answers if you have sufficient time. All Members will be started in the Seventh Step and their answers will serve as a guide to the successful analysis of each Member's progress in Self-Realization.

Note: For your reference and convenience, we suggest that you keep a duplicate copy of your Examination Answers submitted to us, as we shall preserve in our files your answers sent to us.

Q U E S T I O N S

PRAECEPTUM NO. 131   1. Briefly define Reincarnation.
            2. Quote two scriptural passages which refer to reincarnation.
Explain why a mixed diet is necessary to health.

PRAECEPTUM NO. 138   1. Explain why the soul is not released when the physical body dies.
2. Of what is the spiritual or idea-body composed?
3. What is the difference between the astral senses and the physical senses?
4. Why does desire cause rebirth?
5. What is the moral of the story, "The Discontented Man?"

PRACEPTUM NO. 134   1. Metaphysically define: "Disembodied soul."
2. Briefly explain the purpose of human love in its various relationships.
3. Name the limitations which mar love's divine purity.
4. What is the moral of the story, "Sage Byasa and the Gopinees?"

PRAECEPTUM NO. 135   1. Where do disembodied souls dwell?
2. (a) Briefly outline the technique for contacting physically disembodied souls.
(b) Name the two most essential requirements in this technique.
3. What lesson is illustrated in the story, "The Wishing Tree"?
4. What symptoms indicate too much acid in the system?

PRAECEPTUM NO. 136   1. What is Karma?
2. What are the springs of human actions?
3. How can one win freedom from Karma?
4. Tell how you can apply the moral in your own lives, of the story, "King Kuvera and Buddhiman."
5. Name the foods containing a predominance of acid-forming elements.

PRAECEPTUM NO. 137   1. Name two principal factors which determine one's state of health or prosperity in this life.
2. What lesson is contained in the story, "The Culprit and the Judge."

PRAECEPTUM NO. 138   1. What is the actual nature of the human body.
2. Explain the source of rejuvenation of the body.
3. What should we depend upon to the greater extent for the replenishment of energies?

PRAECEPTUM NO. 139   1. Name several details necessary to the rejuvenation of the body.
2. Give in detail the two techniques of sending healing vibrations of energy through the hands.
3. What is the moral of the story, "The Greatest Lover?"
-Page Two-

PRAECEPTUM NO. 140 – 1. Explain the purpose of physical and mental efficiency. 2. What is true prosperity? 3. Explain the value of money.

PRAECEPTUM NO. 141 – 1. What is the source of Cosmic Delusion? 2. Explain briefly the purpose of evolution.

PRAECEPTUM NO. 142 – 1. Why is temptation tempting? (2) What did you learn from the story, "Krishna, the Ever-Changing yet Changeless one." 3. Why is correct, diet important to expectant mother(s)?

PRAECEPTUM NO. 143 – 1. Name the two factors necessary to good speech and good singing. 2. Name the factors involved in good technique in use of vocal power.

PRAECEPTUM NO. 144 – 1. Name several factors necessary in the training of memory. 2. Name principal purposes of memory.

PRAECEPTUM NO. 145 – 1. Who can lead you to God? 2. What is the meaning of Pantheism? 3. What truth did you glean from the story, "The Saint Who Called a King a Beggar?"

PRAECEPTUM NO. 146 – 1. Name the particular vital quality which the teaching of India contains. 2. What lesson is contained in the story, "How a Saint Satisfied an Emperor's lust for Miracles? " 3. What is the value of honey in the diet?

PRAECEPTUM NO. 147 – 1. Of what use is reason? 2. What part should activity play in our lives?

PRAECEPTUM NO. 148 – 1. What method of Yoga is taught by Self-Realization

Fellowship? 2. Name the foundational principles of all religions. 3. (a) Name the first four steps in Yoga. (b) What is their purpose?

PRAECEPTUM NO. 149 – 1. (a) What is the Fifth Step on the ladder of Realization?

(b) Why is it essential? 2. Name the results which should be attained by each of the Seven steps of Self-Realization.

PRAECEPTUM NO. 150 – 1. From what source has the Kriya technique come to

the Western world? 2. Explain briefly the process by which the practice of Kriya changes the center of consciousness? 3. What is "Prana"?

PRAECEPTUM NO. 151 – 1. Explain why the Kriya technique speeds up the natural evolutionary process of the human body, mind, and soul. 2. What important lesson is contained in the story, "The Man Who Misused Miracles."

PRAECEPTUM NO. 152 – 1. Explain the physical process which takes place in the human body by the practice of Kriya. 2. What is the purpose in quieting the heart? 3. What is the difference in the state of rest caused by the sleep state, and that caused by the practice of Kriya technique? 4. (a) By the process of average evolution, approximately how long would it take the human brain to reach perfection in Cosmic Consciousness? (b) How long by way of Kriya technique?

PRAECEPTUM NO. 153 – 1. Name the special rules in the preparation for practicing the Kriya technique.

PRAECEPTUM NO. 154 – 1. Give the procedure of the Kriya technique point by point. 2. (a) Do you feel the current around the spine? (b) Do you feel any

after-results? 3. What special doctrine is emphasized in the teaching of Gautama Buddha?

PRAECEPTUM NO. 155 – 1. Describe and explain why the Kriya exercise draws the bodily current away from the senses to the spine. 2. How can you, too, gain the perception indicated in the Apologue "I Discover the Sun of Cosmic Consciousness."

-Page Three-

PUBLISHED BY

Yogoda Sat-Sanga

Self-Realization Fellowship & Shyamacharan Mission

Founder—Paramhansa Yogananda
President—Sister Daya.

Yogoda Math, Dakshineswar, P. O. Ariadah.
Dist.: 24, Parganas, West-Bengal, India.

YOGODA SAT-SANGA PRESS

EDITOR'S NOTES

The opening prayer of P-132 is read beautifully by Mrinalini Mataji in one of the recorded Christmas meditations she conducted.

Page three appears to be missing. The story of "John" the accountant is picked up at his sixth incarnation. Yogananda recites this story in one of SRF Inc.'s recordings.

Two Praeceptum 141, page 5, recipes actually show a serving of 2/4 portions of various ingredients. Intriguing...

"Exanthemata" (Page 4 of Praeceptum 142) is a reference to measles, rubella, childhood infectious diseases.